General Rufus Putnam

ALSO BY ROBERT ERNEST HUBBARD

Major General Israel Putnam: Hero of the American Revolution (McFarland, 2017)

General Rufus Putnam

*George Washington's
Chief Military Engineer and
the "Father of Ohio"*

ROBERT ERNEST HUBBARD

McFarland & Company, Inc., Publishers
Jefferson, North Carolina

LIBRARY OF CONGRESS CATALOGUING-IN-PUBLICATION DATA

Names: Hubbard, Robert Ernest, author.
Title: General Rufus Putnam : George Washington's chief military engineer and the "Father of Ohio" / Robert Ernest Hubbard.
Description: Jefferson, North Carolina : McFarland & Company, Inc., Publishers, 2020 | Includes bibliographical references and index.
Identifiers: LCCN 2020027076 | ISBN 9781476678627 (paperback) ∞ | ISBN 9781476640129 (ebook)
Subjects: LCSH: Putnam, Rufus, 1738–1824. | Ohio Company (1786–1796) | Ohio—History—1787–1865. | Frontier and pioneer life—Ohio—Marietta. | United States—History—Revolution, 1775–1783—Biography. | Generals—Massachusetts—Biography. | Military engineers—Biography. | Marietta (Ohio)—Biography.
Classification: LCC F483 .H83 2020 | DDC 977.1/03092 [B]—dc23
LC record available at https://lccn.loc.gov/2020027076

BRITISH LIBRARY CATALOGUING DATA ARE AVAILABLE

ISBN (print) 978-1-4766-7862-7
ISBN (ebook) 978-1-4766-4012-9

© 2020 Robert Ernest Hubbard. All rights reserved

No part of this book may be reproduced or transmitted in any form or by any means, electronic or mechanical, including photocopying or recording, or by any information storage and retrieval system, without permission in writing from the publisher.

Front cover painting of Rufus Putnam by John Trumbull, oil, 3⅞ inches × 3¼ inches, circa 1790 (Yale University Art Gallery)

Printed in the United States of America

McFarland & Company, Inc., Publishers
  Box 611, Jefferson, North Carolina 28640
    www.mcfarlandpub.com

Acknowledgments

First, I would like to thank Dana Parker, author of *Building Victory: Aircraft Manufacturing in the Los Angeles Area in World War II*, for suggesting that I write a biography of Rufus Putnam. He thought it would be a good idea, and he was so right!

At Rufus Putnam's birthplace of Sutton, Massachusetts, several people were especially helpful: Wally Baker, who generously provided photographs and information; local genealogy expert Ross Weaver; and Joyce Smith, of the Sutton Historical Society and its General Rufus Putnam Museum.

At Putnam's long-time hometown of North Brookfield, Massachusetts, I must single out the valuable assistance of Brandon Avery, who is president of the North Brookfield Historical Society. Over the years, I have had occasion to work with many historical society officers, and Brandon is one of the best.

I would like to thank David Alff and the other editors at McFarland. I am grateful to Natalie Foreman for her support and advice on both this book and my Israel Putnam biography. A thank you also goes to Tyler Love, Archivist & Library Manager, at Independence National Historical Park.

At the town founded by Putnam—Marietta, Ohio—I am indebted to Bill Reynolds of the Ohio River Museum and Linda Showalter of Marietta College. Other people who were of assistance in my research include: Daniel A. Piazza, chief curator of philately, Smithsonian National Postal Museum; Mary Root, LS, editor of the Surveyors Historical Society's publication, *Backsights*; Jean M. O'Reilly of the Oxford Massachusetts Historical Commission; and Lisa Welte Herzig of the Anna Warner Bailey Chapter, Daughters of the American Revolution, which covers Groton and Stonington, Connecticut.

Acknowledgments

I am grateful for the incredibly informative tour of West Point's Fort Putnam that was given by Jim Fox, chief, community engagement, Public Affairs Office, West Point United States Military Academy.

I would like to acknowledge the contributions of three direct descendants of Rufus Putnam—Dianne Mueller, who is the owner of the website RufusPutnam.com, Patrick Putnam of the U.S. Bureau of Land Management, and Lisa Welte Herzig of the Anna Warner Bailey Chapter, Daughters of the American Revolution, covering Groton and Stonington, Connecticut. They are justifiably proud of their ancestor's accomplishments.

On my list of people and organizations that helped in my research are: Historic Site Manager Grant E. Miller and Assistant Parks and Recreation Supervisor Peter Cutul of the Fort Montgomery (New York) State Historic Site; Michael J.F. Sheehan, senior historian, Stony Point Battlefield State Historic Site; Nathan Soule of Thomaston, Maine's General Henry Knox Museum; the Independence National Historical Park; the White Plains (New York) Public Library; and the Bedford (Virginia) Museum and Genealogical Library.

Most of all, I would like to thank my wife, Kathleen, for editing this book and providing many valuable recommendations.

Table of Contents

Acknowledgments v
Preface 1
Introduction 3

ONE. Family and Childhood 5
TWO. French and Indian War 11
THREE. Before the American Revolution 28
FOUR. Washington's Chief Engineer 43
FIVE. After the Revolutionary War 79
SIX. Pioneer Leader 107
SEVEN. Father of Ohio 127
EIGHT. A Legend in His Own Time 151
NINE. Legacy 178

Chapter Notes 191
Bibliography 221
Index 227

Preface

A few years ago, McFarland & Company published my biography, *Major General Israel Putnam: Hero of the American Revolution*. While researching that book, I became interested in the life and career of Israel's cousin, Rufus Putnam. Like Israel, Rufus Putnam had served in important capacities in North America's two major 18th century wars, and he was one of the most highly respected people in the early years of the United States.

Before presenting a proposal for a Rufus Putnam biography to the publisher, I spoke with someone who remarked that David McCullough, possibly America's best-known historian, was writing a book about Rufus Putnam. Concerned, I spoke with people who had worked with Mr. McCullough on his research. Apparently, Rufus Putnam would be included as one of five main historical figures in his book.

In 2019, McCullough's book, *The Pioneers*, was released. I was pleased to see that it concentrated on Rufus Putnam's life after his move to Ohio—after he reached the age of fifty. The scope of the book covered very little of Putnam's earlier life.

Incredibly, in the almost two centuries since Rufus Putnam died, only one biography of his entire life has been published. In 1886, Mary Cone of Marietta, Ohio, wrote *Life of Rufus Putnam: With Extracts from His Journals*.[1]

My biography highlights Rufus Putnam's importance in the history of the United States. The reader will see his impact on the fledging nation as a farmer, soldier, scout, explorer, and surveyor. He was well qualified to guide the brave pioneers to the Northwest Territory and to advise them how to make a lasting settlement. Rufus Putnam's legacy is still seen today; it stems from his beliefs and values and from his strength and determination.

He was committed to efforts to populate this new land and transplant time-tested laws and standards from back East; he believed in the value of education—especially for the youth—and was the first to survey land that was set aside for educating the settlers' children. Rufus Putnam was morally convinced of freedom for all. He threw his weight into creating a state constitutional provision that passed by the legislature by one vote—creating an antislavery law that could never be repealed.

Introduction

Rufus Putnam's life encompassed many careers: millwright, farmer, surveyor, soldier, military engineer, pioneer leader, and judge. His most famous achievements came as one of General George Washington's most trusted and competent Revolutionary War officers, and later as the leader of the group that founded the first permanent Northwest Territory settlement.

It is not difficult to see that without Rufus Putnam, American history might have taken dramatically different turns on a number of occasions. If Rufus Putnam had not devised a means by which fortifications could be constructed south of Boston, Massachusetts, in early 1776, the British forces that occupied the city might have been reinforced and then attacked the newly formed Continental Army—stopping the American Revolution in its tracks.

After the Revolutionary War, Rufus Putnam was determined to recompense the veterans who fell on hard financial times. He appealed to the government and his friend, George Washington, to pay the veterans in land vouchers. General Rufus Putnam and General Benjamin Tupper originated the idea of the Ohio Company, and General Rufus Putnam was selected to be the leader and superintendent of its first settlement.

In later years, if Rufus Putnam had not pushed for the Northwest Territory to be free of slavery, the history of the following century might well have been quite different. By the time of the American Civil War, the slave states might have been so numerous and powerful that the Union forces would have found it extremely difficult to defeat the Confederate military. The Northwest Territory consisted of what would become Ohio, Indiana, Illinois, Michigan, Wisconsin, and part of Minnesota. Had these states joined the 11 pro-slavery southern states, the number of slave states could have been 17, and their combined economic and military power in the 1860s might well have been enough to defeat the union of northern states—or at least to force a stalemate.[1]

In addition, the great leader of the anti-slavery states, Abraham Lincoln, and his two most famous generals—Ulysses S. Grant and William Tecumseh Sherman—might have had different values and different worldviews if they had been raised in the slave states of Illinois and Ohio.[2] Rufus Putnam was vehemently against allowing any ownership of slaves in the Northwest Territory.

> *"Rufus Putnam ... possesses more practical knowledge in the art of Engineering than any other we have in this Camp or Army."*
> —General George Washington to the Board of War, 1776[3]

> *"To be a great engineer with only such advantages of education as Rufus Putnam enjoyed is to be a man of consummate genius ... to have planned, constructed, and made impregnable the very citadel and fortress of liberty on this continent, to have turned the mighty stream of current and empire from the channel of slavery into the channel of freedom, there to flow forever and forever,—if this be not greatness, then there is no greatness among the living or the dead."*
> —U.S. Senator George F. Hoar, 1898[4]

> *"Rufus Putnam is the hero. He led the whole thing* [the first permanent settlement in the Northwest Territory] *from the beginning; he is the leader who held it together under these terrible conditions. He was a truly dedicated American pioneer if there ever was one."*
> —David McCullough, 2019[5]

CHAPTER ONE

Family and Childhood

The Spy

The latter half of 1776 was a time of retreat for Washington's Continental Army. Angered by the Declaration of Independence, which was signed by the Continental Congress in July, Great Britain's leaders were determined to put an end to the rebellion once and for all. A huge British Naval fleet from England, and another from Canada, converged on New York City—with them were over 30,000 troops.

The far superior British forces drove the Americans from Long Island to Manhattan Island. From Manhattan, the troops of Commander-in-Chief George Washington, and Rufus Putnam's cousin, Major General Israel Putnam, retreated north to Harlem, then to White Plains. At the latter village, the Continental Army had a major supply depot. Washington was concerned—if the British were to capture it, it might be the end of the war for the American forces.

General Washington needed someone he could trust to ascertain the location of the British forces and the direction in which they were moving. He chose a 38-year-old engineering officer who had proved his worth more than once in a war that was now only a little over one year old. That man—Rufus Putnam—six months earlier had invented a way for the American forces to successfully drive the British Army and their high command from Boston, Massachusetts.

In August 1776, Rufus Putnam, on the recommendation of Washington, had been promoted to the position of colonel and Chief Engineer of the Continental Army. At White Plains, he would again demonstrate how valuable he was to the patriot cause.

To carry out the mission, Putnam disguised himself, hiding his identity as an officer in the Continental Army. In his words, he took out "my cockade, Loping my hat & Secreting my Sword & pistols under my Loose coat, and then had I been taken under this disguise the probability is that I Should have been hanged for a Spy."[1]

In all likelihood, he was right: it had only been two months since 21-year-old Connecticut soldier Nathan Hale had been captured and hanged for spying. The location of Putnam's spy mission at White Plains was only about thirty miles north of the likely site of Hale's execution.

Putnam discovered that the British forces were in a far different position than Washington had been led to believe. As soon as the General heard Putnam's report, he immediately redirected many of his troops to guard the supply depot. That action prevented a probable British takeover of the depot and possibly saved Washington's army.

Family

In the 1600s, John Wampas, a member of the Nipmuc tribe, deeded thousands of acres of Massachusetts land to Edward Pratt, who later sold interests to several other Englishmen. Subsequently, there were decades of land disputes involving the Nipmucs and the English immigrants. Finally, the General Court of Massachusetts Bay Colony ruled on ownership. In 1704, it granted Pratt and other English settlers the land on which Sutton (meaning "South Town") sits today. Sutton was surveyed in 1715 and the first town meeting was held in 1718.[2]

In 1685, Rufus's father, farmer Elisha Putnam, was born in Salem Village, Massachusetts.[3] In 1713, after the death of his first wife, Hannah Marble, the 27-year-old Elisha married 18-year-old Susanna Fuller of Topsfield. While at Salem Village they had five children. In about 1725, the family moved to Sutton, Massachusetts, where the remainder of their eleven children were born. Rufus was the youngest of six boys and five girls.

In addition to operating the family farm with Susannah, Elisha served as a church deacon, town clerk, town treasurer, and a representative to the Massachusetts general court. He died in Sutton in 1745 at age 59. Elisha and Susannah Putnam's oldest child, Elisha, Jr., was 22 years older than brother Rufus, and was married before Rufus was even four years old.

Some information on the Putnams can be found in town documents. For example, the town records indicate that a month prior to Rufus's birth, his father and his brother Elisha Jr. were given permission to build stables on the common land near the Sutton meetinghouse as long as they "Did not hurt nor Discommode the training field nor the Buring place."[4] At the same time, Elisha Jr. and four other men were permitted to build themselves a seat over the men's stairs at the meetinghouse provided they "Did not hurt nor Discommode the going up the gallery stairs."[5]

Childhood

Rufus Putnam was born on April 9, 1738. When he was five years old a great comet appeared for weeks in the western sky. An entry in the Rev. David Hall's diary for January 23, 1744, stated[6]:

> A blazing star or comet in the West has appeared for near two months; at first small, but now of great length beyond what I ever saw. This is the third that has of late years appeared. I would not be dismayed at ye signe of Heaven, but O ye sinners fear who live in ye neglect of God and O y't I might so far regard it as to trim my lamp and get ready.[7]

On February 16, the Reverend Hall recorded:

> The blazing star from the south-west has appeared near three months. It was small—it passed by north of the sun; when it first appeared its Tail was about a yard long to appearances, was bent towards the Equator. When it came down about north of the sun its Tail was pointed towards the North Pole—Its Tail appeared about 12 Degrees in Length at a farther distance from the sun. Its Body or Nucleous appeared about 3 Inches in Diameter to the naked eye. Feb. 4th. It appeared half an hour after sunset about half an hour high and about an hour and a half to the North of the sun, it being so near in the sun gloss its Tail did not appear above two yards long—next morning it rose before the sun and appeared much in the same shape. Its tail must be several millions of miles long. The Lord sanctify so awful a token of an approaching God, who thus hangs out his ensign in ye skies y't ye nations may tremble before Him.[8]

Known to astronomers today as the Great Comet of 1744, it is the sixth brightest comet in recorded history.[9] On February 18, 1744, the comet was as bright as the planet Venus. Several days later, it was reported to be visible in the daytime. In March, its most distinctive feature appeared—six tails. Although Rufus was very young, there is little doubt he participated with the rest of Sutton in the great sightings.

Rufus Putnam's accomplishments were acknowledged by Sutton, Massachusetts, at their bicentennial memorial. A plaque on the site of Rufus Putnam's birthplace reads[10]:

General Rufus Putnam
Born April 9 1738
Soldier in the War for Independence

Marker at the site of Rufus Putnam's birthplace house in Sutton, Massachusetts. The youngest of farmers Elisha Putnam and Susanna Fuller Putnam's eleven children, Rufus lived in Sutton until he was seven years old (author's photograph).

Companion of Washington[11]
Constructor of Works at Dorchester Heights
that Compelled the Evacuation of Boston
Engineer of Fortifications at West Point
Father and Founder of Ohio
Leader of the Company that Gave the Great
Northwest to Freedom Education and Liberty

This Memorial Dedicated May 17 1904
by the Town of Sutton at its Bicentennial

In 1898, U.S. Senator George F. Hoar noted: "There is nothing left but a few stones of the cellar wall of Putnam's birthplace, as there is nothing left but a few bricks of the birthplace of Washington."[12]

After his father's death in June 1745, seven-year-old Rufus was sent to live with his maternal grandfather Jonathan Fuller in Danvers, Massachusetts, until September 1747. It was there that he attended school and learned some of the basics of reading. Rufus remembers in his *Memoirs*: "to this time I was kept at School as much as Children usually were at that day, and could read pretty well in the bible."[13]

In 1747, Rufus's mother married Captain John Sadler, a tavern keeper of Upton,[14] Massachusetts, and they brought in nine-year-old Rufus to live with them. Sadler was an uneducated man who so little valued education that he refused to allow Rufus to attend school or even to use candles in the evenings for reading. Probably without Sadler's knowledge, Rufus bought textbooks for himself with money from small game he shot and tips he earned when working at Sadler's tavern.[15]

Years later, Rufus recorded in his memoirs: "during the six year[s] I lived with Capt Sadler, I never Saw the inside of a School house, except about three weeks, he was very illiterate himself, and took no care for the education of his family; but this was not all I was made a ridicule of, and otherwise abused for my attention to books, and attempting to write, and learn Arithmetic, however, amidst all those discouragements I made Some advances in writing and Arithmetic, that is I could make Letters that could be under stood, and had gone as far in Arithmetic as to work the rule of three (without any teacher but the book)."[16]

The effects of these experiences on Rufus are evident in his next line: "Oh! my Children beware you neglect not the education of any under your care as I was neglected."[17]

When Sadler died in 1753, Rufus was fifteen years old. In March 1754, he was apprenticed to his 19-year-old sister Huldah's 28-year-old husband, Daniel Matthews, Jr., as a millwright apprentice in North Brookfield, Massachusetts.[18] Five years earlier, Matthews had purchased land and mill privilege on Sucker Brook near the town line with New Braintree.[19]

Rufus notes: "by [Matthews] my education was as much neglected, as by Capt Sadler, except that he did not deny me the use of a Light for Study in the winter evenings—I turned my attention chiefly to Arithmetic, Geography, and history."[20]

In those pursuits, Rufus did well on his own. But there was one area in which he always regretted that he did not have formal, systematic training. In his seventies, he wrote:

> Had I been as much engaged in Learning to write well, with Spelling, and Grammar, I might have been much better qualified to fulfill the duties of the Succeeding Scenes of Life, which In providence I have been called to pass through. I was zealous to obtain knowledge, but having no guide I knew not where to begin nor what course to pursue,—hence neglecting Spelling and grammar when young I have Suffered much through life on that account.[21]

In an address on the life of Rufus Putnam in 1898, U.S. Senator George F. Hoar noted: "It was to those winter evenings in North Brookfield and the studies by the light of the tallow candle that his country owed the ablest engineer officer of the Revolution, and the wise, farsighted intellect that decided the fate of America."[22]

In the same year 16-year-old Rufus's millwright apprenticeship began, the French and Indian War broke out.[23] In 1754, Rufus's 36-year-old Connecticut cousin, Israel Putnam, volunteered to serve with the British as a member of the Connecticut provincial forces. Rufus and Israel are usually referred to as cousins—and will be in this biography—but actually Israel's father Joseph and Rufus' grandfather Edward were half-brothers.[24]

The two men had much in common. Both were around six years old when their fathers died. Israel was the 11th of 12 children. His sister Mary was born about 28 years before Israel. Rufus was the last born of 11 children. His brother Elisha was 22 years older than him. Neither man had much of a formal education. Both, however, were very creative, with Israel inventing military defensive and offensive devices in both the French and Indian War and the American Revolutionary War, and Rufus becoming the most important military engineer of the Revolution's Continental Army.

Until 1754, the two cousins were not close. The only town they both resided in was Danvers, Massachusetts. However, 22-year-old Israel Putnam left Danvers for Connecticut in 1740, which was five years before seven-year-old Rufus moved there to live with his grandfather. But when 18-year-old private Rufus traveled to the Lake George region of New York with the Connecticut troops in 1757, he encountered Israel who was by then a 38-year-old captain in charge of his own company of rangers.

During part of the next few years Rufus served as one of Israel's rangers. The future would find the two men's lives intersecting on a number of important occasions—especially at a pre–Revolutionary War expedition up the Mississippi River, and during their years of service as high-ranking officers in Washington's Continental Army. For years, Israel was a role model for Rufus and much of the latter's success in military matters can be traced to lessons learned from his cousin.

Chapter Two

French and Indian War

The North American phase of the Seven Years War between Great Britain and France was known as the French and Indian War. The latter began in 1754 and concluded with the Treaty of Paris in 1763. The main area of dispute between the two European powers was the ownership of the Ohio River Valley. In the war, settlers of English heritage from the American seaboard colonies, along with the British military and Indian allies of the British, confronted French troops, French settlers, and Indian allies of the French.

Rufus Putnam served with the British-allied colonial forces from age eighteen to twenty-two. Undoubtedly, one factor in Rufus's decision to volunteer to fight was the example set by his cousin, Captain Israel Putnam. In the war, Israel was quickly promoted from private to captain. Throughout his life, his promotions were based almost exclusively on his battlefield performance. At the time of Rufus's Massachusetts enlistment, Israel had already been serving with the Connecticut provincial forces for three years and was well on his way to becoming a legend in his own time.

On March 15, 1757, Rufus Putnam, three weeks shy of his nineteenth birthday, joined Capt. Ebenezer Learned's Massachusetts company with the promise to serve through February 2, 1758. During this year of Rufus Putnam's military service, he recorded events in his journal. Some of his entries described the harsh life of a militia private and the perilous life of being a scout. His journal depicted the dangerous uncertainty while on maneuvers, having limited provisions, the immediate consequences for those who broke rules, the deadly accidents, the barbarous encounters when scouts got caught while on missions, and the gruesomeness of war.

From April 30 to May 6, the company marched from Brookfield, Massachusetts, to Kinderhook, New York. At Kinderhook the men were lodged in two barns and were furnished with stores that were "very mean and scanty."[1] In his journal, Putnam wrote, "during our stay at Kenderhook, Capt. Learned prayed with his company morning and evening, and on the Sabbath read a Sermon."[2]

Leaving Kinderhook, they passed to Greenbush where they stayed in another barn and were each given nine rounds of ammunition. They were also supplied with kettles, bowls, platters, spoons, and, perhaps most importantly of all, tents—affording them some protection while sleeping.[3]

Rufus noted in his journal that about an hour after sunrise, one of the company, a Jededial Winslow, was shot in the hip. The ball was taken out and he appeared "likely to do well."[4] This portended the dangers they would be facing,

The next day they marched to Seacook, and later joined Colonel Joseph Frye's Massachusetts Regiment of Foot at Stillwater on June 9.[5] Two days afterwards, they arrived at Saratoga and stayed there for three days. The seventeen companies of the regiment then departed for Fort Edward, arriving on June 15.[6] The following day, Rufus's cousin Captain Israel Putnam came into the fort with a prisoner.[7]

In July 1757, when Rufus undertook a dangerous assignment, he saw first-hand how some officers were either incompetent or "caved" under pressure. Rufus volunteered with the rangers and was sent as a scout on a mission with almost a dozen other soldiers under Lieutenant Collings.

During the first two days, they marched 20 miles. Collings then ordered Rufus and two other men to determine the distance to the nearby bay. To make better time, they left their food and blankets behind. Afterwards, they returned to the camp later than expected only to find the rest of their party gone—along with the supplies.[8]

The lieutenant had apparently assumed that Rufus and his companions had been killed or captured and consequently he and his men made a quick retreat. The three stranded men fired a gun to attract attention but received no reply. Putnam found his situation unpleasant—"having nothing to cover us from the Natts & Mosquitoes (with which that country abounds beyond description) but a shirt and breech clout." The three men returned to Fort Edward on July 11 after having spent 48 hours without food.[9]

The following day Lieutenant Collings and the rest of the company arrived at Fort Edward. Collins "confessed they heard our evening gun, but supposed the Indians had gotten us and were after them." Rufus Putnam offers his opinion of the "extremely unsolder-like" actions of the officer: "he ought to have withdrawn but a small distance, and placed himself in ambush and to have posted two men under cover to watch our return, or the approach of the enemy had any appeared."[10]

Rufus notes in his journal that on July 1 two of his cousin Israel's men came into camp with news that Israel, who had left with 68 men, were fighting between three and four hundred French and Indians on Lake Champlain's South Bay. When the enemy reached shore they came close to overwhelming Putnam and his men. Putnam needed help immediately.[11]

General Phineas Lyman took about 400 or 500 men out to assist Captain Putnam. Rufus didn't go because he had been assigned to picket guard duty. Sometime later, Israel Putnam came into camp and related how at about 3:00 a.m. his men had fired on enemy boats, doing great damage. With difficulty the latter landed, wounded three of Putnam's men, and forced Putnam to retreat. After Israel's men returned to camp, Mohawk allies of the British came in with two scalps.[12]

On July 4 General Lyman returned with his men. They related that two of Israel's men had been wounded and taken away as captives. A third man was found "barbecued at a most doleful rate, for they found him with his nails all pulled out, his lips cut off down to his chin and up to his nose, and his jaws lay bare; his scalp was taken off, his breast cut open, his heart pulled out and his bullet pouch put in the room of it; his left hand clenched round his gall, a Tomahawk left in his bowels and a dart struck through him; the little finger of his left hand cut off and the little toe of his left foot cut off."[13]

During this summer of 1757, Rufus notes in his diary the dangers of military life and the type of infractions that were severely punished. For example, on July 15 Capt. Learned ordered that any man found playing cards would receive 500 lashes.[14]

Accidents and military punishments could be deadly. On July 21 one soldier was executed for desertion and hours later returning scouts brought news that one of the lieutenants, by the name of Dormit, had been shot to death near South Bay.[15] Eight days later they found and buried his body. Rufus relates that "his head and arms [were] cut off and his body cut to pieces."[16] On July 26, one soldier's gun accidentally discharged and shot a man in an adjacent tent. The only words the dying man was able to speak were "I am a dead man. The Lord have mercy on me."[17]

It wasn't only the fighting men who were in continuous danger. The following October, three butchers went out after some sheep. One was found dead at the brick kilns, another was found dead with two musket balls in him about 300 yards away, and the third man was missing.

Scouting assignments were especially risky. On July 27, 1757, after the men complained that they wanted more compensation for the dangerous missions, the commanding officer of the fort, Major Fletcher, gathered everyone together and promised an extra three dollars a month and a half-pint of rum whenever they scouted. Rufus remarked in his journal: "The Rum we got sometimes; but the money we never see."[18]

Attack on the Carpenters

Four months into Rufus Putnam's enlistment, he was gaining valuable experience from the French & Indian War that became ingrained in him as a soldier and a future officer in the American Revolution. One such event happened two weeks later, on July 23, 1757, at eight o'clock in the morning. A large party of Indians fired at carpenters who were within a half-mile of Fort Edward, killing thirteen men.[19] After gathering up their dead and wounded, the Indians left. By afternoon, Rufus's cousin, Captain Israel Putnam, had assembled about 250 men and initiated a pursuit. After following the Indians' trail until sunset, Captain Putnam ordered Rufus and two other men to go on about a mile ahead, hide out, and watch to see if the Indians turned around.

Israel said: "if they do not embark in their boats tonight they will send a party back to see if they are pursued." Rufus and the other two men did not observe any Indians returning, but he remarked in his journal "Capt. Putnam's precaution struck my mind very forcedly, as a maxim always to be observed whether you are pursuing or

Rufus Putnam's cousin Israel Putnam, who served as a ranger during the French and Indian War and a major general during the American Revolutionary War. At times, Rufus Putnam served under him in both wars, as well as accompanied him on a 1772–1773 expedition up the Mississippi River. Print from William Farrand Livingston's 1901 biography, *Israel Putnam: Pioneer, Ranger and Major General, 1718–1790*.

are pursued by an enemy: especially in the woods. It was the first idea of generalship, I recollect to have treasured up."[20]

Fort William Henry

In 1757, the French correctly believed the number of British forces at Fort William Henry, on the southern shore of Lake George, to be at vulnerable level. They gathered French, Canadian and Indian troops for an attack—as many as 14,000 men.

The William Henry garrison had fewer than 2,500 soldiers. Rufus Putnam described the fort as: "a regular square with four bastions, the walls consisted of timber and earth, with ditch &c capable for a time of resisting a cannonade & bombardment."[21]

William Henry's commander, Lieutenant Colonel George Munroe, asked for reinforcements from General Daniel Webb at nearby Fort Edward and was refused.[22]

In his journal Rufus writes that on August 3 he was out on scout with Capt. Learned when they heard cannon fire from the direction of Fort William Henry. Upon returning to Fort Edward, they found that Israel Putnam had dispatched three spies to ascertain the situation. The following day word came in from William Henry that the French had landed there with nearly 12,000 troops. The next day, they heard that the French had not begun an attack on the fort and its garrison was "in good spirits and of good courage."[23]

On August 8, 1757, the men at Fort Edward saw:

> the signals that were flung up for signals of distress at Fort William Henry. The Post also said that they had split most of their Cannon, and that they must be obliged to give up the Fort, except they had relief from this Fort. This Express arrived in about ten o'clock, and before he came in, the Cannon ceased, but we knew not the meaning of it. Just at night there came in a Frenchman that belonged to Capt. Thaxter, and he said that the French flag was hoisted in Fort William Henry at eight o'clock this morning; and as soon as he saw it, he jumped over the Breast work and made his escape.[24]

After bombardment by French artillery, Fort William Henry surrendered. The following day, in perhaps the most infamous massacre of 18th century North America, about 1,600 of the Indian soldiers butchered the occupants of the fort, as well as unarmed British soldiers who the French had allowed to leave the fort. The victims included children, women, African Americans, and British-affiliated Native Americans. Rufus Putnam describes the tragedy: "the Indians fell on them, and a most horrid butchery ensued, those who escaped with their lives were striped almost naked. many in making their escape were lost in the woods where they wondered [wandered] several days without food, one man in particular was out ten days, and there is reason to believe some perished, in particular the wounded, but the number murdered & missing was never known to me."[25]

Regarding General Webb and his refusal to send aid to Fort William Henry, Rufus wrote:

> It was the opinion of many officers that he might have relieved the fort, and that he was much to blame for not attempting it, the general idea among us soldiers was that he was a coward, nor did he express more humanity then [than] courage, for he took no care to bury the men butchered in the manner above mentioned, or to seek after the wounded should there be any lying among the dead,—I was on the ground a short time after, and saw the dead bodies lying as neglected as if they had been wild beasts.[26]

Webb's behavior had another effect. Putnam wrote: "The provincials lost all confidence in General Webb, and many of them deserted. I was at one time on the point of deserting but was providentially prevented."[27]

The British army's punishments for desertion were severe. On September 5, 1757, Rufus notes in his journal that two "Royal Americans" were shot for desertion, a Connecticut man whipped 500 lashes, and three Yorkers each given 600 lashes of a total of 1,000 for desertion. The following day, September 6, 60 men from Rufus's camp were sent out on six-day-long scouting missions. It was also the day that on the other side of the Atlantic a boy named Marie-Joseph-Paul-Yves-Roch-Gilbert du Motier was born. About two decades later, Rufus would know him as a fellow officer in the Continental Army—the Marquis de Lafayette.[28]

In October 1757, the provincial rangers at Fort Edward were dismissed. On October 21, Rufus joined a group of carpenters who for another three weeks set about finishing work on the fort. In his journal, Rufus described the structure: "Fort Edward stood on the easterly bank of the Hudson or North River about 66 miles above Albany. The river washed one side of its wall. Its form was somewhat irregular: having two bastions and [two] half bastions. The walls were high & thick composed of hewed timber & earth. A broad rampart, with casement ... a deep ditch with a draw bridge, a covered way."[29]

In November 1757, Rufus and about 360 other troops, were severely disappointed. They would not to be allowed to return to their homes for the winter—instead they were formed into four companies and ordered to posts in the area. Even though their enlistments ran until February 2, 1758, they had expected to be home before the winter snows set in. Rufus related that on January 1, 1758, "we kept the day with joy and wished for Chandlemass [Candlemas]."[30] Still, as he states, the men were "jealous there was a design to hold us in the service longer then our engagement; and being determined to get away if possible."[31]

By this time, concrete plans were being made by the troops to desert. As Rufus states:

> [we knew] that if we attempted it by the common road through Albany we should probably be stopped by the Regular troops in that quarter—our plan was to march by the way of Hoosick; and the snow being now deep and daily increasing, the month of January was employed in preparing snow shoes for the journey. [They hid the snowshoes under the snow.] We lay in huts a small distance from a stockade fort garrisoned by one company of Regulars commanded by Capt. Skene (afterwards Major Skene proprietor of Skenesboro South Bay).[32]

On January 5, Capt. Learned returned from a furlough to his home. He approved of the plan to desert a month later—on February 3—and "pledge[d] himself to head us in the retreat unless he could obtain our discharge." Enlisted man Rufus was impressed—but at age nineteen he was easily influenced by a senior officer. Later, he would change his mind about the man. Putnam wrote: "I then thought much of him, but I have since learned to despise him, for an officer to desert is unpardonable."[33]

On February 2, a letter from General James Abercrombie to Captain Skene was read to the assembled troops. Rufus remembered that it included: "you are hereby required to persuade the Massachusetts men under your command to tarry a few days longer until I Shall hear from their government, and know what their government intend to do with them," and "we were then threatened with death if we went off without a regular discharge; and then ordered to our huts."[34]

At about 3:00 a.m. the next day, about 70 men led by Capt. Learned and a Lt. Walker, silently left the camp. They left at night because they were concerned that if they were discovered leaving, they would be fired upon by the fort's cannon; they weren't concerned with a man-to-man confrontation with the rest of the garrison, because they had the advantage of numbers. Only a Lt. Brown and "a few invalids" stayed behind.[35]

The party was only able to save up food from their "daily allowance," but since they only expected to be traveling about two days on a 30-mile trip to Massachusetts's Hoosick fort, they weren't too concerned.[36] The only problem the first day was the snow—it was deeper than they had expected. As Rufus described, they all wore snow shoes and the first man in line "sunk in half leg deep; about the tenth man had good traveling."[37]

Frostbite and Starvation

The second and third days of the journey, the party was hit with a snowstorm and missed their way to the Hoosick fort. As Rufus writes: "provisions nearly exhausted, weather exceeding cold and stormy. Several men froze their feet, one man fell in the river, and lost one of his snowshoes, by which he suffered much."[38]

On the fourth day, it became clear that they were lost. Capt. Learned spoke to the party: "It evidently appears that we are on a wrong stream and we must be at least 30 miles north of Hoosick Fort ... if any man has a mind to turn back to Stillwater he may go in welcome; for my part, I will sooner die in the woods." Everyone followed him. They were now, unknown to them, at Bennington, Vermont. They climbed several steep hills, the weather was "extremely cold," and the snow was five feet deep.[39]

The fifth day since leaving their camp at Stillwater was February 7. For the past couple of days, the party had been living on a few wild turkeys. Breakfast on this day for 30 of the men, was one "little poor turkey." The remainder of the day they subsided on "beech buds and a few high cranberries."[40]

By the 6th day, most of the men were "feeble, or lame with frozen feet." Only a few of them were fit enough to press down the snow with their snowshoes to create a track for the rest of the party. Starvation is now a real possibility, and as Rufus would later write: "we had one, and but one, dog along with us; he was large and very fat, and this evening he fell a sacrifice to our necessities. Our custom on this march was to encamp ten men at a fire; the dog was carefully butchered and divided into seven parts, except the guts which the butcher had for his fees, these he brought to our fire, and ten of us made a very good supper of their fat without bread or salt."[41]

The 7th day, the ten men of Rufus's group made breakfast of one of the dog's hind feet and part of its leg. Then, their fortunes began to change as the snow was less deep, and they spotted trees that had been cut for shingles. When at sunset they approached a small steam, one of the corporals said it was called Pelham Brook and they were less than three miles from Hawks Fort, on the Deerfield River, which empties into Connecticut River.[42]

Capt. Learned ordered a corporal & two privates to go on ahead to the fort to prepare for the whole party's arrival in the morning. The rest built fires and the ten men at Rufus's fire made a soup from the dog's thigh bone and part of a back bone of pork that they had saved. Rufus remembers: "Seasoned with ginger which relished exceeding well." And notes, "With respect to the meat of a dog I have ever since I had the experience, believed it to be very good eating, and that I could at any time eat it without disgust."[43]

Fifty-two years after this trek, Rufus received a letter dated February 21, 1810, from Stephen Jones, one of the 70 other soldiers. Jones mentions that he had just entered his 72nd year of age and wrote: "I believe your age is not much different from mine." [Rufus was to reach his 72nd birthday on April 9.] In the letter, Jones states:

> For I presumed it would not be unpleasant to you to hear from an old friend, who had been your messmate during the campaign of 1757, and who had waded through the deep snow on the banks of the Hoosick river, and over the lofty mountains of that name, in the cold month of February, 1758, and reduced to the sad necessity of eating dog. Friendships formed on such trying occasions are not easily obliterated, and I assure you that I still feel a lively friendship for you, and have often thought of writing you; but no direct opportunity offering, have hitherto neglected it. You are the only one of my old comrades that I know of who is living. There may be others yet alive, but I do not know where they dwell.[44]

It was the eighth day since the party had set out from Stillwater and as they approached Fort Hawks, several people came out to meet them with bread and sliced meat. Rufus notes that not only was it a friendly act but that "it served to check that rage of appetite by which many have injured themselves by a full meal after long starvation." In his journal Rufus writes: "we arrived at Hawks Fort about ten o'clock, where we were kindly entertained."[45]

Rufus, who at the time was not yet 20 years old, did not fare as badly as most of the rest—many of whom suffered from frostbite. In fact, only Rufus and two other men did not acquire the malady. During much of the journey, Rufus carried fellow soldier Ichabod Dexter's pack because Dexter's feet were frozen. A resident of Hardwick, Massachusetts, Dexter would become an officer in the American Revolutionary War, and part of Shays' Rebellion, for which he was pardoned.[46]

Rufus gives a reason for his relative good health: "yet I was among the foremost in the march, and although hungry yet never failed in vigor and activity, and this I have always thought was owing in a measure to the following circumstance, we had in my mess perhaps a pound of honey in a wooden bottle and after our provisions failed we dipped the end of a rod (not into a honey comb like Jonathan [The son of King Saul in the Bible's first book of the prophet Samuel]) but into the honey bottle and put it to our mouth."[47]

About five days later, Rufus returned to his home in Brookfield, Massachusetts.[48] He notes that Capt. Learned was much blamed for "bringing off his company in the manner he did, nor was he ever able afterward to obtain a commission during that war."[49] He goes on to relate that in the American Revolutionary War, Learned "entered as a colonel, in 1776 resigned, in 1777 was made a Brigadier & resigned soon after the capture of Burgoyne. I never doubted his courage but otherwise he never displayed the Soldier or General."[50]

Given that Ebenezer Learned's hometown of Oxford, Massachusetts, borders Putnam's birthplace of Sutton, and the two men both fought at Dorchester Heights in 1776 and Saratoga in 1777, there are possibly other reasons as well why Putnam held Learned in such low esteem.

The Campaign of 1758

Two months after the long trek in the snow, Rufus was back in action. In April 1758, he volunteered to join Capt. Joseph Whitcomb's company of Colonel Timothy Ruggles's regiment.[51] The political allegiances of Whitcomb and Ruggles in future years could hardly have been more different. While five of Whitcomb's sons were American officers during the Revolutionary War, Ruggles formed a militia company loyal to Great Britain. Forty-six years old at the time Rufus joined his regiment, attorney and Harvard graduate Timothy Ruggles served as a Massachusetts colonel from 1755 through 1757. In 1759 he was promoted to brigadier general. During the Revolution, he left Boston along with the British troops in 1776 and led a company of loyalist militia on Long Island. His Massachusetts estate was confiscated by colonial forces and he settled in Nova Scotia, Canada, where he died in 1795 at age 83.

Ruggles's regiment begin marching from Northampton, Massachusetts, to Albany, New York, on June 3, 1758. Five days later, it arrived opposite Albany. Rufus notes: "From Northampton Street to this place was through a wilderness but one house in whole distance, except [Pantoosuck Fort, on Housatonic River]."[52]

Rufus, now twenty years old, took part in the most important event of his life so far—the British attack on French-occupied Fort Carillon (later renamed by the British, Fort Ticonderoga) in July 1758. His cousin Israel led one of the Ranger units and served as a scout for General George Howe.

On June 12, Rufus was "with the other carpenters of Col. Ruggles Regiment (about 80 in number) detached and sent forward under the command of Lt. Pool. We arrived at Lake George the 22d and were employed in various works there until the army were ready to embark."[53] In his journal, Rufus relates that he helped build two picket forts, floating batteries, and repaired boats.[54]

Disaster at Fort Carillon

Rufus Putnam wrote that on July 5, 1758, "the Army embarked this morning, in Bateaux [flat-bottomed boats], consisting of about 17,000 men, under the command of General Abercrombie, commander in chief, Lord [George Howe (1725–1758)] Howe the Second in command [Howe was the older brother of military commanders Admiral Richard Howe (1726–1799) and General William Howe (1729–1814)], Gen. Thomas Gage the Third, and Col. (John) Bradstreet Qr Master general."[55]

Rufus's descriptions of the commanders are interesting. He describes General Abercrombie as "an old man and frequently called Granne." At least the 52-year-old general appeared that way to Rufus—who was 32 years his junior.[56]

Rufus refers to 33-year-old Lord George Howe as "the idol of the army, in him they placed the utmost confidence, from the few days I had to observe his manner of conducting, it is not extravagant to suppose that every Soldier in the army had a personal attachment to him. He frequently came among the carpenters, and his manner was So easy and familiar, that you lost all that constraint or diffidence we feel when addressed by our superiors, whose manners are forbidding."[57]

"General Gage was a man who never acquired a high reputation, and the furious [43-year-old] Bradstreet was hated by all the Army." Up until that time, this statement was true of the 39-year-old Gage. However, five years later he was put in command of all British military forces in North America and remained in that position until the first months of the American Revolution in 1775.[58]

Rufus continued his narrative regarding the army's maneuvers in July 1758:

> The army moved down the lake until evening when the boats put a shore at Sabbath day point, and after refreshing, put off & rowed all night. July 6th the army landed at the lower end of Lake George, on both sides of the outlet, on our approach, a detachment of French posted on the right or east of the outlet retired without making any opposition—however as soon as a part of the army began to advance into the woods on the west side of the outlet, they were met by a party of the enemy, and a skirmish ensued in which Lord Howe was killed. His death struck a great damp on the army.[59]

Just before the fight, Rufus's cousin, ranger leader Israel Putnam, had cautioned his commander, George Howe, not to place his life in danger. Rufus later learned that Howe died in Israel's arms.[60]

According to David Humphry's biography of Israel Putnam, on the morning of July 7, Capt. Robert Rogers came to the field where Howe had been killed and found that taking the wounded men along with him would be a burden "dispatched every one of them to the world of spirits."[61] Humphreys goes on to comment: "[Israel] Putnam's was not the only heart that bled: The Provincial and British Officers who became acquainted with the fact were struck with inexpressible horror." The evening before Rogers murdered the wounded prisoners, Israel Putnam had comforted them, giving them "all the liquor and little refreshments which he could procure; he furnished each of them a blanket."[62] The differences between Rogers and Israel Putnam were astounding.

Cowardice, Bravery and Honesty

After Howe's death, Rufus was "so panic struck" that he readily agreed to help guard the boats. He remembered only that morning he would have been unwilling to have been assigned that task—he would have wanted an active role in the battle. Soon, he "recovered, at least in a measure, so that I volunteered myself to join the regiment."[63]

Two days after Howe's death, Rufus sought to redeem himself. He notes:

> Late in the after[noon] there was a party called for to carry ammunition forward to the army, then in action, and feeling a little concerned lest my character might suffer for having willingly remained with the boat guard, I volunteered myself on this service (I have heard that some men should say they loved to fight as well as to eat, I never had any such feelings, So far as I am able to judge of myself it was pride and a wish to excel, or at least to come behind none which influenced me at that period of life, to be among the foremost on all locations that offered) when we came to the army we found they had been repulsed at the breastwork in an attempt to storm the enemies' lines, but I had not the least idea of a total defeat—our regiment remained in there breastwork until about midnight and then marched back to the Shore of Lake George where we landed on the morning of the 6th.[64]
>
> July 9th as soon as light appeared we discovered that our regiment was the rear of the army who had all retreated in the night, except the rangers and one regiment of provincials, left near the French lines. about 9 o'clock the army were all embarked, and returned back to the south end of Lake George, and thus ended Abercrombie's expedition with disgrace, and the loss of 1500 men killed, and wounded—at that time I was uninformed of the situation of the works or of the mode of attack, and had I been informed of all this, considering my youth, and inexperience it would have been arrogance to have given an opinion. However afterwards viewing the works and being

informed of the mode of attack, I have judged it the most injudicious and wanton sacrifice of men that ever came within my knowledge, or reading.⁶⁵

Nothing more of consequence was attempted in this quarter this season, except the army commenced building a fort at this place on the ground occupied by the provincials in 1757 during the siege of Fort William Henry, which they called Fort George.⁶⁶

July 22d Col. Ruggles with his regiment marched to Fort Edward, and were employed in repairing the roads from thence to Albany until the 29th of October when they were discharged.⁶⁷

Rufus's journal entry for November 9, 1758, states: "Arrived at Brother Amos Putnam's."⁶⁸ Rufus's memoirs, written decades later, state: "arrived at Sutton, my native Town, where I made it my home for some time thus was I carried through a second campaign enjoying uninterrupted health, the friendship of my officers, and never charged with any crime. But alas in my journal I cannot find any acknowledgment to my Divine benefactor & preserver. Nor do I recollect that I had any serious reflection on the subject."⁶⁹

Campaign of 1759

In April 1759, at age 21, Rufus signed up for his third military campaign. He was assigned to Captain William Paige's company, which was in Lieutenant Colonel Joseph Ingersol's battalion of Colonel Ruggles's regiment.

For almost four months, Rufus had nothing of significance to add to his journal, but then at the end of July, the army under General Jeffrey Amherst (1717–1797) set off for Fort Carillon. The movement went so well and was so different than the disaster of the previous year, that Rufus later wrote it convinced him of the previous "improper mode of attack" and that the soldiers under Abercrombie "who were sacrificed, fell through the want of judgment in the General or the rashness of Colonel Bradstreat."⁷⁰

On July 22, 1759, Rufus writes in his journal, "The army landed this morning about 6 o'clock. The Artillery landed about 10 o'clock on the same wharf that the French Army put theirs off Board in the year 1757." Rafts carried 22 four-pounders, 6 six-pounders and several swivels.⁷¹

Rufus relates the events: "The first Column, part of them with Col. Ruggles (marched) to a point of land Southwest of the Fort. The other part, viz: Major Rogers' Grenadiers and Light Infantry marched on to the Hills between the Mills and the Breast-work, and kept a guard advanced. Ye 2nd column marched and lay to cover the roads from the Landing to the Mills in order to keep the communication clear."⁷²

On July 23, the British took the French breastworks and began entrenching. Rufus relates that the enemy continually fired cannon with little effect. That night, however, one British officer was killed and 12 men were wounded.

At Fort Carillon on July 24, under fire from French cannon, Rufus and the rest of Amherst's men dug trenches outside the fort and prepared their own artillery. On July 26, 1759, the remaining 400 or so French troops left the fort. They attempted to blow it up, but only the gunpowder magazine was destroyed.

The British repaired the fort, renamed it Ticonderoga, and held it until the first year of the American Revolutionary War (1775).

Immediately after the Ticonderoga success, in a move that would be repeated throughout Rufus's military career, he was asked to help construct a sawmill near Lake George. Although he sought to remain with his regiment, the skills he acquired as a millwright continued to be highly prized by his commanding officers. The situation was resolved when "the Brigadier Sent an officer to tell me if I would not undertake or go to work, I Should go to the guard house."[73]

Rufus later wrote: "the Brigadier knew me very well, and I had known him for many years, and I knew it was in vain to contend, nor did I Like to offend an officer whom I So highly respected, and therefore Submitted, however I always esteemed it an arbitrary act, and by no means justifiable to compel a Soldier who is a mechanic to work at his trade against his will."[74]

As soon as the sawmill was completed, Rufus was allowed to rejoin his regiment at Fort Crown Point, which was under construction about a dozen miles north of Ticonderoga. Rufus immediately noticed that one of the carpenters who was working on a block house didn't know how to do "Dovetailing the Corners." As he was instructing the man, the officer in charge, Major Skene, asked who he was. After learning of Rufus's experience, he suggested Rufus work on the Crown Point fortifications. Since it would mean that Rufus would stay with his regiment and go with them if they, as expected, moved to Canada, he enthusiastically agreed. After Skene received permission from General Amherst, he told Rufus that he would be "amply rewarded as a carpenter."[75]

Much to Rufus's dismay, the engineer of the works back at Fort Ticonderoga came to Crown Point and convinced General Amherst to send Rufus back to supervise the sawmills, to see that they were kept in working order. Major Skene told the engineer that Rufus should receive the same pay (one dollar a day) as he would have received working for him at Crown Point.[76]

Two. French and Indian War

Soldier barracks at the Crown Point, New York, fortifications. Militia soldier Rufus Putnam served with the British here during the French and Indian War (author's photograph).

When the provincial troops were discharged a few weeks before their enlistments expired, the quartermaster general, Colonel Robertson visited the sawmills with the engineer in charge. Robertson agreed that Rufus would stay and be paid a dollar per day. At the end of November, Rufus approached the engineer for back pay only to learn he would only be given the dollar rate for his first three days. He was told that he "had Served, but three days over" his enlistment even though the rest of his regiment had been dismissed weeks before. For the rest of his time, he would only receive fifteen pence per day in New York currency.[77]

Years later, Rufus would regret that he "was not so prudent" as Captain Jacobs, a Mohegan officer serving with Rogers Rangers, who requested that the commander put everything in writing.[78]

On December 1, 1759, Rufus, Colonel Miller, Captain Foote and about nine other men set off across Lake George in two boats. Miller brought along two horses and a two-wheeled carriage. Expecting to reach Fort George the following day, they brought along little food. The day started nicely with a breeze to propel them along, but by evening the wind stopped, the temperature plummeted, and they sought refuge near a small island.

The second day, with gale force winds and "waves running mountains high,"[79] they pulled up on the mainland. Rufus wrote: "it never was colder in my remembrance."[80]

On the third day of the expected one-day trip, the food supplies were exhausted and "the cold continuing and hunger increasing." Just then, one of the men found an old black bag on one of the boats with about a dozen pounds of salt pork. Combining this with damaged flour that Colonel Miller had brought along for his horses, they ate boiled pork and dumplings.[81]

On the fourth day, they were pleased to find the wind died down and the lake's surface turn smooth. However, one of the boats began to leak and half-a-foot of ice formed in it, which couldn't be removed. The horses and carriage were transferred to the other boat and, along with chests and baggage, the sides of the boat were only two or three inches out of the water. They were still 20 miles from Fort George, but with calm water they arrived just after sunset.[82]

When Rufus arrived home at Brookfield, Massachusetts, on December 16, he was determined not to volunteer for military serve again. His journal states: "Arrived home to Brother Daniel Mathew's at Brookfield."[83] He was "disgusted at being compelled to leave" his regiment and work at the sawmills. As he explained, it was at a time "when I was ambitious of, and supposed I had a fair prospect of distinguishing myself as a soldier."[84] Since there was no work for a millwright at that time of year, Rufus stayed the winter in nearby New Braintree where he worked on land he had previously purchased.[85]

Campaign of 1760

Three months later, Rufus apparently forgot his resolution to never again enter military service. When in March 1760, a call went out for provincial troops for the new year's campaign, Rufus enrolled in New Braintree's militia company. Captain Paige of Hardwick. Massachusetts asked Rufus to help him raise a new company of troops.[86]

At first Rufus objected. He was not over "the disgust I felt for my treatment the last campaign had not wholly worn off" and he understood some of the "older settlers in town ... appeared very angry and complained that the town was insulted by my appointment, therefore I had very little reason to expect much success in recruiting among them."[87]

After Capt. Paige persisted, Rufus accepted the orders, and eight or nine men signed up immediately. Unfortunately for Rufus, Paige recruited few men himself, and Rufus's men were taken by him to fill his own company. In his memoirs, Rufus states: "From the circumstances I have related let all but especially those unexperienced youth Such as I was, be cautioned how far they trust the friendship of those whose interest it may be to dupe them."[88]

Three weeks later, Col. Abijah Willard presented Rufus with an ensign's commission in his own regiment.[89] Although he had expect to be commissioned a lieutenant given the men he had recruited, Rufus knew it was too late "to refuse an ensign, and I was really obliged to Col. Willard for the appointment."[90]

On June 18, 1760, Rufus joined his company at Fort Ticonderoga, and they were stationed in the area until the end of the year. Rufus later wrote that he regretted that he was unable to be part of the British capture of Montreal on September 8, which marked the British conquest of Canada and the effective end of the French and Indian War.

During this time, Rufus was engaged in engineering work. As he relates: "I was invited by the engineer at Ticonderoga (not the one who abused me the last year as before related) to take the oversight of the mills, and also the erection of a blockhouse where our company was stationed. I agreed with him for at a stipulated price per day which was honorably paid at the close of the campaign."[91]

On November 19, the men of Rufus's company were discharged and they headed back to their homes. Rufus arrived at New Braintree, Massachusetts, on December 1, his service in the war completed.[92]

Chapter Three

Before the American Revolution

Millwright

When Rufus Putnam returned to civilian life, he decided to profit from his background as a millwright. His first step was to buy land with an operational mill. J.H. Temple in his *History of North Brookfield, Massachusetts*, states that Joseph Bartlett sold part of his North Brookfield farm, including "mill privilege, [saw]mill, and tools" on Horsepond Brook to "millwright" Rufus Putnam "on March 3, 1761."[1]

Putnam wrote in his Memoirs: "1761 in March I commenced the Millwright business which I pursued as my chief employment for Seven or eight years, and after that until the revolutionary war commenced in 1775 my business was pretty much confined to farming and Surveying & I also studied Navigation."[2]

Millwrights in the late 18th century were highly skilled people who were much respected in their communities. Scottish millwright and civil engineer Sir William Fairbairn (1789–1874), a millwright in the following century, wrote in his *Treatise on Mills and Millwork*:

> The millwright of the last century was an itinerant engineer and mechanic of high reputation. He could handle the axe, the hammer, and the plane with equal skill and precision; he could turn, bore, or forge with the ease and despatch of one brought up to these trades, and he could set out and cut in the furrows of a millstone with an accuracy equal or superior to that of the miller himself.[3]
>
> He could calculate the velocities, strength, and power of machines: could draw in plan and section, and could construct buildings, conduits, or watercourses, in all the forms and under all the conditions required in his professional practice; he could build bridges, cut canals, and perform a variety of work now done by civil engineers.[4]
>
> The whole mechanical knowledge of the country was centred amongst them, and,

wherever sobriety was maintained and self-improvement aimed at, they were generally looked upon as men of superior attainments and of considerable intellectual power.[5]

With the invention of the steam engine, water was no longer the only source of power and the millwright's job changed. Most of the planning and redesigning began to be performed by engineers, with the millwright's role limited to implementing the engineer's plans.[6]

Rufus Putnam's Family

Soon after returning from the war (on April 6, 1761), Rufus married Elizabeth Ayres, who was the daughter of William Ayers of Brookfield, Massachusetts.[7] A few weeks later, Rufus became ill: "May 14th I was taken Sick of the bilious fever by which I was brought very low but it pleased god to spare my life and in about three months I recovered my health."[8]

Soon his young wife and their son died. Two diary entries tell the story:

> November 16th it pleased god to remove my wife by death, leaving me an infant Son to take care of my feelings on that occasion may be easier conceived then described. however if I did not deceive myself I bore this trial without murmuring against the providence of God[9]
>
> 1762 September 29th God was pleased in his holy providence to remove my little Son (Ayres) by death. thus was I in Less then a year deprived of Mother and Child, and in them as I then thought of all earthly comfort: but I hope I was in Some good measure enabled to ascribe righteousness to my maker[10]

In 1762, father-in-law William Ayers sold 65 acres (which had been in his family since 1720/1721) to Rufus Putnam. Putnam had already built a house on it.[11]

On January 10, 1765, at age 26, Rufus married Persis Rice, daughter of Zebulon Rice of Westborough. Situated east of Worcester, Massachusetts, Westborough was a few miles north of Upton. Born on November 11, 1737, Persis (Rice) Putnam was five months older than Rufus.[12]

In 1768, Joseph Bartlett sold the rest of his farm (not including the mill privilege) to Persis's father Zebulon Rice. On January 4, 1775, Rice sold it to Putnam, who lived there with his family until he moved to Rutland, Massachusetts, in 1781.[13]

In 1770, Rufus Putnam officially joined the First Congregational Church in North Brookfield. While in the town, he served town government and, in 1774, was a member of the local Committee of Correspondence.[14] Between 1765 and 1780, Rufus and Persis had nine children:

This stone marks the location of Rufus Putnam's North Brookfield home, where he lived from 1761 through 1781. All of his children were born during these years (author's photograph).

- Elizabeth Putnam (November 19, 1765–November 8, 1830) who never married.
- Persis (Putnam) Howe (June 6, 1767–September 1822) who was married in 1798 to Deacon Perly Howe (1768–1855) of Belpre, Ohio.
- Susanna (Putnam) Burlingame (August 5, 1768–1840) who was married to Christopher Burlingame (1753–1841). She died in Harmar, Washington County, Ohio.
- Abigail (Putnam) Browning (August 7, 1770–1805) who was married to William Browning (1768–1823) of Belpre, Ohio.
- William Rufus Putnam (December 12, 1771–1855), who was married to Jerusha Guiteau Putnam (1777–1845).
- Franklin Putnam (May 27, 1774–April 1776).
- Edwin Putnam (January 19, 1776–1843) who was married to Eliza Davis.

Martha [Patty] (Putnam) Tupper (November 25, 1777–1842) who was married to Benjamin Tupper, Jr., (1775–1814).

Catharine (Putnam) Buckingham (October 17, 1780–March 1808) who was married to Ebenezer Buckingham.

Referring to Persis Putnam's life in about 1777, Rufus Putnam's biographer, Mary Cone, wrote:

> Mrs. Putnam, with her family of small children, the oldest not more than twelve, lived on a small farm of fifty acres, and those were not of the best or most productive. Colonel Putnam's salary was meagre and not promptly paid. When it was paid, the currency in which it was done, was so greatly depreciated in value that it did not go far toward supplying the wants of the family. Mrs. Putnam eked out their scanty income by the diligent use of the distaff and the needle. Rigid economy prevailed in the household, and industry that would be a marvel to some of the matron's descendants. If the fathers of the Revolution were patriotic, the mothers were no less so. Much they did and more they endured; and inasmuch as patient waiting is more difficult and harder to bear than active serving, they are worthy to be held in grateful remembrance as having had a large share in securing for us a free country, in which the inhabitants are blessed with civil and religious liberty.[15]

Mississippi Expedition

At the end of the French and Indian War, land in the lower Mississippi River area had been transferred from France and Spain to Great Britain in 1763's Treaty of Paris. Land on the east side of the lower Mississippi became part of the British province of West Florida.

In 1763, British King George III issued a proclamation that land grants would be made to veterans of the French and Indian War. The highly respected general Phineas Lyman and other provincial officers who were veterans of the war, applied to the Governor of New York (and possibly the Governor of Virginia) for grants of land. They were informed that the proclamation only applied to regular army troops—not provincials.[16]

Representing a number of New England–area militia veterans, General Lyman traveled to England to seek a grant of land on the lower Mississippi River.[17] The author of the history of Lyman's birthplace put it well when he wrote that Lyman waited "for many long, weary, unrequited years on the British ministry, which put him off from time to time till he learned how disastrous it was for a New England man to seek redress at an English court. He tasted the bitter and ruinous cup to the dregs, and after eleven long years of patient waiting, he returned wasted in health, spirit and fortune and deeply in debt."[18]

Lyman had been reluctant to return without success. He finally was persuaded to leave for home by his eldest son, Capt. Thaddeus Lyman (1746–1812), who traveled to Britain in 1772 and accompanied his father back to Connecticut.

Arriving back home, General Phineas Lyman announced that he had obtained from the British Crown a grant of land east of the Mississippi River between latitudes 32 degrees N and 34 degrees N. Today the Mississippi River border of the State of Mississippi runs from the 31 degree N line to the 35 degree N line. Natchez, Mississippi's latitude is about 31.5 degrees N and Vicksburg, Mississippi's is about 32.3 degrees.[19]

According to Rufus, Lyman assured the veterans that "there was not the least doubt" that the governor of West Florida had orders to grant the land to the provincials. He stated that the British government had assured him that the orders would reach Governor Peter Chester before Lyman could reach America.[20] Although General Lyman had not brought back any written documentation, his fellow veterans (many of whom had served under him during the French and Indian War) believed him.

In response to Lyman's claims, a group of French and Indian War veterans formed what they called the Company of Military Adventurers to scout out the Mississippi lands. Their most famous members were General Lyman and Rufus Putnam's cousin—war-hero Israel Putnam. They chose Rufus to accompany them. Since the French and Indian War, Rufus had taught himself surveying and, in addition to running his farm, had worked as a surveyor during the previous four years.

On December 10, 1772, 34-year-old Rufus Putnam left his Brookfield, Massachusetts, home for his cousin Israel Putnam's house in Pomfret, Connecticut. Rufus left behind his 35-year-old wife Persis, and five children under 8 years old: 1-year-old son William, and 2-year-old Abigail, 4-year-old Susanna, 5-year-old Persis, and 7-year-old Elizabeth. With the benefit of his experience in the French and Indian War, Rufus apparently was not concerned that he would not return. In addition, leading the expedition would be Israel Putnam, who was believed by many to be the most skilled fighting man in the American colonies. Rufus arrived at Pomfret the following day. After making preparations for their trip, Rufus, Israel, and Israel's 13-year-old son Daniel set off for Norwich, Connecticut, arriving on December 16.[21]

The details of the expedition come from two main sources: journals kept by Rufus and by his cousin Israel. Either Israel discontinued writing his journal before trip concluded or the last portion of Israel's was lost. His existing journal entries total only about 6,000 words. Two Rufus Put-

Three. Before the American Revolution 33

nam journals of the expedition still exist. The long one, of about 22,000 words, was apparently written on a daily basis during the trip; the shorter one totally only about 5,700 words is better written and was probably completed at a later time.[22]

The explorers began their journey on December 18, 1772, when the Lyman-Putnam party bought a whale boat in New London, Connecticut, and lashed it to their ship. On the 19th, they sailed for New York City. Arriving there the next day, they prepared for their long sea voyage.

During the period of waiting in New York, Rufus notes business stopped for Christmas, but he didn't attend religious services for "Diverse good Reasons." Possibly the reason was the ongoing smallpox epidemic. Two days later, he stayed indoors "for fear of the Smallpox" and spent the day reading a book that was published first in Denmark. On the 29th Rufus wrote: "lying still at New York but why No Body knows. Walked about 5 mile for my health." That day painting of the sloop was completed, with Rufus noting it had a black bottom and rails, green stern and sides, and the word "Mississippi" printed in gold letters between the cabin windows.[23]

On New Year's Day all business ceased in New York City and "Divine Service attended in the several Churches."[24] The party left New York City for the Caribbean on January 5, 1773. In addition to Rufus Putnam, the company consisted of Israel Putnam, who in two days would reach his 55th birthday, Israel's son Daniel, General Phineas Lyman's son Thaddeus, who was about 26 years old, former French and Indian War militia officer Roger Enos, who was about 43 years old,[25] and a hired man, William Davis. The ship was manned by Captain Wait Goodrich, Mate Samuel Foster, and ship hands Joseph Sheald, Joseph Bickford (Bigford), John Repples, and John Hall.[26]

Rufus writes: "Soon after we Sailed I was taken ... Sea Sick and Continued So many days. Lost much flesh and Strength and have not been able to write till this day being Monday the 25 of January."[27]

Rufus's sea sickness abated by January 30, 1773, when they arrived at Cape Nichala Moles,[28] which was a port on the mountainous northwest part of Hispaniola Island. Nearby was a town of about 300 houses. After five days and some trading with the local inhabitants, they left and headed toward Montego Bay, a port on the north shore of Jamaica. There, Israel confronted a vicious dog as it was attacking another man, but he escaped without injury. They left the island on February 9.[29]

On February 18, they reached the west end of Cuba and spotted a pirate vessel, which they sailed away from, avoiding a confrontation. On

March 1, they arrived at Pensacola in West Florida. There, British Governor Peter Chester (c.1717–1799)[30] and his council welcomed them but informed them that they had not received any orders from London regarding the dispersal of land to veterans of the French and Indian War. Rufus states in his journal: "however the possibility of its yet arriving, with the proposal made for granting Lands to the company, on terms within the power of the governor and Council induced the Committee to resolve on proceeding on the business of reconnoitering the country, on the Mississippi and to make Such Surveys as we might think proper."[31] Rufus, the only surveyor of the Company of Military Adventurers, was made Deputy Surveyor for West Florida.[32]

The minutes of the West Florida Council meetings at Pensacola for March 5, 1773, state "concerning a memorial to Chester from Colonel Israel Putnam, Captain Roger Enos, Mr. Thaddeus Lyman, and Lieutenant Rufus Putnam, who have organized an irregular force of 'Adventurers' to support the West Florida colony, which the Council praised."[33]

On March 18, the party left Pensacola for the Mississippi River. The mouth of the latter was described by Rufus as consisting of brown clay-colored fresh water floating on top of saltwater. On March 20 they anchored off the mouth of the river, but the vessel broke free. With much effort they were later able to secure anchor again. On March 22, they started up the Mississippi, where Rufus made a survey of the mouth of the river.[34]

On the 28th, the company stopped at a plantation owned by a "Monsier De laloiras." With 320 acres and 16 enslaved Africans, it was the largest plantation they had passed. The 72-year-old owner stated that he was the first European born in Louisiana.[35] At this time, Rufus's cousin Israel, never a man of letters, either stopped recording in his journal, or the journal's subsequent entries were lost.

On April 8, Captain Goodrich refused to go any further with his sloop, and the company took a small bateau, and with oars and a sail, and went on alone. The next day was Rufus's 35th birthday.[36] On April 11, they arrived at a settlement of Acadian people who in 1754 had been "removed" by the British from Nova Scotia. It was 71 miles north of New Orleans. Rufus notes in his journal, "April 12th tarried among the Acadians all day and were treated with hospitality—they have a Church a few miles above this on the left bank."[37]

On April 17 they passed Baton Rouge.[38] The company proceeded to pass plantations, a French settlement, an Indian village, and several islands. As the party's surveyor, Rufus meticulously kept a record of traveling distances, the width of streams, and water levels. On April 26, they reached

Natchez [Mississippi], which Rufus estimated was 288 miles north of New Orleans. They came across the ruins of a fort called by Putnam: Rossoline or Rosolen. It was abandoned by the British about four years before and the barracks had been afterwards burned by local tribesmen.[39]

On April 27, 1773, the Putnam party visited settlers on Catherine's Creek. They found the land there good with "Hickory, Walnut, oak, white & yellow ash" and extending from 30 to 40 miles from the river.[40] Unknown to Rufus's party, 4,600 miles away, the British Parliament hours before passed the Tea Act, which triggered American colonist discontent, and led to the Boston Tea Party and the American Revolution. By enacting this law, the British Parliament was attempting to save the failing British East India Company; it was also demonstrating its supreme authority over the colonists by means of imposing a direct tax on their colonies.

Unaware that their expedition would prove fruitless to themselves, the exploring party began to seriously consider the quality of the soils, the available of water, and the other elements that would mark land as promising for settlement. At the home of Thomas James, an Indian trader, Israel Putnam, Thaddeus Lyman, and a Choctaw Indian guide, who they hired, departed by land on an expedition to Walnut Hills on the east side of the Mississippi. Rufus and the others left by boat and arrived at Walnut Hills on May 6.[41]

At one point the Indian guide refused to travel a path from the Yasou to the Big Black River.[42]

Rufus mentions that on May 13 Israel, Lyman and himself:

> Set out by Land, more particularly to examine the high Lands Stretching from the old French Station, before mentioned to the Walnut hills, we Steered our course as near the hills as possible on account of the Cane brakes Saw Several Small Streams issuing from the high Lands, & land very rich, in the afternoon we pursued one of these Streams to Some distance, when we were taken up by a mighty Cane Brake, here Col. Putnam climbed a tree & discovered high Land at about 100 rods distant which we were two hours in gaining, on account of the difficulty of getting through the Cane— here I climbed a tree & had a fine prospect of the Country, the Lands from the Northeast round to the South appear hilly but not Mountainous nor much broken we returned part of the way down the hill & Camped by a very fine Spring.[43]

The three men met up with their boat the next day. Rufus mentions ponds and Cyprus swamps. Exploring the area, Rufus climbed two trees. Going back to the boat, some wanted to again cross a river bend by land but were told that the ponds, swamps and cane made it "impracticable."[44]

When, the party returned to the home of Thomas James's place a week later, James translated for the Choctaw guide. The man related that he had refused to travel the path because he had met two chiefs who "forbid his going" because they did not want the white men to explore lands above the Big Black River.[45] The following day, Rufus, Israel and Lyman set out to explore the lands by the Big Black. They went about 25 miles up the "Six to eight rods wide" river. They found good land, springs and a good location for a mill.

When they again returned to James' place, one of the chiefs of the Choctaw nation was waiting. Showing them his commission from Governor Chester, he said he understood they had been in an area where no white people would be permitted to settle. They met again the next day and the Putnam party asked "how far up the Mississippi their nation had agreed the white people might Settle."[46] He said "at the Last Congress it was agreed the white people Should Settle on the Lousocheto, or BigBlack & not higher."[47]

The Putnam Party then returned down the Mississippi. Rufus provides a "general description" of the country at this time:

> the intervels or bottoms are very rich, with a very deep Soil, but in general & I believe universally Subject to inundation by the waters of the river in high floods. I ground my opinion on this circumstance, that I Saw drift wood Lodged in trees hanging over the Side of the river higher above the Surface of the water then any Land I Saw bordering on the river, except the few hills, or Cliffs, as they are called that join the river. Besides many part of the bottoms are flooded by every considerable fresh in the river, and are also interspersed with many ponds, & Cyprus Swamps, filled with stagnant water, which will be very expensive to drain, & in many instances impracticable.[48]

In the highlands, he found "Hickory & oaks of all kind Bottoms, Locoust, Willow, the Cotton tree—Copalm, Ash, Mulberry, the royal Magnolia, or high Laurel with Cyprus in abundance."[49]

Always the millwright, Rufus saw: "very few Small Streams, none fit for Mills—the Mill Seat on the Big Black is the only one I Saw or heard of in the country."[50]

The birds observed included turkeys, "plenty" of duck, winter geese, and pigeons. Wild game consisted of deer and bear. Several kinds of fish were found and an abundance of alligator was observed in the Mississippi and the streams visited.

On June 12, 1773, they stopped for 16 days about four miles above New Orleans for repairs to the sloop. They then sailed for Pensacola, which they reached on July 5. The governor informed them that during their explorations he had received letters from England, but nothing in them referred to the granting of land to militia veterans of the French and Indian War.

Minutes of the West Florida Council meetings at Pensacola for July 9,

Three. Before the American Revolution

1773, state: "concerning petitions of 'Colonel Israel Putnam, Roger Enos, Rufus Putnam and Thaddeus Lyman on behalf of themselves and the Company of Military Adventurers' and of the same persons 'and their associates' relating to exploration up the Mississippi River and proposed settlement at the confluence of the Mississippi and Yazoo rivers; concerning petition of Wait Goodrich and his associates relating to the Company of Military Adventurers' settlement plans."[51] The men were dispirited/disappointed that no word came from England regarding a land grant that would compensate these veterans for their military service during the French and Indian War. The exploration party decided to return home; Rufus Putnam was unaware that his initial survey of these uncharted lands as recorded in his maps and journal would become valuable to others in the future.

On June 22 the hired man of the expedition, William Davis, was taken ill to the hospital. Each day for a week the others would visit him, but when they left on the 29th, he decided that he might have a relapse and stayed behind. On July 5, the Company presented to the West Florida governor and his Council their plan for nineteen townships off the Mississippi River. Four days later, the Council informed them they were limiting "the time of reservation to the first of March."[52]

The Party headed back home, but Rufus was so seasick at the end of the month that he was unable to keep up with his journal. He remarked it "always attacked [him] whenever we had a fresh Breese of wind, or a rough Sea."[53]

They arrived at New York on August 6 and the three Putnams boarded another sloop for the trip to New London, Connecticut, where they switched to a rowboat for the short stretch to Norwich. On August 12 they arrived on horseback at Israel Putnam's farm. Rufus returned home to Massachusetts the following day.

The two Putnam cousins had gone on the longest journey of their lives, but the future held more important challenges. In less than two years, Israel's reputation for patriotism and courage would reach new heights with his inspirational leadership at the Battle of Bunker Hill, and in less than three years, the engineering brilliance of Rufus Putnam would lead to all British troops evacuating Boston without a fight.

Based upon reports of the Putnam Party, a meeting was held in Hartford where it was resolved to initiate settlements on the Mississippi area lands. According to Rufus: "several hundred families left from Massachusetts, Connecticut, and 'other places.'" However, the next parties traveling to West Florida found that about six months earlier the "King in Council" had sent an order to the governor prohibiting him from granting any more lands either "on settlement or purchase."[54]

Subsequently, the land office in Florida was shut down before most other New England settlers arrived, and it was never reopened. Any settlers who did appear in West Florida were told they could "Set down on any vacant Land they could find."

The captain of the Military Adventurers' ship was apparently one of the people who went back to the Mississippi lands. The *Connecticut Courant* issue of December 14, 1773, stated: "Last Sunday sailed from Middletown [Connecticut] the Sloop *Adventurer*, Wait Goodrich Master, with about Thirty Passengers to settle on the Banks of the Mississippi." And the *Connecticut Courant* issue of April 26, 1774, reported that the passengers of the sloop *Adventurer* (with its captain Wait Goodrich of Connecticut) were "all in perfect Health and high Spirits, on the Prospect of … ample Fortunes speedily on the land which they are going to settle on the Mississippi."

In December 1773, General Phineas Lyman, who spent almost a decade in Britain trying to obtain land grants, and who was the driving force behind the Company of Military Adventurers, traveled to Natchez with a few other settlers. Sadly, Lyman died on September 10, 1774. The year after General Lyman's death, a grant of 20,000 acres of land was issued by the Crown to Thaddeus Lyman and two other sons and two daughters of General Lyman. Rufus notes in his Memoirs: "Those who emigrated in 1774 arrived generally too late in the Season, to expect health in such a Change of Climate, Soon fell Sick many died."[55]

Nothing ever came of the nineteen townships Rufus had surveyed in 1773. However, in 1802, some Connecticut men approached the United States Congress with a claim for at least some of these townships on the grounds that they had settled them in 1774. Congress rejected the claim.[56]

Rufus and his cousin Israel never received any land along the Mississippi River from the British government. Twenty months after they returned to New England, the American Revolutionary War began as colonial militia solders and British troops battled each other at Lexington and Concord Massachusetts. The subsequent military service of the Putnam cousins in support of American freedom made it certain that the British government would never give them, or any of their close relatives, any land. At the end of the war, the land they had surveyed passed from Great Britain to the new American government.

Rufus Putnam lamented in his journal: "the result to my self was the Loss of more than eight months time in the tour, besides two journeys to

Hartford."⁵⁷ However, the expedition would prove to be the longest he would take in his life, and it served as a valuable preparation for the explorations he would take 15 years later—to virgin lands west of the Ohio River.

Although Rufus never received any land as a result of the Mississippi expedition, he never forgot the possibility of war veterans receiving "military bounties" in the form of land grants. After the Revolution he would pursue that idea with the new American government.

Forty-three years after the Mississippi expedition, in 1816, the issue of land grants to veterans of the "Old French War" was again in the news. A southern U.S. newspaper had run an advertisement that stated a Captain Irwin had a "certified copy" of the King's Proclamation which granted lands to Provincial veterans of the French and Indian War. It excited much interest among the surviving veterans and their descendants. To get to the facts of the matter, Timothy Whiting of Massachusetts wrote to 78-year-old Rufus Putnam. Replying from his Marietta, Ohio, home, Putnam wrote that the advertisement "contains a gross imposition on the public" and related the events preceding, during and after his Mississippi expedition.⁵⁸

Appearance and Personality

In 1806, at age 23, future historian and physician Samuel Prescott Hildreth (1783–1863) traveled by horseback from his home in Massachusetts to Marietta. Rufus Putnam was 68 years old at the time. Within two years, Hildreth married Rhoda Cook in nearby Belpre and they settled in Marietta where he opened his medical practice. In 1852, Hildreth's *book Biographical and historical memoirs of the early Pioneer Settlers of Ohio* was published. In it he described Rufus Putnam's appearance:

> In person, Gen Putnam was tall, nearly six feet; stout, and commanding: features strongly marked, with a calm, resolute expression of countenance, indicating firmness and decision, so peculiar to the men who figured in the American revolution: eyes grey, and one of them [his right eye] disfigured by an injury in childhood, which gave it an outward, oblique cast, leaving the expression of his face strongly impressed on the mind of the beholder.⁵⁹

Almost all portraits of Rufus Putnam that were made by people who knew him are left-side profiles that do not show his right eye. An exception is a miniature portrait made by John Trumbull for his painting *Surrender of General Burgoyne*. Both the miniature and the final large painting (which shows 26 identifiable officers in addition to Putnam) show Putnam's right eye from an angle. Interestingly, Trumbull himself suffered an injury in childhood that left him blind in his left eye.[60]

British artist James Sharples, Sr. (1751–1811), created a portrait of Rufus Putnam in the late 1790s. Appearing in uniform, Putnam is painted with a green sash denoting his former rank of colonel. Later, an unknown person(s) added two items: a one-star epaulette to Putnam's shoulder signifying his promotion to brigadier general and a Society of the Cincinnati eagle medal on his lapel.[61]

Dr. Hildreth, who knew Putnam for the last 18 years of the latter's life, describes the general's personality and his impact on his fellow citizens:

> His manner was abrupt, prompt, and decisive; a trait peculiar to the Putnam family, but, withal, kind and conciliating. In conversation, he was very interesting; possessing a rich fund of anecdote, and valuable facts in the history of men and things with which he had been familiar; delivered in a straightforward, impressive manner, very instructive and pleasant to the hearer. The impress of his character is strongly marked on the population of Marietta, in their buildings, institutions, and manners; so true it is, that new settlements, like children, continue to bear through life, more or less, the impressions and habits of their early childhood.[62]

Using Hildreth and many other sources, historian David McCullough was able to write in his *The Pioneers:* "Rufus Putnam was said to have had a stormy temper—it was thought to have been one of his few human flaws—but seldom if ever seen."[63]

In a September 17, 1898, address, U.S. Senator George F. Hoar stated:

> Rufus Putnam was one of those men, rare in all generations, perhaps more rare now than formerly, who seem to be almost absolutely without care for self. He seems to have been indifferent to fame. He had little use for the first personal pronoun in his speech or his writings. He was content to accomplish useful results. He was intent upon the goal, not upon the prize. If he could accomplish useful results, he cared nothing for the pride or glory of the achievement. Among the chief elements of his greatness is his great unconsciousness. So much the more is it the duty of posterity to guard his fame and pay him his due meed [a deserved reward] of credit and honor.[64]

Sarah Cutler Dawes (1809–1896) was the granddaughter of Ohio Company leader the Rev. Manasseh Cutler, and the "seat mate and special friend" of Sophia Tupper, Rufus Putnam's granddaughter. When they both attended school in Marietta, Sophia would live at Putnam's house. [This is the Rufus Putnam house that is today enclosed within Campus Martius Museum in Marietta]. Sarah Dawes states:

> I was often at his house with Sophia, and I remember staying there once all night. I often saw Gen. Putnam and talked with him. Once Miss Betsey introduced me as Ephraim Cutler's daughter. He shook my hand a long time and said, "You are Ephraim's

daughter." He was quite deaf; he seemed to me a very fine looking man, but feeble with age. He was very erect in his carriage and dignified in manner, and I thought he walked like a soldier. He asked a blessing at the table standing himself at the head of the table, while we all stood behind our chairs. At night he had family prayers. We all stood up during the service which was conducted by the General. The house was well furnished but not better than others of the same class.[65]

Sarah Dawes continues with other observations:

I often saw him in church; he would walk up the aisle with great dignity and all the people seemed to pay him great deference. Liquor was used in Gen. Putnam's house as was the case everywhere else. Rufus P. Browning told me that he once took a drink of liquor and his grandfather, Gen. Putnam, saw him and said, "Do not touch another drop of liquor," and this had a great influence over him for he never did. General Putnam dressed like other people.[66]

In 1836, twelve years after Rufus Putnam's death, Jonas Reed used the word "genius" to describe Rufus Putnam in his *A History of Rutland: Worcester County, Massachusetts*: "General Putnam was a valuable officer in the American Revolution—of a solid and penetrating genius; one whose judgment and plans, his fellow officers valued and relied on."[67]

Two years later, John Wilson Campbell (1782–1833), judge of the United States Court for the District of Ohio,[68] wrote "In person, he was tall, and of commanding appearance; muscular, bony, and athletic; eminently fitted for the hardships and trials of war. His mind, though not brilliant, was solid, penetrating, and comprehensive, seldom erring in conclusions."[69]

It is difficult to reconcile the "though not brilliant" with other descriptions of Putnam, especially the "brilliant" elements of his life as a military commander and statesman. Campbell's short biographical account of Putnam's life was found by Campbell's widow among his papers and published five years after his death. The depth of Campbell's knowledge of Rufus Putnam is open to question. Campbell was a notable figure in early 19th century Ohio, and thus must have had many occasions to encounter the elderly general. However, Campbell was not yet born during the key moments of Putnam's service in the American Revolutionary War. And when 50-year-old Rufus Putnam led the party of 47 pioneers to found Ohio's first settlement in 1788, Campbell was only six years old.

Was Putnam both a genius and "not brilliant"? As a member of the Democratic-Republican Party which was co-founded by Thomas Jefferson, it's possible that Judge Campbell took Jefferson's blatant libel of Putnam back in 1803 (see Chapter Eight) at face value. In order to justify the firing of the long-time Washington-appointed U.S. surveyor general, Jefferson, as was sometimes his custom, was harsh and unfair.

Writing 62 years after Rufus Putnam's death and 53 years after Judge Campbell's death, Mary Cone in her 1886 Rufus Putnam biography stated [bold print added]:

> It is scarcely necessary to sum up the character of this man, whose life has been thus imperfectly sketched. His work is his best epitaph and eulogium. He was **not brilliant**, he was not quick, but he was richly endowed with that best of gifts—good, sound, common sense, and he had, in unusual degree, that prescience that enabled him to skillfully adapt means to ends, so as thereby to accomplish what he wished. Always modest, he "leaned not to his own understanding," but constantly recognized his need of help from on high. His judgment was sound, he was patient and had great power of endurance. His integrity was never questioned; he was always found on the side of the right, and no good cause was ever brought before him from which he willingly turned away.
>
> His personal appearance was imposing. He was courtly in his manners, after the old style of gentlemen, though oftentimes a little abrupt, after the manner of the Putnams. Being a much experienced man, he was very interesting as well as instructive in conversation. He had a large fund from which to draw, for he had seen much of distinguished men, and of many important events he could say, if he would, quorum magna pars fui [in which I played a large part].[70]

Perhaps one way to assess the phrase "not brilliant" is to look at what has been said of some of America's greatest individuals. Writer Peter H. Gibbon in a 1998 *Baltimore Sun* article on George Washington, stated [bold print added]: "Washington also inspired respect from those who knew him best. He was **not brilliant** like Hamilton nor eloquent like Jefferson. He lacked Franklin's originality and Madison's insight. But our first president had character."[71]

During Franklin Delano Roosevelt's first campaign for the U.S. presidency, one Groton [college preparatory school] graduate mentioned to another that he remembered Franklin as [bold print added]: "a quiet, satisfactory boy of more than ordinary intelligence, taking a good position in his form but **not brilliant**."[72]

Chapter Four

Washington's Chief Engineer

Brewer's Regiment

On the eve of the American Revolutionary War, in 1774, Rufus Putnam was commissioned Captain Lieutenant of Grenadiers in the Massachusetts militia.

On April 19, 1775, the American Revolutionary War began when British troops fired upon Massachusetts militia units at the battles of Lexington and Concord. Subsequently, British forces were confined to the Boston peninsula and surrounded by land-based American forces.

The site of the Battle of Concord was only about 60 miles northeast of Rufus Putnam's North Brookfield home. Putnam volunteered to serve as a Lieutenant Colonel in Colonel David Brewer's regiment,[1] which was under General John Thomas.[2] Rufus didn't know it at the time, but he would remain in that position from June 17, 1775, to December 1775,[3] and he would serve in the American forces until the end of the war—seven years later.[4]

On June 17, 1775, the Committee of Safety at Cambridge, Massachusetts, recommended that Rufus Putnam be commissioned by Congress.[5] Brewer's regiment was stationed at Roxbury a few miles south of Boston, which was a relatively exposed location. General Thomas and his staff gave priority to fortifying their position in case of a surprise attack, and also to protect the town itself.

Rufus wrote that on June 17 "The general [General Thomas][6] and field officers ... met in Council, to advise what was best to be done in our exposed Situation. It was the unanimous advice of the officers convened, that Some Lines of defense should be immediately commenced for the Securing the troops from surprise & protection of the town."[7]

General Thomas attempted to obtain the services of Continental Army's Chief Engineer, Col. Richard Gridley,[8] but he was fully occupied with the defenses of Cambridge, Massachusetts. Rufus Putnam's name was raised as someone who had military engineering experience in the French and Indian War. Rufus at first objected that he had "never read a word on the subject of fortification" although he had worked "under British engineers in the last war."[9]

Nevertheless, he was convinced to undertake the work. As Putnam would later write, the American forces had: "No lines to cover us better than a board fence in case the enemy advanced upon us, and that was what we had every reason to expect." He "immediately began tracing out lines in front of Roxbury, towards Boston, and various other places on the Roxbury side, particularly at Sewell's Point."[10]

One day, Commander-in-Chief Washington and Major General Charles Lee arrived to examine the troops and fortifications "on the Roxbury side of the river." Putnam wrote: "I was much gratified and encouraged by their approbation of the plan of the works I had laid out. General Lee said much in favor of the works at Sewell's Point, compared with those that had been constructed on the Cambridge side." Putnam proudly relates: "The works laid out at Roxbury, Dorchester and Brookline were all of my constructing, and late in the fall I laid out the Norton Cobble Hill, near Charleston mill pond."[11]

But this was just the beginning. As Rufus says, he went on and "surveyed & delineated the courses, distances and relative situation of the enemy's works in Boston & Charlestown with our own in Cambridge, Roxbury, etc."[12]

General Lee was so impressed that in December he asked Putnam to accompany him to Providence and Newport. That trip led to Putnam laying out fortifications there, "particularly a battery from whence to command the harbor, and some works near Howland's Ferry to secure the command."[13]

In October 1775, Col. Brewer faced a court martial for "procuring a Lieutenant's Commission for his son, an inexperienced boy of 16 or 17 years of age" and for accepting his son's pay while the boy was not serving. Brewer was also charged with ordering more blankets than were required by his regiment and using soldiers under his command "in his own private business, in Labour on his farm." He was found guilty of the supplies and labor charges and dismissed from the Continental Army as of October 23, 1775.[14] As Brewer's senior officer, Rufus Putnam took over command of the regiment, and headed it up until December 1775.

At the end of 1775, Putnam was commissioned a lieutenant colonel in the 22nd regiment under Colonel Samuel Wyllis. However, his engineering skills were too much in demand, and he never joined the regiment.

It was then that Putnam was instructed by General Charles Lee to construct fortifications in Rhode Island. Even more important was Putnam's upcoming work for the American Commander-in Chief.[15]

Dorchester Heights

On June 17, 1775, the British troops won the Battle of Bunker Hill, but they suffered great casualties and in the following eleven months were unable to move inland from the city of Boston. Their existence in the city depended upon support and resupply from the sea. The siege ended when the British left Boston for Halifax, Nova Scotia on March 17, 1776.

George Washington didn't play a part in the Battles of Lexington and Concord, nor in the first days of the Boston confrontations—he was not commissioned Commander-in-Chief of the Continental Army until June 19, 1775. However, his leadership was critical in ending the siege of Boston.

In November 1775, General Washington sent 25-year-old Colonel Henry Knox and his men to Fort Ticonderoga, New York, to bring back cannon that had been captured earlier in the year from the British. Using "80 yoke" of oxen, Knox's men delivered 59 cannon to Boston, an incredible wintertime journey of 300 miles. It's impossible to determine exactly how many militia and volunteers he engaged, since many only helped out on part of the journey.[16]

At the beginning of 1776, Washington was concerned with driving the British forces from Boston. It had been about six months since the Battle of Bunker Hill and Washington had them bottled in with only two avenues of escape: to leave by sea or to plow through the American forces which surrounded Boston.

The low hills south of Boston, known as Dorchester Heights, were so barren that neither the British nor the Americans had dared to erect fortifications there. The British, in particular, remembered when less than a year earlier they had suffered heavy casualties when they attacked the Americas on another Boston hill—Breed's Hill, in what would come to be known as the Battle of Bunker Hill.

The Americans under Washington were reluctant to attempt occupation of Dorchester Heights—they were fearful the enemy would notice and immediately demolish the American positions. In addition, by the time

Knox arrived with the cannon, it was the last week of January 1776 and winter weather was at its coldest and the first two feet of ground were frozen. Also, the harbor below the Heights was iced up and ships carrying food and supplies would need to wait for weeks before deliveries could be made to Boston.

In January 1776, it might have been possible for Colonial troops to cross the ice to attack Boston. Washington still considered the feasibility of occupying the highest points just south of the city—Dorchester Heights, so that the British might be drawn out of the city and be open to Washington's larger forces. General officers were asked to solicit the opinions of their officers.

At this time, Rufus Putnam was invited to dinner at Washington's headquarters. During the meal, Washington asked Putnam to stay behind after the others left. As Putnam later wrote: "when we were alone he entered into a free conversation on the subject of storming the town of Boston."[17]

Perhaps the best alternative would be to occupy Dorchester Heights and achieve a towering presence over the city of Boston as well as the British ships in Boston Harbor. In that situation, the enemy might actually find it best to sail away without a fight.

However, it was a two-edged sword. As Rufus wrote, he and Washington considered that: "the cold weather which had made a bridge of ice for our passage into Boston, had also frozen the earth to a great depth, especially in

Monument at Dorchester Heights. It was here that Rufus Putnam's fortifications were placed to drive the British troops from Boston in early 1776. The American forces held the city for the remaining years of the war (author's photograph).

Four. Washington's Chief Engineer

the open country such as was the hills on Dorchester Neck—so that it was impossible to make a lodgment there in the usual way." Washington asked Rufus to consider the situation and if he came up with a solution to report it to him "immediately."[18]

After leaving headquarters with another officer, Rufus Putnam passed General William Heath's quarters. As Putnam noted: "I had no other motive but to pay my respects to the general." While there Putnam spotted a book on a table. Its title caught his eye—*Muller's Field Engineer*. He was curious, but General Heath wasn't the kind of man to loan out his books. As Putnam relates it:

> I immediately requested the General to lend it me. He denied me. I repeated my request. He again refused, & told me he never lent his books. I then told him that he must recollect that he was one, who at Roxbury in a Measure compelled [me] to undertake a business which at the time I confessed I never had read a word about, & that he must let me have the book. After some more excuses on his part, close pressing on my part, I obtained the loan of it.[19]

When Putnam arrived back at his place after dark, he didn't have time to read the book—workmen were waiting to report the day's progress to him. In the morning, Putnam took out the book and the word "chandeliers" caught his attention. He had no idea what it meant. In Putnam's words: "but no sooner did I turn to the page where it was described with its use but I was ready to report a plan for making a lodgment on Dorchester Neck."[20]

Shortly afterward, Putnam met with the Continental Army's Chief Engineer, Colonel Richard Gridley, and its chief artillery officer, Henry Knox. They supported Putnam's plans, and Washington approved them.

Putnam's idea was to build the "chandeliers"—above-ground fortifications that could be set up on the frozen soil of Dorchester Heights. Soldiers prefabricated wooden frames composed of ten-foot-long timbers and five-foot-high posts. The frames that would be filled with bundles of fascines [brushwood].

On March 4, 1776, General Washington directed his troops to place the Ticonderoga cannon on Dorchester Heights. Critical to his plan were the prefabricated fortification devices that Rufus Putnam had constructed. Putnam, Washington and the generals were confident that they would work.

At the beginning of March 1776, American troops dragged the cannon from Roxbury, Massachusetts, to Dorchester Heights. They probably saw the lifting of the cannon up the icy sides of Dorchester's hills as a relatively minor task compared with the incredibly arduous journey that

Knox and his men had made across Western Massachusetts' Berkshire Mountains.

On the night of March 4, 1776, General John Thomas and about 2,000 men with 360 oxcarts of fortification materials ascended Dorchester Heights. They installed Putnam's chandeliers, and positioned many of the cannon that Knox and his men had retrieved from Fort Ticonderoga. They even painted logs black to appear from a distance to be additional cannon.

In the morning, the British were shocked. Their commander, General Howe, is believed to have said that the Americans had done more in one night than his army would have done in six months.

Faced with cannon overlooking them, within days about 11,000 British troops under General William Howe, along with about 1,000 colonial residents who were loyal to the British, boarded the fleet of British ships, left Boston to the American forces, and headed to Halifax, Nova Scotia, Canada.

In the 19th century, the Dorchester hills were razed to provide fill for Boston Harbor. In 1898, the state legislature funded the construction of a monument on the last remaining hill—a white marble tower to mark the 1776 fortifications.[21]

After Putnam's remarkable success at Boston, General Washington had more than enough work lined up for him. On March 31, 1776, the Commander and Chief wrote:

> You are hereby Order'd to march to New York, by the way of Providence—When you arrive at Providence you are to deliver Governor Cooke the Letter directed for him and afford him your best advice and assistance in the Construction of the Works there. At New York you are to apply to the Commanding Officer of the Continental Forces & follow such Orders & directions as you may from time to time receive from him.

At the same time, Washington sent along this note to Governor Nicholas Cooke:

> The Bearer Colo. Putnam, who has been employed as an Engineer in the Army under my Command, is now on his Way to New York; I have order'd him to wait upon your Honor to afford you such advice & assistance in the Construction of your Works as his time will permit. You will find him capable and ingenious, & I am happy in having this opportunity of sending you an Officer of such experience.

George Washington

After the success of the Dorchester Heights fortifications, Washington understood the value of an officer like Rufus Putnam.

Four. Washington's Chief Engineer

Virginian George Washington was six years older than Rufus Putnam, who until the Revolutionary War had lived his whole life in Massachusetts, but they had many things in common. Both were veterans of the French and Indian War. Both were Freemasons and descendants of 17th century English immigrants.

They both owned farms, although Washington's was vastly larger. They were both surveyors. According to the Geography and Map Division of the Library of Congress, "Between 1747 and 1799 Washington surveyed over two hundred tracts of land and held title to more than sixty-five thousand acres in thirty-seven different locations."[22]

Washington and Putnam even had deficiencies in common. Both were notoriously poor spellers. Fortunately, it was an age when many of the most respected people were poor spellers and a deficiency in spelling, punctuation and grammar was not a serous handicap for an intelligent, talented, and industrious person.[23]

Most importantly of all, Rufus was like a younger brother to Washington. He was a man Washington could rely on to undertake a wide variety of military missions—and complete them successfully. Over the course of his service in the Revolutionary War, Rufus commanded regiments at major battles (including Saratoga), risked his life as a spy (Westchester County, New York), and provided his Commander-in-Chief with information that was of the highest importance to the success, and sometimes even the existence, of the Continental Army.

While undertaking research for his book, *The Pioneers*, historian David McCullough stated: "If I were doing a biography of Washington and I could interview two or three people, [Rufus] Putnam would be one of the first people I would interview."[24]

On this trip to Rhode Island, Putnam worked on construction at Newport and then moved on to New York to layout and oversee "the works which were erected during the campaign, at New York, Long Island & their dependencies with Fort Washington, Fort Lee, King Bridge &c." Many years later, Putnam remembered, "this was a service of much fatigue, for my whole time was taken up from daylight in the morning until night in the business, besides sometimes going in the night by water from New York to Fort Washington."[25]

In July, Washington found new work for Putnam—in New Jersey. The Commander in Chief wrote to Congress:

> General Mercer is now in the Jerseys for the purpose of receiving & ordering the Militia coming for the Flying Camp, and I have sent over our Chief Engineer, to view the Ground within the Neighbourhood of Amboy and to lay out some necessary works for

the Encampment, and such as may be proper at the different passes in Bergen Neck and other places on the Jersey Shore, opposite Staten Island, to prevent the Enemy making impressions & committing depredations on the property of the Inhabitants.[26]

But the Washington letter that would most change Rufus Putnam's life was this one to the Board of War on July 29, 1776:

> Rufus Putnam acts here as a Chief Engineer, by which means the Regiment is totally deprived of his services, and to remove him from that department, the public would sustain a Capital Injury: for although he is not a man of scientific knowledge, he is indefatigable in business and possesses more practical knowledge in the art of Engineering than any other we have in this Camp or Army. I would humbly submit It therefore to Congress, whether It might not be best to give him (Putnam) the appointment of Engineer with the pay of sixty dollars per Month: less than which I do not suppose he would accept as I have been obliged in order to encourage him to push the business forward in this our extreme hurry to give him reasons to believe that his Lt. Colo. pay would be made equal to this sum.[27]

When in August 1776, Congress appointed Putnam as Engineer, Washington wrote to him. As was often the case throughout Rufus's life, Washington was his chief supporter and advocate.

> To Colonel Rufus Putnam
>
> New York Augt 11th 1776.
>
> Sir,
>   I have the pleasure to inform you that Congress have appointed you an Engineer with the Rank of Colonel, and pay of Sixty Dollars per Month.
>   I beg of you to hasten the Sinking of Vessels and other obstructions in the River at Fort Washington as fast as it is possible—advise Genl [Israel] Putnam constantly of the kind of Vessels you want and other things that no delays that can possibly be avoided may happen. I am Sir Yr assur'd friend & Servt.
>
>   Go: Washington
>
> P.S. Congress have just sent two French Gentn here as Engineers will either of them be of use at Fort Washington or Kings Bridge?[28]

In his Memoirs, Rufus looked back on these days:

> My being appointed engineer by Congress was wholly unexpected—I had begun to act in that capacity through pure necessity and had continued to conduct the business more from necessity & respect for the general then from any opinion I had of my own abilities, or knowledge of that art; true it is that after my arrival at New York I had read some books on fortification & I knew much more then when I began at Roxbury but I had not the vanity to suppose that my knowledge was Such as to give me a claim to the first rank in a corps of engineers, yet my experience convinced me that such a corps was necessary to be established, therefore near the last of September, I drew up a plan for such an establishment & presented it to General Washington, and which he transmitted to Congress.[29]

That October 5, 1776, letter by Washington to Congress included this section:

Four. Washington's Chief Engineer

I have taken the liberty to transmit a plan for establishing a Corps of Engineers, Artificers &c. sketched out by Colo. Putnam, and which is proposed for the consideration of Congress. How far they may incline to adopt It, or whether they may choose to proceed upon such an extensive scale, they will be pleased to determine; However I conceive it, a matter well worthy of their consideration, being convinced from experience and from the reasons suggested by Colo. Putnam, who has acted with great diligence and reputation, in the business, that some establishment of the sort is highly necessary and will be productive of the most beneficial consequences.[30]

General George Washington as he appeared in 1776. During the American Revolutionary War, Washington relied on Rufus Putnam to undertake a variety of military missions. When he became U.S. president, Washington appointed Putnam the first Surveyor General of the United States (courtesy White House Historical Association).

By this time, Rufus Putnam was certainly proving his worth. About two weeks before this Washington letter, Rufus had ridden with General Thomas Mifflin to reconnoiter "the country between Kingsbridge [Located about seven miles north of Harlem, today it is part of the northwestern Bronx.] & Morrisania [Located about three miles north of Harlem, today it is part of southwestern Bronx.] & eastward on our return we met with General Washington near Harlem heights, where we made our report to him in consequence of which a council of general officers was convened, whose advice was the withdrawing the army from the city ... this measure was the Salvation of the army, and which probably would not have been but for the discoveries made by Mifflin & myself."[31]

In November, Washington gave Putnam a series of orders:

To Colonel Rufus Putnam

                        Headquarters Whiteplains November 5th 1776

Sir
    you are directed to repair to wrights Mills, & lay out any work there you conceive to be necessary in case it is not already done; from thence you are to

> proceed towards Croton Bridge, and post the two Regiments of Militia in the most advantageous manner, So as to obstruct the enemies' passage to that quarter. you are also to give what directions you think are proper to those regiments, respecting the breaking up the roads Leading from the North river [Hudson River] eastward. after this you are to go up to Pekes Kill and direct Lashers detachment to break up the roads there, you are likewise to Lay out what works will be advisable there & order them to be Set about. Given under my hand at [headquarters]. Go Washington.[32]

Although Rufus Putnam's work for Washington was of great importance, he still sought to actively fight for his country. He remembered well how disappointed he had been when he was sidelined to work on construction during the French and Indian War.

On December 8, 1776, Rufus wrote the Commander-in-Chief that he had accepted command of a regiment in the Massachusetts line of the Continental Army, and was commissioned a colonel. Washington responded with: "Your Letter of the 8th Instant from Peakskill came duely to hand. your acceptance of a Regiment to be raised on continental establishment by the State of Massachusetts bay, is quite agreeable to me, and I Sincerely wish you success in recruiting & much honor in Commanding it;—your professions of attachment are extremely pleasing to Dear Sir your most obedient Servant Go WASHINGTON."[33]

On December 20, 1776, Washington mentioned Putnam in a letter to Congress:

> I have also to mention, that for want of some establishment in the department of Engineers agreeable to the plan laid before Congress in October last, Colo. Putnam who was at the Head of it, has quitted and taken a Regiment in the State of Massachusetts. I know of no other man tolerably well qualified for the conducting of that business. None of the French gentlemen whom I have seen with appointments in that way, appear to me, to know anything of the matter. There is one in Philadelphia whom I am told is clever, but him I have never seen.[34]

It is believed Washington was referring to Polish military engineer Thaddeus Kosciuszko (1746–1817). Thomas Jefferson once called Kościuszko "As pure a son of liberty, as I have ever known."

In January 1777, Rufus traveled to Massachusetts to recruit his regiment and was "pretty successful." By May, three of the regiment's company's marched from Worcester, Massachusetts, to Peekskill, New York, and in June to Fort Ann, which lay east of Lake George, New York. In July, Rufus marched with the rest of his regiment to a spot near Fort Edward, which was south of Lake George.

The last time Rufus had seen Fort Edward was in 1760—the final year of his service in the French & Indian War. Putnam wrote: "the last time I saw it when standing, it appeared as it really was a very strong fortification—but now alas its remaining walls & ditch would afford no cover in case of an attack." Now, in 1777, with years of military engineering experience from two wars behind him, Putnam knew as well as anyone how to evaluate military fortifications.[35]

Fortifying the Hudson River

Early in 1776, months before the Battle of Brooklyn, the Americans built Fort Stirling on Brooklyn Heights next to the East River as Washington began moving troops to Brooklyn, New York.[36] On the east side of the village, Washington built three forts to support Fort Stirling: Forts Putnam, Greene,[37] and Box.[38]

The northernmost of the three forts, star-shaped Fort Putnam, with its five guns and five companies of soldiers, was surrounded by a ditch with pointed stakes. It was named for Rufus Putnam.[39] The Americans also "set up a mounted battery on Governors Island" and constructed nearby Fort Defiance.

In 1776, American troops fortified a site on the west side of the Hudson River opposite the north end of Manhattan Island, calling it Fort Constitution. Later, the name was changed to Fort Lee to honor Major General Charles Lee. Opposite the fort, (on Manhattan Island's highest point—a 230-foot cliff), they built a second fortification in the summer of 1776—Fort Washington. Most of the construction of Fort Washington was performed by Pennsylvania soldiers under the supervision of Rufus Putnam.[40]

Rufus Putnam was fulfilling Washington's directive "to hasten the Sinking of Vessels and other obstructions in the River at Fort Washington as fast as it is possible" to slow down the passage of British ships, so that they could be fired upon by the artillery in the forts. Putnam directed the sinking of old ships in the Hudson River. In addition, he constructed sharp wooden stakes in Brooklyn and floated them to a spot between the forts.[41]

Regarding Putnam's Fort Washington, a 1901 article in the *New York Times* stated "everything that could be done to destroy it has been done." It goes on to say "The City has blasted a modern carriageway through the two eastern bastions, and has destroyed the southerly breastworks." The article lamented the neglect of the site: "even the flagpole which once marked the site has been removed, and the place left to a melancholy solitude and natural decay."[42]

Fifty-five individuals have held the title Chief Engineer of the Army between 1775 and 2019. That is an average tenure of almost four and a half years. Richard Gridley (a colonel when appointed) was the first, Rufus Putnam (a lieutenant colonel when appointed) was the second. Three other men were appointed in the late 1700s: a major, a lieutenant colonel, and a brigadier general. Only colonels were appointed in the 1800s up until the Civil War. Since then all Chief Engineers have held the rank of general.

The Battle of White Plains

The second half of 1776 was a time of setbacks for General Washington's forces as they were pursued by the British through New York, and into New Jersey.

After Washington's main army was forced to retreat from western Long Island, Manhattan and Harlem, it ended up north of Harlem in the fall of 1776. Although at the Battle of Harlem Heights the American forces were able to successfully stop the British frontal attacks, it was mostly the British who won the battles.

An officer in the British 64th Regiment wrote to a friend: "The rebel army are in so wretched a condition as to clothing and accoutrements, that I believe no nation ever saw such a set of tatter-de-mallions [ragged wretches]: there are few coats among them but what are out at elbows, and in a whole regiment there is scarce a pair of breeches; judge then how they must be pinched by a winter campaign."[43]

The British officer did find one thing not lacking on the American side: "As to provisions they have been pretty well supplied; more care has been taken of their bellies than their backs."[44]

As Washington moved north from Harlem, British General William Howe attempted to cut off the American retreat. He sent about 4,000 thousand British and German soldiers by boat up the East River to the marshy peninsula of Throgs Neck (in the southeastern Bronx). However, Washington cut off connections to the mainland, effectively stopping him.

On October 19, Howe's troops returned to their boats and landed further north at a place called Pell's Point. It was there that 44-year-old Colonel John Glover of Massachusetts was able to delay the enemy long enough for Washington to move the main body of his army out of harm's way.[45]

North of Manhattan, at the village of White Plains, New York, there was a key American supply depot. Its loss could prove catastrophic to the

Four. Washington's Chief Engineer

American effort. On October 20, Washington dispatched Colonel Rufus Putnam on a mission to ascertain the location of the British forces.

The next morning Putnam set out from Kingsbridge to reconnoiter the enemy position. With him were Colonel Reed, the adjunct general, and a foot guard of about 20 men. When they arrived on the heights of East Chester, they saw a small body of British near a church, but they could obtain no intelligence. Nearby houses were deserted.[46]

Colonel Reed told Putnam that he needed to return to camp to issue general orders. Seeing how they had not discovered anything important on their mission, Putnam told Reed to take the guard back with him, because he wanted "to go alone." It was then that Putnam undertook one of the most dangerous roles of his military career—as a spy. He explained:

> I then disguised [hid] my appearance as an officer as far as I could, and Set out on the road to White Plains. However, I did not then know where White Plains was, nor where the road I had taken would carry me. I had gone about 1½ mile, when a road turned off to the right, I followed it perhaps a mile & came to a house, where I learned from the woman that this road Lead to New-Rochelle that the British were there & that they had a guard at a house in Sight.[47]

After obtaining directions from the woman, Putnam continued on to White Plains. Finding all of the houses along the way deserted, he approached a house with men next to it about three or four miles before White Plains. Through his spyglass, Putnam could see that they were not British soldiers. Cautiously, he approached them and asked for oats for his horse. As he sat down, he listened carefully to their conversation. Satisfied that they were "friends to the cause of America," Putnam "began to make the necessary enquiries—& on the whole I found that the main body of the British Lay near New Rochelle."[48]

Given that New Rochelle was only about nine miles of "good roads" and "in general level open country" from White Plains, it would not take long for the British to reach the depot. At White Plains they would find "a large quantity of Stores, with only about three hundred militia to guard them." In addition, a detachment of British troops was positioned only six miles from White Plains at Mamaroneck, and "five or Six of the enemies' Ships & Slops, tenders &c" was only five miles away on the Hudson River.[49]

With this knowledge, Putnam needed to return to his lines without being discovered. He continues:

> having made these discoveries I Set out on my return, the road from Wards across the Bronx was my intended route unless I found the British there, which happily they were not, but I Saw American on the heights west of the Bronx, who had arrived there after I passed up—I found it to be Lord Stirling's Division. it was now after Sunset. I gave My Lord a short account of my discoveries took Some refreshment, & Set off

> For headquarters, by the way of Philips, at the mouth of Sawmill river, a road I had never traveled, among tory inhabitance & in the night. I dare not enquire the way, but providence conducted me.[50]

Putnam arrived at Army headquarters near Kingsbridge at about 9:00 p.m. He had ridden more than 50 miles.[51]

He immediately sought out the Commander-in-Chief:

> I found the General [Washington] alone. I reported to him the discoveries I had made, with a Sketch of the country. he complained very feelingly of the Gentlemen from New York from whom he had never been able to obtain a plan of the country—that from there information he had ordered the stores to White plains as a place of Security.[52]

Hearing that British General Howe was invading Westchester, Washington immediately sent for Generals Nathanael Greene and George Clinton.[53] Putnam recalls: "as Soon as General Clinton came in my sketch and Statement was Shown to him & he was asked if the Situation of those places were as I had reported,—genl Clinton Said they were."[54]

But Rufus Putnam's work that day wasn't over. Washington gave him an additional order—to see to it that Lord Stirling moved his men south to reinforce Washington's army. Rufus detailed the situation: "I had but a Short time to refresh my Self & Horse when I received a Letter from the General with orders to proceed immediately to Lord Stirling's, and I arrived at his quarter about two o'clock in the morning."

Putnam then proceeded with Lord Stirling's Division to White Plains, where they arrived at about nine o'clock a.m. and established an adequate guard over the critical supplies. Putnam wrote about the "stupidity of the British general in that he did not early on the morning of the 20th send a detachment and take possession of the post & stores at White Plains for had he done this we must then have fought him on his own terms."[55]

Looking back years later, Putnam recognizes the critical importance of their actions:

> October 21st 1776—Lord Stirling Division Marched before daylight & we arrived at the White Plains about 9 Clock AM—and thus was the American army Saved (by an interposing providence) from a probable total destruction. I may be asked wherein this particular interposition of providence appears. I answer, First in the Stupidity of the British General in that he did not early on the morning of the 20th Send a detachment and take possession of the post & Stores at White plains for had he done this we must then have fought him on his own terms, and such disadvantageous terms on our part as humanely Speaking must have proved our overthrow.[56]

While Rufus was joining Stirling, General Washington traveled to White Plains to check on the safety of his supplies and to examine the terrain in preparation for an expected battle.

Four. Washington's Chief Engineer

In his old age, Rufus Putnam looked back on his foray into spying with perhaps a greater realization of the risks he confronted than he had in 1776:

> when I parted with Col. Reed on the 20th as before mentioned, I have always thought I was moved to So hazardous an undertaking by foreign influence—on my rout I was Liable to meet with Some British or tory parties, who probably would have made me a prisoner, (as I had no knowledge of any way of escape across the Bronx but the one I came out) hence I was induced to disguise myself by taking out my cockade, Loping my hat & Secreting my Sword & pistols under my Loose coat, and then had I been taken under this disguise the probability is that I Should have been hanged for a Spy.[57]

Rufus Putnam's spying mission is not as well-known as those of other Revolutionary War American spies, such as Benjamin Tallmadge, who created a spy ring for Washington, tavern owners Austin Roe and Robert Townsend, and African American double agent James Armistead Lafayette.

Washington moved his headquarters to White Plains on October 23. Soon afterward, he sent Colonel John Haslett[58] and Virginian Major John Green with 600 and 150 men respectively to attack and defeat Robert Rogers' Loyalist troops on Heathcote Hill in Mamaroneck.[59] French and Indian War legend Rogers had earlier been denied a Continental Army command by Washington and chose to fight for the British instead, forming a ranger unit he named the Queen's Rangers.

In the days before the battle. Washington's commanders arrived with their troops: Major General John Sullivan's division, General George Clinton's brigade, and General John Morin Scott's brigade.

On October 28, General Howe moved his British and Hessian forces toward White Plains. The morning of October 28 he sent columns under General Henry Clinton and Hessian commander Leopold Philip de Heister against the American defenses. The American soldiers had dug entrenchments across the line of hills above the town.

Washington moved about 1,000 men under Major General Joseph Spencer of Connecticut toward the British, giving Washington time to occupy Chatterson's Hill. Spencer's men barely made it back to the American defense line. Washington stationed himself at a location he expected to be at the heart of the upcoming battle. At another location—Purdy's Hill—Rufus Putnam's cousin, Major General Israel Putnam, was in charge.

With approximately 3,000 men, Washington was faced with about 5,000 enemy troops. As this was going on, Rufus Putnam was supervising the fortification of 180-foot-high Chatterson's Hill for the right wing of the American Army. He explains:

They commenced a severe cannonade but without any effect.... General McDougall about this time arriving with his Brigade from Burtises, & observing the British to be crossing the Bronx below in large bodies in order to attack us, our troops were posted to receive them in a very advantageous position. [In 1890, a Revolutionary War cannon was found in White Plains and put on display next to Chatterton Hill in 1926. After it was stolen on two separate occasions, a replica cannon was mounted onto a boulder at the foot of Chatterton Hill, where it sits today. A plaque on the side of the monument reads: "Near this spot the British under Howe forded the Bronx River and attacked the right wing of Washington's Army located above on Chatterton Hill. Erected by act of Congress, May 18, 1926."][60]

The British forded the Bronx River [At the time, it was far wider and deeper than in the 21st century] and moved about 4,000 men and artillery up against between 1,600 and 2,000 American troops on the hill. Commanded by Brigadier General Alexander McDougall,[61] the American forces consisted of Continental Army soldiers from Connecticut, New York, Delaware, and Maryland, as well as militia from Massachusetts, Connecticut, New York, and New Jersey. Although they possessed only two pieces of artillery, many of the American soldiers were seasoned—within the past few months, they had gained an incredible amount of experience at the Battles of Long Island and Harlem Heights, as well as at Throg's Neck and Pell's Point. The two artillery pieces on Chatterton Hill were commanded by a future American Founding Father—Alexander Hamilton. Although only about twenty years old, Hamilton was already an artillery captain.

Putnam later explained:

> The British advanced in front of our Lines at White plain about 10 Clock AM—I had just arrived on Chatterton hill in order to throw up Some works when they hove in sight. As Soon as they discovered us they commenced a Severe cannonade but without any effect of consequence. General McDougall about this time arriving with his Brigade from Burtises, & observing the British to be crossing the Bronx below in Large bodies in order to attack us, our troops were posted to receive them in a very advantageous position.[62]

The British moved at least a dozen cannon to a hill neighboring Chatterton. The Americans were successful in stopping the first British advances. Only the addition of Hessian forces and British cavalry turned the tide. The absence of bayonets among the American troops was a key factor in their confrontation with the British horse soldiers.

Although the American militia was forced to retreat, it was an orderly retreat—not the kind of action the British had come to expect of inexperienced militia soldiers. Rufus Putnam relates the situation:

> The British in their advance were twice repulsed, at length however their numbers were increased so that they were able to turn our right flank. We lost many men but

from information afterwards received there was reason to believe they lost many more then we the rail & Stone fence behind which our troops were posted proved as fatal to the British as the rail fence & Grass hung on it did at Charlestown the 17th of June 1775 [the Battle of Bunker Hill].[63]

Washington led his retreating men to Purdy Hill, where he and General Israel Putnam prepared for another British assault. However, General Howe did not follow-up after his taking of Chatterton Hill, and the Americans were able to make a clean retreat from White Plains. Three days after the battle, an anonymous American soldier wrote:

> The scene was grand and solemn, and the adjacent hills smoked, as though on fire, and bellowed and trembled with a perpetual cannonade and fire of field pieces, hobits [small mortars on gun carriages], and mortars; the air groaned with streams of cannon and musket shot; the air and hills smoked and echoed terribly with the bursting of shells; the fences and walls were knocked down, and torn to pieces, and men's legs, arms, and bodies, mangled with cannon and grape shot, all round us.[64]

At White Plains, each side suffered about 50 fatalities and between 150 and 200 wounded or captured. Perhaps more significant than anything else, the Battle marked the last chance the British Army would have to surround Washington's army and end the Revolution in one battle.

After the battle, Rufus was given new orders by General Washington:

> After the affair of the 29th of October my time was employed in examining the nature of the country in a military point of view in our rear towards North Castle, Croton River &c until about the 5th of November when I received the follow order from the general which I Shall take the liberty to transcribe.[65]

From his headquarters at White Plains, General Washington wrote to Putnam:

> Sir
>
> you are directed to repair to wrights Mills,[66] & lay out any work there you conceive to be necessary in case it is not already done; from thence you are to proceed towards Croton Bridge, and post the two Regiments of Militia in the most advantageous manner, So as to obstruct the enemies' passage to that quarter you are also to give what directions you think are proper to those regiments, respecting the breaking up the roads Leading from the North river [Hudson River] eastward after this you are to go up to Pekes Kill [Peekskill][67] and direct Lashers detachment to break up the roads there.[68] You are likewise to Lay out what works will be advisable there & order them to be Set about.[69]

Heavy rain for days after the Battle of White Plains turned roads into muddy ravines, slowing the British pursuit of Washington's main army. Not able to catch it, Howe returned south and captured Fort Washington on November 16, taking close to 3,000 prisoners. Four days later, he took Fort Lee, which was across the Hudson, but by then the American troops had already evacuated the facility on orders from General Washington.[70] Washington's quick evacuation of Fort Lee had barely saved that portion of his army.

On November 11, 1776, Washington arrived at Peekskill and Rufus Putnam accompanied him to Fort Montgomery. Afterwards, Washington "crossed the North river" [Hudson River] and left instructions for Rufus to "ascertain the Geography of the country with the roads & passes through, & about the high lands, a report of which I afterwards made with a Sketch of a plan."[71]

The Battle of Saratoga

After the Americans failed to capture Quebec in 1775–1776, thousands of British soldiers remained in Canada. In 1777, a decision was made to move many of these troops south to join up with General William Howe's force that would move north from New York City. If successful, the combined British force could control the Hudson River and isolate New England from the rest of the colonies.

In the summer of 1777, 55-year-old British General John Burgoyne led about 10,000 soldiers, loyalists, and Native American allies south. They captured Fort Ticonderoga on July 6, 1777, and Fort Edward on July 31.

General Burgoyne stopped at Saratoga, New York, with a little over 7,000 troops, while the commander of the American forces, 50-year-old Major General Horatio Gates, camped only four miles away. Gates had about 9,000 soldiers. The American army built fortifications on Bemis Heights—a ridge of bluffs that overlooked the Hudson River on its west side.

The Battle of Saratoga included two battles: one on September 19 and one on October 7. At the First Battle of Saratoga, also named Battle of Freeman's Farm, Burgoyne divided his forces into three columns—two of British Solders, one of German troops. The center column was confronted with Virginian Colonel Daniel Morgan's light infantry and riflemen.[72] The battle raged on until late in the day when Burgoyne ordered his German soldiers to support his central column. Although the Americans retreated, the British suffered twice as many casualties.

After retiring from the field, Burgoyne waited for General Henry Clinton to come up from the south with reinforcements. Clinton never showed up. Dangerously short on supplies, Burgoyne couldn't wait any longer and attacked the American forces. Thus began the Second Battle of Saratoga, also called the Battle of Bemis Heights.

When on October 7, Burgoyne attacked, the American forces had reached a strength of over 12,000 fighting men. After the casualties the British suffered less than three weeks earlier, they had fewer than 7,000.

Major General Benjamin Lincoln headed the Right Wing of the American Army and Horatio Gates had the left wing.[73] At the Battle of Bemis Heights, General Lincoln commanded brigades that were under brigadier generals John Glover (1732–1797), John Nixon (1727–1815), John Paterson (1744–1808), and Jonathan Warner (1744–1803).

Colonel Rufus Putnam commanded the 5th Massachusetts Regiment in Nixon's brigade.[74] Putnam was familiar with the Saratoga area. He had been there in June 1757 when serving in Capt. Ebenezer Learned's company during the French and Indian War. Now, two decades after that war, at the second battle of Saratoga, that same Ebenezer Learned, was now a brigadier general, and commanded one of the three brigades in Major General Horatio Gates' left wing of the army.

As the fighting raged on, Simon Fraser, one of Burgoyne's top generals, fell mortally wounded. American General Benedict Arnold, then 36 years old, was instrumental in capturing the British's Breymann Redoubt, which enabled the Americas to move behind British lines.

At the Battle of Bemis Heights, Colonel Rufus Putnam, then 39 years old, was positioned with the Massachusetts 5th and 6th regiments. When the orders were given to storm the German reserve troops, Putnam's men raced across an open field and entered the front of the German works. Putnam moved his regiments out of the works toward the "enemy's enclosed redoubt" on the right flank of their main camp. As Putnam relates in his memoirs, "General Learned, as soon as he had secured and sent off all the plunder taken in this camp, withdrew all the other troops without bidding me a good night." That night General Glover joined Putnam "with three regiments from the right wing of the army."[75]

On October 8, Burgoyne attempted to retreat north, and reached the village of Saratoga. However, the American forces, now over 15,000 men strong, surrounded him. Burgoyne surrendered his troops on October 17. It was the first time the British had surrendered an army during the American Revolutionary War, which at the time of Saratoga, had been raging for two-and-a-half years. Burgoyne returned to England after Saratoga, resumed his position in the House of Commons and was not given another command in the remaining 15 years of his life.

The Battles of Saratoga are considered by many the turning point of the American Revolutionary War. When the leaders of France heard of the American victory, they decided to support the latter's cause financially and militarily.

Rufus Putnam's map of the Saratoga battlefield, "An Orthographical View of the American and British Armies on the 7th & 8th of October 1777," is "the only known contemporary American map of the battlefield and the American fortified camp."[76]

The Putnam map showed both British and American positions. A copy of it, likely made in the 1950s, exists today, but the location of the original map is not known.[77] Detailed maps of the British and German positions do exist. They were made by British engineer William C. Wilkinson.

John Trumbull's 1821 painting *Surrender of General Burgoyne* portrays 27 American, British, and German officers, including Rufus Putnam. Putnam is pictured in the group of five officers to the immediate right of the central figure, General Gates. Around Putnam are: Colonel William Prescott of Massachusetts (1726–1795) (who is best known as an American commander at the 1775 Battle of Bunker Hill, and who, along with Rufus Putnam's cousin Israel Putnam, is often credited with arguably the most famous command of the Revolutionary War: "Do not fire until you see the whites of their eyes."); Colonel Daniel Morgan of Virginia (1736–1802), who as much as anyone, was responsible for the success at Saratoga,[78] Lt. Colonel John Brooks (1752–1825) who was known for leading an successful Assault on Hessian positions at Saratoga and later serving as governor of Massachusetts; and Chaplain Enos Hitchcock (1744–1803) of Rhode Island. Like Rufus Putnam, the Reverend Hitchcock's life after the war was noted for his support of religion and education, and his opposition to slavery.

The Trumbull painting is on display in the United States Capitol's rotunda in Washington, D.C. A smaller version by Trumbull hangs in the Yale University Art Gallery in New Haven, Connecticut. A 1994 U.S. Postal Service one-dollar stamp featured the Capitol's version.

Putnam's Rock

An article in an 1822 issue of *The American Journal of Science and Arts* mentioned the incident of New York's "Putnam's Rock," which occurred in June 1778.[79] At the time of this article's publication, Rufus Putnam was still alive, and living in Marietta. In a February 5, 1822, letter

Four. Washington's Chief Engineer

to the editor, James Freeman Dana, the first professor of chemistry and mineralogy at Dartmouth College, referred to an account given to him by his friend Col. Tucker of Gloucester, Massachusetts, who had been a Lieutenant in Rufus Putnam's regiment in 1778.

It seems there was a well-known rock on the top of 1380-foot-high Butter Hill, which was a few miles north of West Point on the Hudson River. It was described by Tucker as appearing in the morning fog as like "a horseman's tent or hospital marquee riding on the cloud."[80]

It was common for off-duty officers to amuse themselves by climbing the hills and rolling down large rocks. They often hit up against other rocks causing tiny avalanches. This caused "great terror to those persons who were below." One day after

Rufus Putnam appears in the rear center of this portion of the John Trumbull painting *The Surrender of General Burgoyne*. At Saratoga, Colonel Rufus Putnam commanded the 5th Massachusetts Regiment in John Nixon's brigade. Completed in 1821, this painting hangs in the Capitol Rotunda in Washington, D.C. (courtesy Architect of the Capitol).

officers came down from a "rolling," Putnam proposed they check out the horseman's tent rock. It was found to be sitting on a large flat rock "near the brink of a considerable precipice." Putnam expressed the belief that it could be moved and would tumble all the way down to the river.[81]

A few days later, Putnam led a party of officers (including Tucker), and their servants, to the top of the hill, bringing with them axes and ropes. They cut trees for levers and attached ropes to them. Putnam ordered the men to pull the ropes at his cry of the word "Congress." As the huge rock rolled off its platform and down the hill, the men "had the satisfaction of seeing the most majestic oaks and loftiest pines bowing down in homage and obedience to this mighty traveler which never stopped till it reached the bed of the river."[82] The rock landed far enough from the shore for ships to sail around it.

Tucker continues: "The party followed after in its path and were astonished to see that rocks of many tons weight and trees of the largest size were ground to powder."[83] In celebration of their feat, between sixty and seventy men of the party gathered on the rock as Col. Putnam broke a bottle of whiskey, christening it "Putnam's Rock."[84]

In the 1800s, the entire mountain was renamed Storm King, with Butter Hill now the name of its eastern summit.[85]

West Point

At the beginning of 1778, Rufus was asked by his cousin, Major General Israel Putnam, and New York Governor (and General) George Clinton to supervise construction on fortifications at West Point on the west bank of the Hudson River. Washington also brought in a brilliant Polish engineer, Col. Thaddeus Kosciuszko, who devised a system of small forts.

In March 1778, Rufus was ordered with his regiment, to proceed to West Point to design and supervise new fortifications. Prior to this, a "French" engineer had worked on the West Point plans, but in the words of Rufus Putnam, "his plans were entirely disapproved of by Governor Clinton & the General officers."

It was determined that a battery along the river "to annoy the shipping" was more appropriate than the Frenchman's design. It was decided to build a chain of small fortifications on the high ground bordering the West Point plain. Rufus predicted that it was capable of being made a "very strong place."

Rufus Putnam directed his men, as well as troops of General Alexander McDougall, to build a major fortification on 500 feet above sea level hill that commanded the West Point plain. Gen. McDougall wrote "The hill which Col. Putnam is fortifying is the most commanding and important of any that we can now attend to ... the eastern-most face of this work must be so constructed as to command the plain on which Colonel Putnam's regiment is now encamped."[86]

General McDougall named it Fort Putnam after Rufus. Putnam remained at West Point until June 1778 and was then sent with his regiment to join General Horatio Gates army at Peekskill, New York. From there the army proceeded to White Plains.

Four. Washington's Chief Engineer

View of the Hudson River from Fort Putnam at West Point. This fort was not designed to fire on ships on the Hudson River; its main function was to protect the lower-lying forts beneath it from an overland attack. Constructed in 1778 by Rufus Putnam and his men, the fort was named for Putnam by General Alexander McDougall (author's photograph).

Before President Thomas Jefferson signed legislation establishing the military academy in 1802, the West Point plateau on the Hudson River's west bank was only known as a critical military location. Before 1778, it was not even known as that—since it lacked fortifications. During the American Revolutionary War, the Continental Army's Commander-in-Chief, General George Washington, considered it to be the most important strategic position in America.

In 1775, somewhat less than one-half of the two-and-a-half million people in the 13 colonies—lived in New England. The rest lived in the Middle Atlantic and southern states. The only large cities—today they would be the size of towns—were Boston, Massachusetts, New York, New York, Philadelphia, Pennsylvania, and Charlestown, South Carolina.

For the American patriots to win a war with Britain, it was necessary that its armed forces be well supplied. Anything less and the war could

Interior of West Point's Fort Putnam. A bronze plaque at the fort recognizes the contribution of Rufus Putnam: "Fort Putnam, Built In 1778 by Colonel Rufus Putnam's Regiment of Massachusetts Infantry. Rebuilt and Enlarged 1794. Restored 1909" (author's photograph).

be lost in months or even weeks. Since different colonies produced different combinations of material items, it was necessary that the supply lines between the colonies, as well as between the colonies and the Continental Army be open and free of obstructions. For example, the factories of New England were primarily responsible for furnishing the army with clothing, armaments, and ammunition.

If the Hudson River, which runs parallel with the western border of Connecticut, Massachusetts, and Vermont, were to fall entirely into British hands, with the Continental Army stationed in New York or New Jersey, there would be a serious problem. (The bulk of the Continental Army usually was in New York or New Jersey from early in 1776, when the British troops left Boston, through 1779–1780 when the fighting shifted to the southern states.) The British could then close off river crossing sites, which usually had ferry service. They could also run the length of the river with their naval force.

Four. Washington's Chief Engineer

There were many times Washington quickly led his army away from dangerous situations. If he had been prevented from crossing the Hudson or not able to have access to it to move troops swiftly, he might not have been able to survive during those times. General George Washington called West Point the "Key to the Continent" and sought to fortify it to prevent British ships from sailing north or south along the Hudson River. He even spent a good deal of his time during the war in the vicinity of West Point.

Another consideration involved British troop positions. With the American army controlling the Hudson above New York City—in the Hudson Highlands—the British couldn't afford to move too many men from Canada to the American colonies. If they did, Washington might attempt another invasion of Canada. He was unsuccessful before, but with a larger number of troops, he might succeed the next time. It was especially significant since most of his soldiers—both the regulars in the Continental Army and the state militia troops—were now far more experienced in warfare.

Fortifications had already been started on the east side of the Hudson River opposite West Point by Netherlands-born engineer, surveyor, cartographer, and soldier Bernard Romans. However, given the commanding position of the terrain on the west side of the river, Romans' works were deemed inadequate. Romans was well-know at the time as an active patriot, and the surveyor of what are now the U.S. states of Florida, Alabama, and Mississippi.[87]

In order to prevent the British from traveling up and down the Hudson River (or even worse, occupying the West Point location), in 1778 Washington arranged for Thaddeus Kosciuszko to design fortifications at West Point.[88] Continental Army troops were directed to construct forts, batteries, and redoubts[89] at the location. Meanwhile, a massive iron chain was stretched across the river from West Point to Independence Island on the east bank of the Hudson.

In 1779, Washington moved his headquarters to the now well-defended location. For the rest of the war, the British never captured West Point. The American forces, however, did come close to losing it on one occasion—through treachery. Continental Army general Benedict Arnold, who was in command of the West Point fortifications, made arrangements to turn them over to the British. He failed, his accomplice, Major John André, was executed by the Continental Army as a spy, and West Point continued to serve as an important military position. Today, West Point is the oldest continuously occupied military post in the United States.

Fort Putnam was constructed of large logs. The parapets were made of fascines [brushwood] and packed earth. In 1794, the fort was strengthened, and in 1910 it was restored as an historical site. It was restored even more completely at the time of the 1976 bicentennial, when 14 replica cannon—some iron, some brass—were installed.

Located on Crown Hill, Fort Putnam's main function was to protect the forts beneath it from overland attack. It was not designed to fire on British ships on the Hudson River. The forts below it included: Fort Arnold (with its batteries and Sherborne's Redoubt) were to the northeast of Fort Putnam, and the closer Fort Webb, Fort Wyllis (Wyllys), and Fort Meigs, which were to the southeast of Fort Putnam. The latter three forts protected Fort Arnold from a ground-level assault along the Hudson River, covered the ground going from the three forts to Fort Putnam, and protected each other.

Fort Clinton, first named Fort Arnold after American general Benedict Arnold, on the West Point plain, was named after General James Clinton, whose brother George was the colonial governor of New York. It was designed and partially constructed by Louis de La Radiere of Washington's corps of engineers[90] and completed under the supervision of Thaddeus Kosciuszko (1746–1817) between 1778 and 1780.

Fort Wyllis was named after Colonel Samuel Wyllis of the 3rd Connecticut Regiment. Wyllis was an almost exact contemporary of Rufus Putnam, born the year after Putnam (January 7, 1739—Gregorian Calendar) and dying the year before Putnam. He is often referred to by his Connecticut militia title of "Major General."[91]

Fort Meigs was named after Connecticut-born Col. Return Jonathan Meigs, Sr. (1740–1823), who had a distinguished record during the American Revolutionary War: he was on the Benedict Arnold expedition to Canada, where he ended up a prisoner of war, he was with General Anthony Wayne's force at Stony Point, and he conducted a 1777 raid on British forces at Sag Harbor, New York, where his forces destroyed 12 ships and captured 90 of the British without the loss of a single man.

Sherburne's Redoubt was built in 1778 by Colonel Henry Sherburne's regiment to protect the back approach to Fort Arnold, western approaches to the West Point Plain and "northern approaches to Fort Putnam."[92]

Redoubt 4 was located on Rocky Hill to the west of Fort Putnam. After its 1778 construction, Fort Putnam's garrison included about 420 soldiers as well as artillerymen.

Today, West Point is known world-wide as the location of United States Military Academy. West Point graduates have included generals Ulysses S.

Four. Washington's Chief Engineer 69

Grant, William Tecumseh Sherman, Robert E. Lee, John J. Pershing, Dwight Eisenhower, Douglas MacArthur, George Patton, Norman Schwarzkopf, 20 astronauts, and 74 recipients of the Medal of Honor.

Rufus Putnam's fortifications at West Point are mentioned in James Kirke Paulding's 1818 poem "The Backwoodsman":

> A lovelier landscape caught the gazer's view,
> Softer than nature, yet to nature true.
> Now might be seen, reposing in stern pride,
> Against the mountain's steep and rugged side,
> High Putnam's battlements, like tow'r of old,
> Haunt of night-robbing baron, stout and bold,
> Scourge of his neighbour, Nimrod of the chase,
> Slave of his king, and tyrant of his race.
> Beneath its frowning brow, and far below,
> The weltering waves, unheard, were seen to flow
> Round West Point's rude and adamantine base,
> That call'd to mind old Arnold's deep disgrace,
> Andre's hard fate, lamented, though deserv'd.[93]

Today, the U.S. Army Corps of Engineers counts Rufus Putnam as the first District Engineer for its New York District. A bronze plaque at the U.S. Military Academy at West Point's Fort Putnam recognizes the contribution of Rufus Putnam to the Continental Army's defenses:

> FORT PUTNAM
> BUILT IN 1778 BY
> COLONEL RUFUS PUTNAM'S
> REGIMENT OF
> MASSACHUSETTS INFANTRY
> REBUILT AND ENLARGED 1794
> RESTORED 1909

Installed in 1778, the 600-yard-long West Point Chain stretched on rafts from West Point on the west bank of the Hudson River to Constitution Island on the east bank.[94]

Designed to prevent the passage of British ships north from New York City, the chain was removed each winter to prevent it from being damaged by the ice. The West Point location was chosen because the Hudson narrows and turns sharply at that place. This made it necessary for ships to slow down. The chain further impeded their progress, making them sitting ducks for onshore cannon fire. Each of the two-foot-long links weighed about 100 pounds. A section of the original chain is on outdoor display at the United States Military Academy at West Point.

The West Point Chain was not the first Revolutionary War chain to be installed to prevent British ships from freely navigating the Hudson River. About two years prior to its installation, the Continental Army had installed a similar chain further to the south at Fort Montgomery. Stretched from Fort Montgomery on the west bank to Anthony's Nose mountain peak on the east side, construction was supervised by Captain Machin. On October 6, 1777, British forces under General Henry Clinton overran Fort Montgomery and the adjacent Fort Clinton, and removed that chain. It was only six months after the removal of the Fort Montgomery chain that Rufus Putnam put his regiment to work on the chain at West Point.

In September 1780, Benedict Arnold while still apparently an Amerian Patriot, ordered that a copy of the following assessment of Fort Putnam be transmitted to General Washington.[95] "Fort Putnam, Stone, wanting great repairs, wall on East side broke down, and rebuilding From Foundation. At the West and South side have been a Chevaux-de-Frise; on the West side broke in many Places. The East side open; two Bomb Proofs and Provision Magazine in the Fort, and Slight Wooden Barrack. A commanding piece of ground 500 yards West, between the Fort and No. 4—or Rocky Hill."[96]

Two years after its construction. Fort Putnam was known to have the following cannon and mortars: five 18-pounders, two 12-pounders, two 6-pounders, one 4-pounder, and four 5½-inch mortars. In 1794, the casements were constructed at the fort. Eight years later, the United States Military Academy was founded at West Point.

A November 11, 1894, *New York Times* article on Hudson River forts built during the Revolutionary War states: "The most interesting fort at West Point is Fort Putnam ... in Revolutionary days [it] was considered impregnable." At the end of the 19th century it consisted of "the broken casemates, the ruined ramparts, the yawning chasms in the once-turreted walls, make up a picture that is extremely interesting."[97]

In 1907, Wallace Bruce described West Point, including Fort Putnam:

> West Point, taken all in all, is the most beautiful tourist spot on the Hudson. Excursionists by the Day Boats from New York, returning by afternoon steamer, have three hours to visit the various places of history and beauty. To make an easy mathematical formula or picturesque "rule of three" statement, what Quebec is to the St. Lawrence, West Point is to the Hudson. If the citadel of Quebec is more imposing, the view of the Hudson at this place is grander than that of the St. Lawrence, and the ruins of Fort Putnam are almost as venerable as the Heights of Abraham.[98] The sensation of the visitor is, moreover, somewhat the same in both places as to the environment of law and authority. To get the daily character and quality of West Point one should spend at least twenty-four hours within its borders, and a good hotel, the only one

Four. Washington's Chief Engineer

on the Government grounds, will be found central and convenient to everything of interest. The parade and drills at sunset hour can best be seen in this way.[99]

Bruce goes on to describe Fort Putnam's history and its physical state at the beginning of the 20th century:

> Old Fort Putnam was erected in 1778 by the 5th Massachusetts Regiment under the direction of Col. Rufus Putnam. It was originally constructed of logs and trees with stone walls on two sides to defend Fort Clinton on the plain below. It was garrisoned by 450 men, and had 14 guns mounted. In 1787 it was dismantled, and the guns sold as old iron. Its brick arch casements overgrown with moss, vines, and shrubbery are crumbling away, but are well worth a visit. It is 495 feet above the Hudson. A winding picturesque carriage road leads up from the plain, and the pedestrian can reach the summit in 20 minutes. On clear days the Catskill Mountains are visible.[100]

In 1909 stone walls were built around the 18th century remains of Fort Putnam in an effort to restore the fort to its 1794 condition. In celebration of the American bicentennial in 1975–1976, replica cannons and mortars were installed at Fort Putnam in an attempt to duplicate the fort's artillery of 1780. During restoration, foundations of the fort's original barracks were found and a museum was built upon them. Today, Fort Putnam, on the northwest corner of West Point, is administered by the West Point Museum.

In July 1778, Rufus led his regiment to White Plains where they joined Washington's main army. In September General Gates division of the army, including Rufus and his regiment, were sent to Danbury, Connecticut.[101]

While at White Plains, Putnam was ordered by Washington to "explore" nearby country, and when Putnam moved with Gates' army to Danbury, Connecticut, General McDougall assigned him the task of examining eastbound "roads and passes" from New Milford, Connecticut. Later, he received a letter from the Commander-in-Chief.

> Sir
>
> I have perused your Report of this day to Genl McDougall. You will continue your examination of the different roads, and reconnoiter the most convenient halting places on each—allowing the interval of an easy days march from one to the other—and make a report of the whole to me, that I may be enabled to regulate the different routes.
>
> The Road towards Litchfield appears from your account of it to be [worth] attention—and Col. Hale should be directed to proceed on it accordingly. I am Sir Your most obedt Servt, Go: Washington.[102]

Less than a week later, after having traveled through much of central and western Connecticut, Putnam wrote back. He detailed the number of miles between key places, the condition of roads, and the available of wood, water and forage. He finds a river between Waterbury and Woodbury that is "about 40 Feet Wide has no Bridge And in Low water the Forde is rather Deep and Since the Late Rains—would wet the Baggage in Wagons" and discusses the advisability of building a bridge.

The Battle of Stony Point

The location of West Point was considered by both the British and the Americans to be a vital position for the colonies. Since it was the strongest natural formation on the Hudson River, whoever possessed it was in a position to prevent ships from moving south from Canada or north from New York City. And the party that controlled the river could allow—or prevent—passage across the river by boat or ferry. General Washington knew and appreciated this fully—his troops, horses, and supplies often crossed the river, and important messages frequently needed to be transmitted between New England and the rest of the colonies/states.

In 1777, the army of British general John Burgoyne tried to pass down the Hudson from the north, but was stopped at Saratoga, New York.[103] Given that the fortifications at West Point were too strong to attack directly, the British developed a plan to "draw" many of the 9,000 American troops out of West Point by setting up their own fortifications to the south, as well as by initiating attacks on Connecticut towns.

On May 30, 1779, 6,000 British troops left New York City and headed north by both land and the Hudson River. They next day, they took the forts on Stony Point (on the west side of the Hudson) and Verplancks Point (on the east side), which were about 13 miles south of West Point.

Stony Point was connected to Verplancks Point by a ferry. The river is only about one-half mile wide at that location, providing a prime location for a ferry service that handled the transport of civilians, their livestock and goods. In the American Revolutionary War, it also afforded a way for the Continental Army and state militia forces to quickly and efficiently move men, horses, and supplies across the river.

Proceeding with the Connecticut phase of the strategy, the troops of British general William Tyron (who at the time was also the British governor of New York), raided that state, burning 240 houses and seven churches, and destroying farms, mills and water vessels. Several months before, General Tryon had raided Horseneck, Connecticut (today part of the Town of Greenwich) with 1500 troops to destroy a salt works. By chance, Rufus Putnam's cousin Major General Israel Putnam was in town as part of a review of his troops along the Connecticut coastline. In the

Four. Washington's Chief Engineer

last major heroic event of Israel's fabled military career, he plunged down a hill on his horse—a hill that was so steep that none of the scores of British horsemen dared to follow him.[104] At that time, General McDougall, upon hearing of the raid, sent regiments under Rufus Putnam to Connecticut to aid his cousin's troops. Shortly after leaving his position at Croton, New York, Rufus learned that the Tryon excursion was over and Rufus turned his men around. (It would have been an interesting turn of events if the 38-year-old Colonel Rufus Putnam had arrived in time to aid his 58-year-old cousin's troops. It had been almost two decades since, in the middle of the French and Indian War, in the wilderness north of Albany, New York, Captain Israel Putnam had instructed young private Rufus in the basics of warfare.)[105]

At almost the exact time his cousin Israel was being attacked in Connecticut, Rufus was informed that a British galley was spotted heading north on the Hudson River. One of his Croton Landing patrols intercepted eleven men after they landed at Teller's Point and attempted to steal livestock. The ten British soldiers, as well as their Native American pilot, were captured without casualties.[106]

The British proceeded to reinforce the captured positions at Stony Point, and, by that action, threaten West Point, as well as control of the Stony Point–Verplanck ferry.

One hundred-fifty-foot-high Stony Point was almost an island since it was surrounded by water on three sides and connected to the west bank of the river by marsh land, which flooded daily. Once in control, the British had constructed barricades of sharpened logs (known as an abatis) to prevent an attack and protected the abatis with artillery. At Stony Point, under the command of Lt. Col. Henry Johnson, were four companies of the Seventeenth Regiment of Infantry, one company of Tories, and a detachment of the Royal Artillery. Two companies of the Seventeenth Regiment and two companies of Grenadiers defended at the second line of abatis about a third of the way down the hill. In addition, the British stationed warships on the Hudson River.

General Washington's response to the British takeover of Stony Point was to plan a top-secret military attack. He met with Brigadier General Anthony Wayne of Pennsylvania, who he wanted to lead the attack. According to one account of the meeting, Wayne, not fazed by the potential of defeat, told Washington: "General, if you will only plan it, I will storm hell." It's said that Washington replied, "Perhaps, General Wayne, we had better try Stony Point first." It's also been said that a soldier who overheard this conversation passed on word that Wayne must be "mad."

That was one possible explanation for the origin of Wayne's famous nickname—Mad Anthony Wayne.[107]

Wayne's attack force was composed of four regiments of about 340 men each. One was filled with Pennsylvania and Virginia soldiers under Col. Christian Febiger (1749–1796), one of Pennsylvania Maryland, and Delaware troops led by Col. Richard Butler (1743–1791), one with Connecticut soldiers led by Col. Return Jonathan Meigs, Sr. (1740–1823), and the fourth of Massachusetts and North Carolina troops "temporarily" commanded by 26-year-old Major William Hull. (The following month, Hull's regiment would be permanently assigned to Rufus Putnam.) However, in early July, Washington had other plans for Rufus Putnam.

Several days before the expected attack, Washington assigned Rufus Putnam the task of conducting detailed surveys of the surrounding terrain, including the nearby hills. On July 9 Washington gave Putnam a note that stated: "Colonel Putnam has permission to take as many men as he chooses of his own regiment, or any other for Special Services—and to pass all Guards."[108]

In the afternoon of July 10, Putnam left Constitution Island at West Point with 50 soldiers to observe the enemy's fortifications at Verplanck's Point. At about sunset they reached Continental Village.[109] They then traveled at night by backroads and hid in the woods. Heavy rain delayed Putnam's plans to surveil enemy positions. They found shelter in a barn, but their ammunition was wet and useless. They found an abandoned house where they were able to build fires and dry out and clean their weapons and ammunition. When in their "disarmed & defenseless State," they were "apprehensive the enemy might have got knowledge from Some of the inhabitants, who probably must have Seen us I marched the party directly along the great road (in Sight of the enemies' block house) towards Peaks kill."[110]

When he was able, Putnam hid his men in the woods again, and in the morning, they were able to get close enough so Putnam could make his "observations." They returned to their camp on July 13—three days after they had set out.[111]

Putnam's findings were contained in a July 13 letter from him to General Washington. They would be vital to the stealth operation where one slipup could well cause its failure. Washington also discovered from a deserter that it was possible to approach West Point from the south along a stretch of sandy beach.

On July 14, Putnam met with Washington, who told him he had decided not to attack Verplanck's Point at the same time as Stony Point, but that

Four. Washington's Chief Engineer

Looking toward the east bank of the Hudson River from the Stony Point battlefield. Rufus Putnam and his men's "faint" at Verplanck occurred across the river on the right side of this photograph (author's photograph).

the former should only be a "faint." Putnam later recalled that Washington instructed him to "take as many men from that Brigade as I thought proper, & make my arrangements to be on the Ground ready to fire on the enemy at Vanplanks point the moment I found Wayne had attacked Stony point."[112] The evening before the attack most of the men were not allowed to load their muskets in case an accidental discharge might alert the British to the attack. Also, the American soldiers were threatened with instant execution if they violated the orders for complete silence. Guards were sent to nearby homes to detain anyone who might leave to alert the British and, according to some sources, all dogs in the immediate area were killed to prevent their barking from alerting the British.

The march to Stony Point from the north began on July 15, 1779, at Sandy Beach, which was five miles south of West Point. The troops traveled west, then south, over mountain roads to minimize the chances of being seen by the British. Two columns were armed only with bayonets,

The "Central Bowl" of the Stony Point battlefield. It was here on July 16, 1779, that the American forces under Brigadier General "Mad Anthony" Wayne achieved a much-needed victory (author's photograph).

while a center column alone would do the firing. Historian Henry P. Johnston would write of this action: "it taught the enemy that the 'rebels' could use the bayonet with a boldness and effect which even their own infantry could not easily surpass; it increased the confidence of the American troops at large in their own prowess; it was, in fact, one of those events in war which count for much, and which in our Revolutionary struggle especially had an important influence in bringing it to a successful termination."[113] Just after midnight on July 16, the right column moved across marsh. After the attack on Stony Point began, Rufus Putnam led a small force toward Verplanck Point in the diversionary action. It worked, with the British believing there would be a full-scale attack on the eastern fort.

At Stony Point, the American light infantry charged, tore down the first line of abatis and pushed forward. Furious hand-to-hand combat ensued. At the second abatis, a bullet grazed General Wayne's head, but he survived. Within less than two hours, the Americans succeeded in taking Stony Point, with most of the British surrendering. Recovering from his wound, at two o'clock a.m., Wayne asked for a sheet of paper and wrote to General Washington: "The fort and garrison, with Col. Johnson, are ours. Our Officers and men behaved like men who are determined to be free."[114]

Washington arrived at Stony Point on July 17—the day after the battle—to inspect his troops, the British prisoners, and the captured guns, ammunition and supplies. He ordered the fortifications to be destroyed and the position abandoned.

The battle was a morale builder for the Patriot army, and it made the British think twice before they again underestimated the competence and determination of their opponents. On July 21, Washington wrote to the Continental Congress: "The event will have a good effect upon the minds of the people—give our troops greater confidence in themselves and depress the spirits of the enemy proportionally."[115]

The American forces killed at least 20 British and Hessian soldiers, wounded 74, and took 472 prisoners. Only fifteen American soldiers were killed, with eighty-four wounded. It would be the last major battle of the Revolutionary War in the northern states. After the Americans left Stony Point, the British reoccupied the position, only to abandon it themselves a few months later.

The importance of the ferry between Stony Point and Verplanck was highlighted two years later when the American forces under Washington and their French allies under the French general the Comte de Rochambeau (1725–1807) crossed the Hudson at that point with 8,000 troops. They were on their way to Yorktown, Virginia, where they would defeat the British in the decisive battle of the war.

On August 11, 1779, American Major General Charles Lee, a multilingual student of history,[116] wrote that the assault on Stony Point "is not only the most brilliant, in my opinion, through the whole course of the war on either side, but that it is one of the most brilliant I am acquainted with in history."[117]

As mentioned, after the Battle of Stony Point, Rufus Putnam was given command of a regiment of light infantry, which was part of General Anthony Wayne's corps. They broke up camp in January 1780, at which time Putnam was granted leave to visit his family in Massachusetts.

At the time, Putnam and his wife Persis, had five daughters: 14-year-old Elizabeth, 12-year-old Persis, 11-year-old Susanna, 9-year-old Abigail, and two-year-old Martha, and two sons: 8-year-old William Rufus and 3-year-old Edwin.

Putnam returned to camp in mid–April 1790 and was given command at Croton River. This lasted from early May until July 27. He was then given a leave of absence and didn't return to the army until about December 1, 1780.

Today the site of the Stony Point Battle is preserved as Stony Point Battlefield State Historic Site. On site is a museum and an 1826 lighthouse. One of the interpretive signs near the lighthouse displays Putnam's drawing of the second British fort at Stony Point.

After the Battle of Stony Point, Rufus Putnam did not see any additional action for the remainder of the war. All of the subsequent major battles were fought in the southern states. North and South Carolina saw most of the action, with Virginia being the scene of the climactic battle of the war—Yorktown.

The Battle of Camden in South Carolina on August 16, 1780, was a major British victory. Major General Horatio Gates, who possessed about twice as many troops as the British, ended up with about one-half of his 4,000 men either killed, wounded or captured.

October 7, 1780, at South Carolina's The Battle of Kings Mountain, an American force of somewhat less than 1,000 men defeated over 1,000 Loyalist soldiers. The Loyalist death toll was about ten times that of the Patriots.

On January 17, 1781, American Brigadier General Daniel Morgan faced British Lieutenant Colonel Banastre Tarleton at the Battle of Cowpens. About four times as many British were killed as Americans, and the Americans captured 600 British soldiers.

Chapter Five

After the Revolutionary War

The Rutland Farm

With the war ended, Rufus Putnam returned to his home in Rutland. Years later when he wrote his memoirs for his family, he looked back on his years with the Continental Army. Then in his mid-seventies, he wrote with characteristic humility: "My Character as a Soldier is not for me to give—however that my descendants may know in Some measure what Services I rendered my county, and in what estimation I was held by my superior officers, I propose to give some account of the Special Services I was called to engage in."[1]

Today, the Massachusetts town of Rutland features only one image on its town seal—the home of Rufus Putnam. Although he lived in Rutland for only about eight years, Rufus Putnam held important town and state offices, in addition to managing his farm.

Long before Rufus Putnam became its most famous citizen in 1781, Rutland had a long and interesting history. Settled as Naquag in 1666, the town was incorporated in 1713.

After British general Burgoyne's army surrendered to the American forces at Saratoga, New York, in October 1777, Rutland was chosen as a location to house the prisoners of war. A little over a mile from the meetinghouse, a Capt. Thomas Read built a barracks measuring one hundred and twenty feet by forty feet. Two stories high, it contained twenty-four rooms, each twenty feet square. The barracks contained brick chimneys and was furnished with bunks. The building, along with some temporary barracks, was surrounded by a 12-foot-high enclosure on several acres. A guard house and a jail were erected at its southeast corner. A sturdy gate was placed in the front.

Early 20th century photograph of Rufus Putnam's Rutland, Massachusetts, home. He lived here with his family from 1781 through 1787. It was during these years that Putnam co-founded the Ohio Company of Associates and arranged for Northwest Territory lands to be made available to veterans of the American Revolutionary War. In 1787, he left Rutland to found the first American settlement in the Northwest Territory; in 1790, he returned to bring his family to Ohio (Library of Congress).

Five. After the Revolutionary War

Burgoyne's troops at Rutland were guarded by "two sentries at the gate, one at each corner of the stockade, one at the guardhouse, and one at the storehouse." Non-commissioned officers and soldiers, with their wives, would "by obtaining a permit from the officer of the guard" barter with local inhabitants for potatoes (which were plentiful) and other food items.[2]

The commissioned officers were quartered in private houses, and "in general their conduct was gentlemanlike." As described in the History of Rutland, they "lived in style, kept horses, paid their bills on Saturday; their deportment was mostly in accordance with the articles of convention."[3] At least three of them married local women. After the war, the barracks were used as a private residence, a store, a card factory, a tavern, and a "quarry" for building materials.

In early 1779, the 5,000 enemy prisoners were marched from Rutland and other Massachusetts camps through Connecticut, New York, New Jersey, Pennsylvania, Maryland, and Virginia. For the next few years they were moved around to evade British troops. Many ultimately ended up back in Rutland. Over the course of captivity, about one-half of the men either died, were paroled or exchanged, or deserted.

In 1780, Rufus Putnam bought a large farm in Rutland, Massachusetts, for his wife, Persis, and their eight living children. The oldest, Elizabeth, was about 15 and the youngest, Catharine, was less than a year old.[4] Their house sat about two miles west of the spot recognized as the geographical center of Massachusetts.[5] In addition to working the Rutland farm, Rufus spent most of the winter and spring months of 1781 lobbying the General Court for benefits for Massachusetts veterans.

Putnam's Rutland house was a two-story frame building built in the mid–1700s by Colonel John Murray, a wealthy Scotch-Irish immigrant who supported Great Britain during the American Revolution. Murray, who fled to Canada at the beginning of the American Revolutionary War, gave the house to his second daughter, Isabel, who married loyalist attorney Daniel Bliss of Concord, Massachusetts.

On May 24, 1781, the house, with its 150 acres of land, which had been confiscated by the Massachusetts government, was purchased by Rufus Putnam for 993 pounds.[6] In the town of Rutland, Rufus Putnam "was active and useful,—officiated as constable, collector, selectman and representative to the General Court; with others as a committee in 1786, was chosen to ascertain and report a proper number and arrangement of school plots in Rutland, which service they performed, and made very particular and accurate bounds and descriptions of the number recommended."[7]

In the early 1780s, land was donated by Jewish merchant Aaron Lopez (1731–1782) to found Leicester Academy in Leicester, Massachusetts, which is a few miles east of North Brookfield.[8] Rufus Putnam "subscribed" 100 pounds to the effort and served on the state-chartered school's first board of trustees. The Academy opened on June 7, 1784. Among Leicester's best-known graduates were cotton gin inventor Eli Whitney (1765–1825) and David Henshaw (1791–1852), who was United States Secretary of the Navy under President John Tyler.

Jonas Reed in his 1836 *A History of Rutland* lists some of Putnam's activities during the Rutland years: "he was appointed by Congress one of the Surveyors to lay out the Western Territory; was one of the Committee on the sale of Eastern Lands, a Justice of the Peace, and of the Quorum; was one of the first and principal settlers and characters that commenced the settlement of Ohio."[9]

Putnam lived in the Rutland house until he moved to Ohio in 1788. He sold the building to Stephen Sibley. Owners after Sibley were Benjamin Mead, Deacon William Mead, and Josiah Mead. The latter's widow sold it to three trustees.[10] In 1901 the Rufus Putnam Memorial Association was formed "for the purpose of holding and maintaining the homestead farm of General Rufus Putnam."[11]

Measuring 42 feet wide by 36 feet deep, the main house has four rooms on each floor. On the right side of the ground floor's hallway are a sitting room and a kitchen, while to the left are a parlor and a dining room. A 1934 federal government survey found the clapboarding, interior paneling, and second story floors original. Sometime in the past, the floorboards in three of the ground floor rooms were replaced with 1700s floorboards from the attic. In the early 20th century, a two-story wing was attached to the house's rear. At the time of the 1934 survey, the house included 135 acres.[12]

In 1901, a bronze plaque was installed on the Putnam house by the Massachusetts Society of the Sons of the Revolution. It reads:

> Here
> From 1781 to 1788
> Dwelt
> GENERAL RUFUS PUTNAM
> Soldier of the Old French War
> Engineer of the Works
> Which compelled the British Army
> To evacuate Boston
> And of the Fortification of
> West Point

> Founder and Father
> Of Ohio.
>
> In this House
> He planned and matured
> The scheme of the Ohio Company
> And from it issued the call for the
> Convention
> Which led to its Organization.
> Over this Threshold
> He went to lead the Company
> Which settled Marietta
> April 7, 1788.
>
> To Him
> Under God it is owing
> That the
> Great Northwest Territory
> Was dedicated forever to
> Freedom, Education and Religion
> And that the
> United States of America
> is not now a
> Great slaveholding Empire.[13]

In the 19th and 20th centuries, Rutland was noted for its facilities that cared for tuberculosis patients. They ranged from large to small. The State Sanatorium was built in 1898, and the moderate-sized Jewish Tuberculosis Sanatorium of New England was located on the site of today's Naquag Elementary School. Both of these were non-sectarian nonprofit facilities that cared for all patients.

On December 2, 1782, George Washington wrote to Rufus Putnam to encourage him not to retire from the Continental Army. The letter is a good example of the Commander-in-Chief trying to persuade one of his best officers not to resign. Washington wrote: "I am informed that you have had thoughts of retiring from service, upon the Arrangement which is to take place on the 1st of January—but as there will now be no opening for it, unless your reasons should be very urgent indeed.... I have thought proper to mention the circumstances, in expectation they might have some influence, in inducing you to remain in the Army."[14]

Washington went on to mention that with Colonel William Shepard (1737–1817)[15] now retired and Brigadier General John Paterson (1744–1808)[16] given command of the 1st Brigade, Putnam would now be the second colonel in the Massachusetts line and would have command of a brigade. In addition, Washington told Putnam that there was a good chance Congress would approve two brigadier generals in the Massachusetts line and he would "at least" be a candidate for promotion to brigadier general.

Washington acknowledged that he could not guarantee Putnam the promotion to general officer. He ended the letter by appealing to "upon a view of these circumstances and prospects, the state of your affairs will permit you to continue in the present arrangement (which must be completed immediately) it will be very agreeable to Sir your Most Obedt Servt."[17]

Days after receiving this letter, Rufus Putnam responded to General Washington, explaining that "the peculiar circumstance of my family" and "private reasons" led him to seek to resign before the end of the war. Now, however, he had decided to delay retirement. One reason was that with Colonel Shepard retiring, Rufus's friends "might censure me should I resign at present."[18]

Putnam thanked Washington for information regarding "promotion in the Massachusetts Line being yet before Congress," and asked him if he could mention his accomplishments "in a favorable light" to Congress.[19]

In his Memoirs, Rufus writes: "whether my sentiments expressed as above were communicated to Congress or not I cannot tell, but be that as it may, I received a brigadier's commission dated the eighth of January 1783." Rufus stayed with the army until April 19, 1783, when Congress ratified a preliminary peace treaty and "peace was publicly proclaimed in the army." In June, the Massachusetts line was reduced to three regiments and General Patterson, as the senior brigadier general, took charge of it. On September 3, the United States and Great Britain signed the Treaty of Paris and on November 25, British troops left New York City. The other American officers and soldiers were furloughed and discharged in November.[20]

Rufus closed the Revolutionary War section of his memoirs with a subject that meant a great deal to him—his friendship with George Washington:

> That I enjoyed a good share of the esteem, & confidence, as well as the friendship of General Washington, must appear to all who shall peruse this memoir,—And that his friendship for me continued, during his political existence, will appear from what follows—March 31st 1790, the President appointed me judge of the General Court in & over the territory Northwest of the Ohio, & on May 5th 1792, the President appointed me a brigadier in the army.
> October 1st 1796, he appointed me Surveyor General of the United States.[21]

Writing his memoirs only a few years after his firing by Thomas Jefferson, Rufus states:

> To be able to leave behind me such indubitable evidence of the esteem, friendship, & patronage of so great & good a man as General Washington (continued for more than

twenty years) *is no small Source* of consolation, under the persecution I have suffered from the arch enemy, of Washington's Administration.[22]

The Memoirs continue with: "I Shall next proceed to give Some account of my pursuits and employment after the peace took place until my arrival at Marietta with my family in November 1790—and of the Indian War so far as relates to the Settlement on the Ohio Company Lands."[23]

Before Rufus Putnam left camp in June 1783, the "Northern States" petitioned Congress for a land grant. The object was a large tract of land northwest of the Ohio River. Rufus later was made aware that Congress had done nothing in respect to the petition, so he accepted the task of surveying land "bordering on the bay of Passamaquoddy" in Maine. He was employed on that work for three months—from August 1784 through November 1784.

Newburgh Petition

Rufus Putnam held the rank of brigadier general from January 7, 1783, to November 3, 1783. After the Battle of Yorktown on October 19, 1781, only four other men besides Rufus Putnam were appointed brigadier generals: Maryland's Otho Williams in 1782, Massachusetts' John Greaton and New Jersey's Elias Dayton on the same day as Putnam (January 7, 1783), and France's Charles Armand on March 26, 1783. Also, after October 19, 1781, brigadier generals Henry Knox, Louis Duportail, and William Moultrie were promoted to major generals.[24]

In October 1781, British forces commanded by General Charles Cornwallis were decisively beaten at Yorktown, Virginia, by the combined force of American Continental Army troops under General George Washington and French Army land and sea forces led by the Comte de Rochambeau. It marked the final battle of the American Revolutionary War.

However, the treaty officially ending the war was not signed until almost two years later (September 3, 1783), and was not ratified by the Continental Congress until 1784. In the interim it was necessary to retain a standing army in case hostilities reignited. The Continental Congress found it difficult to raise the funds necessary to pay the soldiers, and state governments had many excuses for not contributing.

Two of the movements at the time used the name "Newburgh"—The Newburgh Petition and the Newburgh Conspiracy. They were radically different.

As we have seen, in 1773, Rufus Putnam, in the role of surveyor, joined with other veterans of the French and Indian War in an expedition up the Mississippi River. They believed they had been promised land by the British king, and they sought to identify and stake claim to the best property. But it was not to be, and Rufus returned home disappointed.

Ten years later, another war ended, and Rufus again sought to acquire land for himself and his fellow veterans. This time it would be the Congress of the United States that would be asked to provide the land, and again it would not be any easy task for Putnam and the other ex-soldiers. This time, however, Putnam was not the 35-year-old farmer that he was in 1773. Since then he had become one of *General* Washington's most respected commanders and was now one of soon-to-be *President* Washington's most trusted advisors and friends.

In 1783, Rufus Putnam led an effort to give Revolutionary War veterans their back pay—not in hard currency or greatly devalued paper currency, but in land in Ohio. Putnam's plan had the endorsement of Washington. Almost 300 Continental Army officers signed a petition—authored in part by Putnam—known as the Newburgh Petition. It reads:

> To His Excellency the President, and Honorable Delegates of the United States of America in Congress Assembled:
>
> The Petition of the subscribers, Officers in the Continental Line of the Army Humbly Showeth
>
> That by a Resolution of the Honorable Congress passed September 20th, 1776, and other subsequent resolves, the Officers (and Soldiers engaged for the War) of the American Army, who shall continue in service till the establishment of Peace or in case of their dying in service, their heirs are entitled to receive certain Grants of Lands according to their several grades to be procured for them at the expense of the United States.
>
> That your petitioners are informed that the tract of country bounded north on Lake Erie, east on Pennsylvania, southeast and south on the river Ohio, west on a line beginning at that part of the Ohio which lies twenty-four miles west of the mouth of the river Scioto, thence running north on a meridian line till it intersects the river Miami which falls into Lake Erie, thence down the middle of that river to the lake, is a tract of country not claimed as the property of, or within the jurisdiction of any particular State in the Union.
>
> That this country is of sufficient extent, the land of such quality, and situation such as may induce Congress to assign and mark it out as a Tract or Territory suitable to form a distinct Government (or Colony of the United States) in time to be admitted one of the confederated States of America.
>
> Wherefore your petitioners pray, that, whenever the Honorable Congress shall be pleased to procure the aforesaid Lands of the natives, they will make provision for the location and survey of the lands to which we are entitled within the aforesaid District; and also for all Officers and Soldiers who wish to take up their lands in that quarter.
>
> That provision also be made for a further grant of lands to such of the Army as may wish to become adventurers in the new Government, in such quantities and on such

Five. After the Revolutionary War

conditions of settlement and purchases for public securities, as Congress shall judge most for the interest of the intended government, and rendering it of lasting consequence to the American Empire.

And your petitioners, as in duty bound shall ever pray.

June 16, 1783.[25]

This petition was signed by 285 officers, including 155 from Massachusetts, 46 from Connecticut, 36 from New Jersey, 34 from New Hampshire, 13 from Maryland, and one from New York. Rufus Putnam's name is third on the list.

One major general—Massachusetts's Henry Knox—signed it, as did six brigadier generals: Rufus Putnam, John Greaton and John Paterson from Massachusetts, Elias Dayton from New Jersey, Jedediah Huntington from Connecticut, and John Stark from New Hampshire.

The other officers who signed the petition included: 6 colonels, 12 lieutenant colonels, 18 majors, 75 captains, 114 lieutenants, 32 ensigns, 13 surgeons, seven surgeon's mates, and one chaplain. Among these men were: Colonel Benjamin Tupper, his son, Lieutenant Anselm Tupper, and Lt. Colonel Ebenezer Sproat, all of whom in a few years would join Rufus Putnam in establishing the first permanent settlement in the Northwest Territory. Also signing were two men who had been George Washington's aides during the Revolution: the great painter Lt. Colonel John Trumbull, and Lt. Colonel David Humphreys, who in five years would publish his biography of Rufus's cousin—Major General Israel Putnam.

In addition to satisfying the veteran's just demands, the presence of hundreds of settlers with military experience on the western frontier would be an incredible deterrent to Indian attacks. It was a valid argument, but Congress refused to do anything.

While, Rufus Putnam and other officers, with the support of Washington, were struggling to obtain land for veterans of the war, a more violence-prone group of the veterans was getting close to taking the law into their own hands—using the weapons of war to force civilian government leaders to give in to their demands. In this case, it would not be waging war on a foreign dictatorial government 3,000 miles away, but rather fighting their own seven-year-old, democratically elected federal government.

The efforts and threats of these men were termed the Newburgh Conspiracy. Continental Army officers stationed at Newburgh, New York, spearheaded the efforts. They had not received their back pay, and the pensions promised by Congress were possibly going to be denied. Many had suffered at Valley Forge five years earlier or had lost their property in the war. Some saw neighbors who did not serve in the American forces profit financially from the war effort.

Newburgh Conspiracy

By March 1783, a group of officers was ready to take action—possibly to march to Philadelphia to confront Congress. Maybe even to stage a military coup. On March 15, 1783, Washington made an appearance before an assembly of these officers at Newburgh, New York, and asked them to support Congress. At first, they were unswayed, but when the Commander-in-Chief spoke, they listened.

"By an anonymous summons," Washington began, "an attempt has been made to convene you together—how inconsistent with the rules of propriety! how unmilitary! and how subversive of all order and discipline—let the good sense of the Army decide."

Washington continued:

> While I give you these assurances, and pledge myself in the most unequivocal manner, to exert whatever ability I am possessed of, in your favor—let me entreat you, Gentlemen, on your part, not to take any measures, which, viewed in the calm light of reason, will lessen the dignity, & sully the glory you have hitherto maintained—let me request you to rely on the plighted faith of your Country, and place a full confidence in the purity of the intentions of Congress; that, previous to your dissolution as an Army they will cause all your Accts to be fairly liquidated, as directed in their resolutions, which were published to you two days ago—and that they will adopt the most effectual measures in their power, to render ample justice to you, for your faithful and meritorious Services.[26]

As Washington reached in his pocket for a letter from a member of the Continental Congress, he fumbled and took out a new pair of eyeglasses. Few if any present had seen him with glasses. Washington looked up at the assembled soldiers and said: "Gentlemen, you will permit me to put on my spectacles, for, I have not only grown gray, but almost blind in the service of my country."[27] Many of the officers cried. Few still wanted to disobey their Commander-in-Chief. The Newburgh Conspiracy effectively ended at that moment.

Washington did more than just end a potential mutiny—he set a precedent that established the supremacy of civilian rule in the United States that would last through the centuries.

Perhaps the most important political question facing the new country was the role of the national government. Under the Articles of the Confederation, the central government was weak—most governmental authority was given to the individual states—and the leaders in those states were jealous of their rights.

A large part of the controversy over the powers of the national government, involved the role of the military. Few Americans wanted to create a national military force that might possibly become as oppressive as the British armed forces. Many believed the existence of state-run militia units was all that the new country needed to maintain order between the states, as well as to handle minor confrontations with other nations. If another major war broke out, troops could assemble at that time to meet the needs—or so they thought.

Washington and most of his officers were concerned. For years, they had experienced the problems that resulted from an untrained, undisciplined, and unreliable soldiers. They knew that the survival of the new nation depended upon its ability to defend itself. That defense not only involved the area of the thirteen states, but as of the passage of the treaty ending the Revolutionary War, it also included the huge Northwest Territory—lands where Native American tribes were coming into conflict with white settlers.

The new nation's future also might well include military engagements with European powers—Great Britain, or other nations. (In a few years, even America's great ally, France, looked like it might become an adversary as revolutionaries executed the French king and initiated the violent and bizarre Reign of Terror.)

Continental Militia Proposal

As one of Washington's key military advisors during the Revolutionary War, Rufus Putnam was in a position to provide advice to the man who would soon become the first United States president. In the following April 1783 letter, Putnam proposed a "Continental Militia" to Washington.[28] At the time, leaders of the new republic were deeply divided on the desirability of a permanent national military force. Many thought that the state militias could handle all defensive needs—up to and including the invasion of the U.S. by a foreign power. Even among the supporters of a standing national military, many desired it to be severely limited in its size and function. Rufus Putnam began his letter to Washington with:

Dear General

Enclosed are Some propositions for the establishment of a Continental Militia— I am aware there are many objection lying against the Scheme, but I See none but what I think may be fairly [ ]—but if I am mistaken and there is in Such an Establishment, as I have hinted anything which the Citizens of America ought to fear as Tending To Undermine their liberties—your Excellency's candor will not Impute to the badness of my Heart—and the Same Candor will excuse the [ ] incorrectness of my Pen in this as well as [ ] other performance—I am Sir with all posable respect your Excellency Most obedient Humble Servant

R. Putnam[29]

The enclosed recommendations were both detailed and practical. Titled "Thoughts on a Peace Establishment For The United States of America," Putnam's proposal begins (with his spellings preserved), "America is by no means to place her principle Security, in walled Towns & the multitude of her Fortresses, nor is She in time of Peace to be at the expense of a reguler Army; Sufficient for the defence of every part of her Territorys, Should they be invaided—yet unless her harbours (at least the principle ones) are Secured by Fortifications and Small Garrisons, her Sea Ports are liable to be Surprized, plundered and burnt or laid under contributions by a few Ships of War; and if Aided by Land Forces an Enimy might in Some of them, So establish him Self, in a very Short time as to render it very defiquelt to drive him out."

Some of Putnam's main recommendations are:

- The frontiers should be secured by "Forts and Garrisons" that can delay the progress of an enemy.
- New York City is the most important seaport to be protected. After that, the rivers and towns between there and Canada are critical, since in Putnam's opinion, an enemy would (as happened in the Revolutionary War) seek to establish a chain of forts that would separate the eastern states from the middle and southern states.
- Falmouth, Maine, is in second place of importance because of its proximity to British-occupied Halifax, Nova Scotia.
- Other seaports deserving protection include: Penobscot County, Maine (which is a major source for ship masts and lumber), Charles Town, South Carolina, and Savanna, Georgia; both of these latter had "Spaniards on their Right" and Indians "in the rear."
- Putnam considered individual states to be fully capable of defending the other harbors and seaports.
- To form West Point as the "Grand Arsenal of America" with a garrison composed mostly of artillery men and artificers. (Stony Point would be "an appendage" of West Point. Other, smaller arsenals would be established throughout the country.)

- To build a fort on Lake Champlain at Windmill Point, which is just a couple of miles south of the International border. (The Treaty of Paris in 1783 established the Canadian/U.S. border at Quebec Province and New York State as being at the 45th parallel.) The objective to be to "forever to shut the British out" of Lake Champlain. Putnam explains: "in case of a War with Great Britain it will prevent their making themselves masters of the Lakes" and "aide us in Introducing an army into Canada whenever that Should be Thought proper." Crown Point was recommended as a backup.
- To support the Lake Champlain fort, Putnam recommends supply posts at Albany, New York, and between Canada and Albany.
- Putnam considers American military supply posts along the Great Lakes, and concludes American forces should be greater in peacetime than the British forces are because the latter only needed to consider Indian attacks, while the United States needed to guard against both the Indians and the British.
- Putnam recommends military strength in Illinois should be at least equal to the Spanish strength. He suggests small forts on or near the Ohio River—particularly at the site of Fort Massac, which was built by the French during the height of the French and Indian War. (Eleven years later, Fort Massac would be rebuilt by the Americans during the Northwest Territory's Indian War. In 1908, the site became Illinois' first state park.)
- Putnam recognizes British naval superiority at Lake Ontario and advises the United States to establish another supply route to Niagara, Detroit, and other places along Lake Erie. He warns that if Niagara is taken, "with it we must lose the whole Western World." (Of course, the definition of the term Western World was very different than it is today; in America of 1783, it referred to the Northwest Territory.)
- Putnam proposes a chain of military posts from Lake Erie down to the Ohio River area. Starting at the mouth of the 100-mile-long Cuyahoga River at Lake Erie where today Cleveland, Ohio, is located, posts are proposed at the portage between the Cayahoga and Muskingum Rivers as well as on the Tuscarawas River, which is a principal tributary of the Muskingum River and at the Forks of Muskingum River. Going south, additional fortifications are recommended at Wills Town, which was the site of an Indian village; at the mouth of the Muskingum River; and near the Hockhocking River, which is a

tributary of the Ohio River. (The Hockhocking River today is called the Hocking River.) The last post mentioned would be on the 100-mile-long Kanawha River, which is a tributary of the Ohio River. (Today, the Kanawha is in the U.S. state of West Virginia.)

Considering these major recommendations, Putnam projects the following military establishment to Washington:

3 Regiments of Infantry

1 Regiment of Artillery of 12 companies

1 Company of Artificers that is attached to the Artillery

Under Putnam's plan one regiment of foot (regiment of infantry) consisting of 1 Colonel, 2 Lieutenant Colonels, 2 Majors, 16 Captains, 16 Lieutenants, 16 Ensigns, 1 Chaplain, 1 Adjutant, 1 Pay Master, 1 Quarter Master, 1 Surgeon, 1 Mate, 1 Lieutenant Major, 1 Quarter Master M. Sergeant, 1 Drum Major, 1 Fife Major, 80 Sergeants, 16 Drummers, 16 Fifes, 1088 Rank & file.

Putnam also proposes the following posts and garrisons manned by the three infantry regiments:

Eastern New York State Area:

- On Lake Champlain—Four Companies
- Albany, Fort Stanwise, Lake George and the Communication in the Northern & Western Quarters—Three Companies
- West Point and Dependencies—Three Companies
- New York—Two Companies
- Maine—Four Companies

Western New York State and Michigan Area:

- Oswego—Four Companies
- Niagara—Four Companies
- Detroit—Four Companies
- Michilimacknac—Four Companies[30]

Elsewhere:

- South Carolina & Georgia—Four Companies
- Illinois and Fort Massac—Four Companies[31]
- Fort Pitt—One Company[32]

Five. After the Revolutionary War 93

- Mouth of Cayahoga—Two Companies[33]
- On the Waters of the Muskingum and Ohio Rivers—Five Companies

The 12 companies in the single regiment of artillery would be dispersed as follows:

At West Point—Six Companies

On Lake Champlain—One Company

Maine—One Company

South Carolina & Georgia—One Company

Oswego & Niagara—One Company

Detroit & Michilemacknac—One Company

Fort Pitt Cayahoga and the Posts on that Frontier—One Company

Putnam proposes that the Company of Artificers be at West Point.

In an attention to detail that would be evident in the subsequent decades when Rufus Putnam headed up the settlement of Ohio, he includes such items as:

> The pay of commissioned and non-commissioned officers (he recommends the present pay levels), the pay of privates (he proposes no more than five dollar per month), and the pay of everyone to be given, if possible, on a weekly basis. Putnam also addressees the question of the proportion of officers from each of the states.

Putnam declares that his proposed military establishment should be sufficient to "guard against Surprise, prevent the progress of an enemy for a Time, especially on the first breaking onto a War, which is all that is to be expected from it, and all that in my opinion Congress ought to attempt by any establishment of Troops, to be always kept in pay."

Next Putnam addresses his plan for a Continental Militia:

1. All able-bodied men between ages 18 (or 20) and 25 be required to enrollment in and be available to serve in the Continental Militia.
2. Each Continental Militia regiment would consist of one colonel, two lieutenant colonels, two majors, one adjutant, one Pay Master, one quartermaster, one Surgeon, one mate, one chaplain, one lieutenant major, one quartermaster sergeant, one drum major, one fife major. Sixteen companies would be divided into battalions. Each company would have one captain, one lieutenant, one ensign, five sergeants, three corporals, one drummer, one fifer, and sixty-five privates.
3. The Continental Militia would have twenty-four regiments totaling up to 26,112 rank and file.

4. Every seven years, Congress would assess the states for the troops on the same basis as the Continental Tax of 1782. Each state shall divide their territory into districts by regiment. Further division should be made by battalions, and then by companies.

5. The commanding officer (usually a captain) of each company district each December shall create a list of all able-bodied men in the district who are eligible to serve in the Continental militia. He will then select 70 of the youngest men and return a list of the remaining men to the appropriate state militia commander. Sixty-five of the chosen seventy men will be enrolled in the Continental militia company, with the remaining five to be on standby as substitutes.

6. Each year the commanding officer will enroll new soldiers as men attain the minimum age or take up residence within his company's district. The oldest men will be discharged.

7. Under the proposed system an enrolled man might serve as a Continental soldier for "5 or 7 years," but Putnam considered it probable that no one would serve more than three years.

8. The officers would be appointed by the governors of the states and commissioned by the Congress.

9. The officers will assume the rank of officers in the Continental Army.

10. The troops would be governed by the same regulations and system of discipline as the "regular establishment."

11. All officers must be residents of the districts to which they are appointed. If they move their residence outside the district they would be considered to have resigned.

12. That there be "one Commander in Chief from whom all orders respecting the Continental Militia as well as the regular Established Service Should Issue; the same in peace as in Time of War."

13. Each regiment's quartermaster will have a supply depot with arms, ammunition, tents, camp equipment and one month's provisions—all paid for by the federal government.

14. On the occasion war breaks out, or Congress orders it, the Continental Militia "Shall take the field and March to any part of the Continent required" and each soldier shall continue to serve until he is 25 years old.

15. When called to serve, the Continental Militia would be entitled to the same pay and clothing as the regular soldiers.

Five. After the Revolutionary War

Putnam also included recommendations on the numbering of regiments, the appointing of major generals and their staffs, military exercise requirements, provisions for substitutes, and the arms and clothing that would be supplied to the soldiers.

> Putnam recommended for peacetime: 24 Regiments of noncommissioned officers and privates totaling 28,066 men, and three regiments of regular foot soldiers, adding another 3,654, for a total of 31,720. For wartime, he suggests increasing this to 35,770 soldiers.

Two months after submitting his military establishment proposal, Rufus wrote to Washington on military fortification of the Northwest Territory. It would be another five years before Putnam would set foot on Ohio soil to establish the first permanent American settlement in the Territory, but this 1783 letter shows he was already considering the need for military protection.

One of the most important points Putnam raises was concerning the relations between the Native American tribes and the new American government. With Great Britain controlling Canada to the north and Spain possessing the area to the west of the Mississippi River, Rufus knew the allegiance of the Indian tribes could be a deciding factor in a future war. He writes:

> One great means of securing the Allegiance of the Natives, I take to be the furnishing them with such necessaries as they shall stand in need of, and in exchange receiving their furs and skins. They are become so accustomed to the use of Fire Arms, that I doubt if they could gain a subsistence without them, at least they will be very sorry to be reduced to the disagreeable necessity of using the Bow and Arrow, as the only means for Killing their game, and so habituated are they to the woolen Blanket &c. &c., that an absolute necessity alone will prevent their making use of them.[34]

Putnam then advocates the construction of factories to supply the native people with necessities; he cautions that "unless they are furnished by the subjects of the United States, they will undoubtedly seek else [where], and like all other people form their attachment where they [have] their commerce."[35] He contends that, in case of war, the Indian tribes could well aid the enemies of the United States.

Putnam then goes on to discuss establishing fortifications in the west, retracing some of the same ground already covered in his earlier proposal for a national military establishment.

Several years later, as Rufus Putnam was occupied in setting up Marietta's military defenses and tackling all the governmental, social and economic issues of the new settlement, President George Washington was urging the newly formed U.S. Congress to create an official U.S. military.

The President of the United States still had the Continental Army at his disposal, but it was not the official army of the new country, and it was beset with inherent weaknesses.

On August 7, 1789, Washington wrote a letter to Congress in which he stressed the need to create a national military.[36] In this letter, Washington also addressed conflicts with Native American tribes, stating, "While the measures of Government ought to be calculated to protect its citizens from all injury and violence; a due regard should be extended to those Indian Tribes whose happiness, in the course of events, so materially depends on the national justice and humanity of the United States." It was read to Congress by Secretary of War Henry Knox. In it, Washington wrote that "the honor, safety and well-being of our Country so evidently and so essentially depend" on a national military and that he was "particularly anxious, it should receive as early attention as circumstances will admit."[37]

When neither the House of Representative nor the Senate took any action, three days later Washington pushed them again to attend to the matter. It wasn't until September 29 that both houses of Congress passed a bill that established "the armed forces of the United States of America."

The Society of the Cincinnati

In May 1783, officers at the Continental Army founded the Society of the Cincinnati. Named after Lucius Quinctius Cincinnatus (c. 519– c. 430 BC), a legendary hero of Ancient Rome, its aims were: "to perpetuate the memory of the War for Independence, maintain the fraternal bonds between the officers, promote the ideals of the Revolution, support members and their families in need, distinguish its members as men of honor, and advocate for the compensation promised to the officers by Congress."[38]

Besides Brigadier General Rufus Putnam, the Society of the Cincinnati's original members included: its founder Henry Knox, George Washington, and major generals Alexander Hamilton, Horatio Gates, Nathanael Greene, the Marquis de La Fayette, Baron Von Steuben, Benjamin Lincoln, and Rufus Putnam's fellow Ohio settler, Arthur St. Clair.[39] Within the Society's first ten years, 2,270 officers became members.

Today, the Society of the Cincinnati is the United States' oldest patriotic organization.

Congress Chooses Surveyors

Two months after Putnam submitted his continental militia proposal to General Washington, army officers petitioned Congress for a land grant northwest of the Ohio River. They learned from Washington in June 1784, that Congress had not acted upon the petition:

"As the Congress who are to meet in November next by the adjournment will be composed from an entire new choice of Delegates in each State it is not in my power at this time to direct you to a proper correspondent in that body."[40]

In 1783, the Commonwealth of Massachusetts owned 17 million acres of land in what one day would become the State of Maine. In 1784, Massachusetts requested that Rufus lead a survey of much of that land.[41]

Rufus later wrote: "I engaged with the committee of eastern lands, to survey certain lands bordering on the bay of Passamaquoddy, [Passamaquoddy Bay is located on the border of Maine and the Canadian province of New Brunswick] and August 2, 1784, I left home for that country. I returned to Boston the eighth of the following November."[42] Between 1784 and 1786, most of Putnam's time was occupied with the Maine surveying work, although he continued in his efforts to convince people— especially Revolutionary War veterans—of the land opportunities in the Northwest Territory. He knew this virgin land had great potential; after he retired from military service, he would guide veterans and other pioneers westward so they could achieve a better life for themselves and their families.

Thirty-one-year-old Park

Portrait of Rufus Putnam. Most paintings and drawings of Rufus Putnam show his left profile. This is probably due to the fact that his right eye was disfigured by an injury in childhood. Print from the 1886 *Journal of Gen. Rufus Putnam Kept in Northern New York During Four Campaigns of the Old French and Indian War.*

Holland,⁴³ was, like Rufus Putnam, a veteran of 5th Massachusetts Infantry in the Revolutionary War. He recounts a humorous anecdote in his journal on a visit he and Putnam made to Judge Stephen Jones in August 1784, as follows:

> Judge Jones treated us very kindly, and politely invited General Putnam and myself to take tea with him that afternoon; said he had some friends from Boston, whom he was expecting, and would try to make our time pass pleasantly. The time came, and we told our men they might get their supper and not wait for us, and proceeded to make our visit. We passed the afternoon very pleasantly indeed. Tea at length arrived with which we had anticipated a good supper, but, alas! it was carried round, as the expression is, and a servant came in with it, poured out, and a slice of bread and butter in each saucer. He came first to General Putnam, who on taking his tea from the tray, upset it the first thing he did, and what was worse, what his saucer did not catch, fell scalding hot on his knees and destroyed his comfort for the evening. I succeeded in lifting mine in safety from the tray and lo ! my bread was thickly spread with butter, an article of which I never partook, in any way in my life. We tried, however, to make the best of our misfortunes, though to eat bread with butter on it, I could not.
>
> We returned to our camp, General Putnam scolding and I laughing, and ordered a supper to be prepared for us. We had eaten in the army for months together, from a clean chip, with a knife and fork among half a dozen of us, and our soup with a clam shell for a spoon thrust into a split stick for a handle, and got along very well; but this carrying round tea was a little too much for us.⁴⁴

In 1785, Rufus had more work than he could handle. He was appointed Superintendent of the Survey of Eastern Lands, Massachusetts, and a member of the Committee for the Sale of Eastern Lands, Massachusetts.⁴⁵ It was impossible for him to perform any surveying work in the West at the time. Putnam explains in his Memoirs:

> In 1785 the general assembly of Massachusetts were so well satisfied with my services the last year that they appointed me one of the committee for the sale of their eastern lands. While I was in Boston, my election as one of the surveyors of the lands in the western territory was announced to me, in a letter of May 20 from the secretary of congress, and requiring an immediate answer of my acceptance. I was considerably perplexed as to what answer to return, for I was not only under engagement to the state of Massachusetts—which I could not with honor disregard without their consent—but surveyors and hands were engaged for the season, provisions laid in and a vessel chartered to take us to the eastern country. At the same time, I was very loathe to relinquish my appointment for the western country. On a view of the circumstances, I wrote a letter of acceptance to the secretary of congress, and a letter to the Massachusetts delegates in congress, requesting their influence that General Tupper might be accepted as a substitute for me in the western country until I could attend to the service in person.⁴⁶

Congress agreed and selected Benjamin Tupper as a substitute for Putnam.⁴⁷ After the Revolution people in the existing states became interested in the opportunities for settlement in the undeveloped lands west of the Allegany Mountains and north of the Ohio River. The states of Connecticut, Massachusetts, and New York claimed rights to Northwest Territory lands. New York surrendered its rights. Connecticut and Virginia did, too, but reserved some lands. On May 20, 1785, Congress appointed surveyors to survey the lands.

On May 27, 1785, Congress chose as Northwest Territory surveyors:

- Nathaniel Adams of New Hampshire (Later replaced by Winthrop Sargent)
- Rufus Putnam of Massachusetts (Later replaced by Benjamin Tupper, since Putnam was already occupied with Maine surveys)
- Caleb Harris of Rhode Island (Later replaced by Ebenezer Sproat)
- William Morris of New York
- Adam Hoopes of Pennsylvania
- James Simpson of Maryland
- Alexander Parker of Virginia
- Absalom Tatum of North Carolina
- William Tate of South Carolina

On July 18, it added Isaac Sherman of Connecticut.[48]

At the time of the surveys, the danger of conflict with local tribes was a possibility. However, the only forts that were in the huge area were Fort Pitt at the mouth of the Alleghany River, Fort McIntosh near the mouth of Big Beaver Creek, Fort Harmar at the mouth of the Muskingum River, and Fort Vincent on the Wabash River.

Bounty Land

Up until 1855, the federal government gave what it called "bounty land" to military veterans (or their heirs) from the American Revolutionary War as payment for their military service or as an incentive to enlist. In addition to the Revolutionary War, bounty lands were issued to many veterans of the War of 1812, the Mexican War, and Indian wars of the late 18th century and first half of the 19th century. When veterans applied for the lands, they were given warrants that could be redeemed for land or could be sold. Some veterans settled on the lands deeded to them; others sold their land to investors or settlers. The pre–Revolutionary War colonies and the U.S. states also were involved in offering bounty lands to soldiers who had served in colony and state militias.

An example of legislation governing bounty lands is the Military Bounty Land-Bill, which was passed by the U.S. Congress on September 28, 1850. It affected "each of the surviving, or the widow or minor children of deceased commissioned and non-commissioned officers, musicians, or privates, whether of regulars, volunteers, rangers, or militia, who performed military service in any regiment, company, or detachment, in the service of the United States" in the wars between 1790 and 1850.[49] For these claimants, the law specified 40 to 160 acres.[50]

"That each commissioned and non-commissioned officer, musician, and private, for whom provision is made by the first section hereof, shall receive a certificate or warrant from the department of the interior for the quantity of land to which he may be entitled, and which may be located by the warrantee, or his heirs-at-law, at any land-office of the United States, in one body, and in conformity to the legal subdivisions of the public lands, upon any of the public lands in such district then subject to private entry; and upon the return of such certificate or warrant, with evidence of the location thereof having been legally made, to the general land-office, a patent shall be issued therefor."[51]

The 1850 act also covered the rights of prisoners of war. An act in 1855 granted bounty lands to additional classes of veterans. Notably, it stated: "The provisions of this act, and all the bounty-land laws heretofore passed by Congress, shall be extended to Indians, in the same manner and to the same extent as if the said Indians had been white men."[52]

Shays' Rebellion

After the Revolutionary War, the United States, as governed by the Articles of Confederation, possessed a relatively weak national government. Problems with the economy and international trade were widespread. Discontent in Massachusetts was especially high because, unlike many other states, it did not pass debt relief laws.

In 1775, Daniel Shays, then about 28 years old, fought the British at the Battles of Lexington and Concord as a Minuteman. After serving at the Battle of Bunker Hill and Fort Ticonderoga, Shays was wounded in 1780 and returned home. Because he was only partially paid for his war service, Shays was unable to pay his debtors. It's been said he even sold an ornamental sword that General Lafayette had given to him for his outstanding war service.

Five. After the Revolutionary War

In the mid–1780s, Shays was not alone in being deeply in debt. The devaluation of currency and unfulfilled promises the government made to the veterans left many, especially farmers, facing foreclosures. While farmers were frantically trying to make ends meet to provide for their families, the courts, and the state and local governments, proceeded to sell their lands to pay off their debts, which included unpaid taxes. After losing part of their land, farmers were even less likely to break free of their economic hardships.

The situation was ripe for a revolt and that's exactly what occurred. In December 1786, Shays and other leaders raised an "army" of farmers and others affected by the land seizures. Shays later insisted he was opposed to violence and had never wanted the revolt to take on his name.

In an attempt to bring peace, Rufus Putnam met with Daniel Shays in January 1787. Putnam knew him well—Shays had served as a captain under Putnam in the Continental Army's Fifth Massachusetts Regiment. Putnam sent a transcript of his conversation with Shays to Massachusetts Governor Bowdoin.[53] It was apparently written at Putnam's Rutland home. According to Putnam, the conversation went as follows.

> RUTLAND, JANUARY 8. 1787. Sir:—As I was coming through Pelham the other day I met Mr. Shays in the road alone,[54] where we had a conversation, some of which was of a very particular kind. I shall state the whole, by way of dialog, as far as I can recollect; but in order to understand the meaning of some parts of it, it is necessary you should know that the week before they stopped Worcester court the last time, I spent many hours with Shays and his officers, endeavoring to dissuade them from their measures, and persuade them to return to their allegiance.[55]
>
> Sitting down with Putnam, Shays asked about a petition that the rebels had sent to the Massachusetts governor, saying "I don't know that it will alter the case, for I don't suppose the governor and council will take any notice of it." Putnam responds that Shays has no reason to expect the governor and council "will grant the prayer of it" and because many things asked for it is out of their power to grant; and besides that since you and your party have once spurned at offered mercy, it is absurd to expect that another general pardon should be ever granted.
>
> At that, Shays cried out "No! Then we must fight it out."
>
> "It's impossible you should succeed," said Putnam. He told Shays that it was not honorable to fight in a bad cause and involve his country in a civil war.
>
> Shays insisted that "the sole motive with me in taking the command at Springfield, was to prevent the shedding of blood." Putnam asks, "If that was the case…. Why did you not stop there?" Shays insists that he heard warrants were issued for him and he "was determined not to be taken."
>
> Putnam asks, "How came you to write letters to several towns in the county of Hampshire, to choose officers and furnish themselves with arms and 60 rounds of ammunition?" Shays denies it, stating "it was done by a Committee … put my name to the copy and sent it to the Governor and Court."
>
> After asking why Shays did not accept offers to give himself up and hearing objections, Putnam told him:

"When offered mercy has been once refused, and the crime repeated, Government never can with any kind of honor and safety to the community pass it over without hanging somebody; and as you are at the head of the insurgents, and the person who directs all their movements, I cannot see you have any chance to escape."

To this, Shays replies, "I at their head! I am not," and he seeks to convince Putnam that he is not the true leader of the movement.[56]

In response, Putnam asks "But how do you get along with these people, having been with them so long; how is it possible they will let you stay behind?" to which Shays says "I tell them that I never will have anything more to do with stopping Courts, or anything else, but to defend myself, till I know whether a pardon can be obtained or not."[57]

When Putnam asks "And what if you cannot get a pardon?" Shays states "Why, then I will collect all the force I can and fight it out; and, I swear, so would you or anybody else, rather than be hanged."[58]

Putnam says he has only one more question: "Had you an opportunity, would you accept of a pardon, and leave these people to themselves?" Shays response is "Yes—in a moment."[59]

Putnam then advised him to "immediately leave for Boston and throw himself upon the mercy and under the protection of Government." The conversation ends with[60]:

SHAYS: "No, that is too great a risk, unless I was first assured of a pardon."

PUTNAM: "There is no risk in the matter, you never heard of a man who voluntarily did this, whose submission was not accepted; and if your submission is refused, I will venture to be hanged in your room."

SHAYS: "In the first place, I don't want you hanged, and in the next place, they would not accept of you."

Putnam concludes his report to the governor with "The only observation I shall make is, that I fully believe [Shays] may be brought off, and no doubt he is able to inform Government more of the bottom of this plot than they know at present."[61]

After reading Putnam's transcript of the conversation with Shays, Massachusetts Governor Bowdoin offered to pardon Shays, but at the same time he continued to raise an army to move against the rebelling farmers. The pardon was nullified by Shays' actions weeks later when he participated along with over 1,000 other men in an attack on the federal arsenal in Springfield, Massachusetts. The rebels were quickly overcome.

The attacks on government and business establishments continued into 1787. The Governor of Massachusetts recruited about 3,000 militia soldiers to oppose Shays' men. Led by General Benjamin Lincoln, they put down the rebellion. Rufus Putnam joined Lincoln as a "volunteer aid" until the insurgents were dispersed. After their final defeat, the movement's leaders escaped to nearby states.

In the summer of 1787, the newly elected governor of Massachusetts, John Hancock,[62] granted pardons to many of the rebels. Shays was pardoned in 1788. He died in near poverty in 1825. Thomas Jefferson said that the motives of the rebels "were founded in ignorance, not wickedness."

Shays' Rebellion was one of the factors leading to a national Constitutional Convention. In February 1787, the Continental Congress called for a Constitutional Convention in May to amend the Articles of Confederation. Faced with the possibility of future attacks on state government facilities, many Americans supported a stronger federal government. They got it—shortly thereafter—by means of the U.S. Constitution.

Unlike the Articles of Confederation, the Constitution provided for executive and judicial branches in the national government as well as a legislative branch; i.e., the Congress. It also included a Bill of Rights that would apply to all United States citizens regardless of which state they might reside in.

History has been relatively kind to the rebels of 1786–1787. On January 13, 1987, acting on a law passed by Congress, President Ronald Reagan proclaimed the week of January 19, 1987, as Shays' Rebellion Week and January 25, 1987, as Shays' Rebellion Day, "To recognize the influence of Shays' Rebellion on the movement for our Federal Constitution."[63]

Ohio Company of Associates

The original constitution of the United States of America, the 1781 Articles of Confederation, designated the Confederation Congress as the legislative branch of the federal government.[64] Three years later, that congress passed the Ordinance of 1784.

Written mostly by Thomas Jefferson, the Ordinance of 1784 specified that land obtained from Great Britain after the Revolutionary War—north of the Ohio River, west of the Appalachian Mountains, and east of the Mississippi River—be divided into territories, and later, when the territories reached a certain population level, into states. The sale of the lands would be used to fund the needs of the federal government, whose taxing powers were severely limited under the Articles of Confederation. The Ordinance of 1784 led directly to the Northwest Ordinance of 1787.

In 1786, the Ohio Company of Associates was founded by Rufus Putnam,[65] Benjamin Tupper,[66] Samuel Holden Parsons,[67] and Manasseh Cutler,[68] with the expressed goal of settling of Northwest Territory land. They met with veterans and other interested parties from eight Massachusetts counties on March 1, 1786, at the Bunches of Grapes Tavern on King Street (today's State Street) in downtown Boston, Massachusetts.[69] The tavern was a block or two east of the Old State House and the Boston Massacre site.

In 1925, the City of Boston placed a bronze plaque on the site of the tavern, which is inscribed with the following[70]:

> Here in 1786 was organized the Ohio Company
> Pioneer in the development of the great west
> Under the leadership of General Rufus Putnam
> First township laid out at Marietta Ohio

In May of 1787, Rufus Putnam was appointed head of the Ohio Company, with the title Superintendent of Affairs of the Ohio Company. Putnam, Parsons, and Cutler were selected as the Company's directors and thirty-three-year-old Harvard College graduate Winthrop Sargent was chosen as its secretary.[71] Later in 1787, James Mitchell Varnum was chosen as a director.[72]

The Ohio Company of Associates sought to purchase land in the Northwest Territory as specified in the Ordinance of 1784. It would thus participate in the first territorial expansion of the new country beyond the lands of the original thirteen states.

Samuel Holden Parsons was selected to approach the new Federal government with the Company's proposals. When he failed, they chose the Rev. Manasseh Cutler. He spearheaded the effort to allow the Ohio Company of Associates to purchase land in what is today the southeastern corner of the State of Ohio. Cutler arranged for more than 1.5 million acres of raw land to be bought at less than 10 cents an acre. This was followed by the Continental Congress passing the Northwest Ordinance on July 13, 1787.

Speaking of Manasseh Cutler, George F. Hoar, who represented Massachusetts in the U.S. Senate, wrote: "He was probably the fittest man on the continent, except Franklin, for a mission of delicate diplomacy. It was said just now that Putnam was a man after Washington's pattern, and after Washington's own heart. Cutler was a man after Franklin's pattern, and after Franklin's own heart. He was the most learned naturalist in America, as Franklin was the greatest master in physical science."[73]

The year of 1787 was a busy one for Putnam—in April he had been appointed a justice of the peace, and in May he was elected to the Massachusetts General Assembly by the Town of Rutland. It was also a time when Rufus and his wife needed to evaluate what it would be like to move from a life as prosperous members of a civilized Massachusetts community to pioneers in a wilderness filled with untold dangers, including Indian attacks.

Not everyone at the time had the foresight of Putnam. One Massachusetts newspaper included a woodcut that depicted "a stout, ruddy, well-dressed man on a sleek, fat horse," with the caption, "I'm going to Ohio." He was speaking to "a pale and ghastly skeleton-like looking figure, clad in tatters, astride an almost inanimate animal" who replied, "I've been to Ohio."[74]

The Northwest Ordinance

The Northwest Ordinance of 1787 arranged the organization and government of "not less than three nor more than five states" from the Northwest Territory.[75] Thomas Jefferson had proposed cutting up the Northwest Territory into a greater number of states with name such as: Sylvania, Michigania, Cherronesus, Assenisipia, Metropotamia, Illinoia, Saratoga, Polypotamia, and Pelispia.[76] Eventually, the territory would be divided up into the states of Ohio, Indiana, Illinois, Michigan, Wisconsin and part of Minnesota. In the long run, the Northwest Ordinance of 1787 established the process by which new states could become part of the United States as equals to the existing states.

The Northwest Ordinance had the official title "An Ordinance for the government of the Territory of the United States northwest of the River Ohio." A total of a little over 2,800 words long, it established religious freedom, public education and the absence of slavery in the new lands. It included many elements that were later incorporated into the U.S. Constitution and its Bill of Rights, such as the prohibition of cruel and unusual punishment, habeas corpus, and the right to trial by jury.

Its last paragraph is usually considered the most important:

> Sec. 14. Art. 6. There shall be neither slavery nor involuntary servitude in the said territory, otherwise than in the punishment of crimes whereof the party shall have been duly convicted: Provided, always, That any person escaping into the same, from whom labor or service is lawfully claimed in any one of the original States, such fugitive may be lawfully reclaimed and conveyed to the person claiming his or her labor or service as aforesaid.[77]

By 1787, Rufus Putnam's home state of Massachusetts (which included what would become the State of Maine) had already adopted antislavery measures. So had Vermont (in 1777, while still an independent entity), New Hampshire in 1783, and Connecticut and Rhode Island (both in 1784).

Nineteenth century Congregational minister Sidney Crawford wrote:

"To him [Rufus Putnam], it may be safely said, without detracting from the fame of anyone else, the country owes its present escape from the bondage of African slavery more than to any other man. Had it not been for his providential leadership, and all that it involved, as is so tersely written on the tablet in the Putnam Memorial at Rutland, 'The United States of America would now be a great slaveholding empire.'"[78]

Part of the reason Congress was able to pass the Ordinance was that the Northwest Territory's southern border was the Ohio River, which was considered an extension of the North/South Mason-Dixon Line, which was surveyed between 1763 and 1767. It originally marked the border of the "Southern" state of Maryland and the "Northern" state of Pennsylvania.[79]

The ordinance also established religious liberty in the new territory:

> And for extending the fundamental principles of civil and religious liberty, which form the basis whereon these republics, their laws and constitutions, are erected; to fix and establish those principles as the basis of all laws, constitutions, and governments, which forever hereafter shall be formed in the said territory....
>
> No person, demeaning himself in a peaceable and orderly manner, shall ever be molested on account of his mode of worship or religious sentiments, in the said territory.[80]

Education was covered as well. It isn't difficult to see these words coming from young, education-starved Rufus Putnam: "Religion, morality, and knowledge, being necessary to good government and the happiness of mankind, schools and the means of education shall forever be encouraged."[81] The Ordinance addresses Native American concerns:

> The utmost good faith shall always be observed towards the Indians; their lands and property shall never be taken from them without their consent; and, in their property, rights, and liberty, they shall never be invaded or disturbed, unless in just and lawful wars authorized by Congress; but laws founded in justice and humanity, shall from time to time be made for preventing wrongs being done to them, and for preserving peace and friendship with them.[82]

The Northwest Ordinance of 1787 was adopted on July 13, 1787, which was almost a year before the U.S. Constitution was ratified. Delegates to the Constitutional Convention signed the U.S. Constitution on September 17, 1787, but it wasn't ratified until June 21, 1788.

In 1830, American statesman Daniel Webster said of the Northwest Ordinance of 1787: "We are accustomed to praise the law-givers of antiquity; we help to perpetuate the fame of Solon and Lycurgus; but I doubt whether one single law of any lawgiver, ancient or modern, has produced effects of more distinct, marked and lasting character than the ordinance of 1787. We see its consequences at this moment, and we shall never cease to see them, perhaps while the Ohio shall flow."[83]

Chapter Six

Pioneer Leader

The First Journey

In 1788, General Rufus Putnam led forty-seven other men, calling themselves the Ohio Company of Associates, on a one-thousand-mile journey west from Massachusetts to the junction of the Muskingum and Ohio Rivers on the western Virginia border. One of the longest rivers in the United States, the 981-mile Ohio River flows westward from Pittsburgh, Pennsylvania, to Cairo, Illinois, on the Mississippi River. Today, it touches the borders of six states: Pennsylvania, West Virginia, Ohio, Kentucky, Indiana, Illinois. The 48 pioneers were seeking to establish the first permanent settlement in the Northwest Territory.

As the Ohio Company started off for Ohio, Manasseh Cutler wrote to Rufus Putnam: "My son [nineteen-year-old Jervis Cutler] is gone on in the company, and I beg you will be so kind as to pay some attention to him, and give him such counsel and advice as you would your own. I feel a satisfaction in the reflection that he is under your care."[1] Decades later, writing a book about her father, Jervis's brother, Ephraim Cutler, Julia Perkins Cutler describes Putnam.

> No man in the territory more entirely deserved and enjoyed the respect and confidence of the people than General Rufus Putnam. He had with General Tupper originated the idea of the Ohio Company, and had been selected as the leader and superintendent of the colony who made the first settlement at Marietta, a position for which he was well fitted by his good judgment, intelligence, and decision of character. He had served as a private soldier in the Old French War, and also, with great distinction, throughout the Revolution, as a military engineer, and as an officer. He was made a brigadier general near the close of the war. President Washington commissioned him, in 1792, a judge of the supreme court of the territory, and in 1796 the surveyor-general of the United States. He was faithful and energetic, a Christian as well as a patriot. He, too, a few months after the close of the convention, was deprived

of his office by the same spirit of proscription which had led to the removal of St Clair as governor.[2]

The dangers the Marietta settlers faced in southeastern Ohio is evident from the journal of General Richard Butler, who passed down the Ohio River with his troops less than three years earlier (the fall of 1785). General Butler had been assigned the task of making treaties with the local Native American tribes.

After Butler encountered scattered, nearly defenseless, families between the Muskingum River and the Pennsylvania border, he made these notes in his journal[3]:

> Friday, Oct. 1st, passed Yellow Creek, and found several improvements on both sides of the River,—put in at one Jesse Penniman's on the North side, five miles below Yellow Creek; *warned him off*; called on one Pry, *who I warned off also*; this appears to be a shrewd sensible man.... Passed on to the Mingo towns, where we found a number of people, among whom one Ross seems to be the principal man of the settlers on the North side. I conversed with him and *warned him and the others away*.
>
> Sunday, Oct. 2. Called at the settlement of Charles Morris, *whose house has been pulled down and he has rebuilt it*. At this place, found one Walter Kean, who seems but a middling character, and rather of the dissentious cast; *warned all these off*, and requested that they would inform their neighbors, which they promised to do. Called at the settlement of one Capt. Hoglan, *who we also warned off; his house had also been thrown down and rebuilt*.
>
> Tuesday, Oct. 4th. I wrote to Col. Harmar for three other men to join these as an escort, and to give Maj. Dougherty *orders to pull down every house on his way to Muskingum, that is, on the North side of the River*.[4]

Before the first group of Rufus Putnam's Ohio Company set off from Massachusetts, arrangements were made for the hiring of four or five surveyors, twenty-two assistants to the surveyors, six boat builders, four house carpenters, nine "common" workman, and one blacksmith. The surveyors were: Colonel Ebenezer Sproat,[5] Anselm Tupper,[6] John Mathews, Colonel Israel Putnam, Jr., and Jonathan Meigs.

The 20 non-surveyor men's leader was 49-year-old Major Haffield White who left Danvers, Massachusetts, on December 1, 1787, and reached Simerill's ferry on the Youghiogheny River, which is thirty miles above Pittsburgh, in late January 1788. The surveyors and their assistants left Hartford, Connecticut, on January 1, 1788; they were led by General Rufus Putnam. General Putnam left the company for New York on business, turning it over to Colonel Ebenezer Sproat. Rufus rejoined them on January 24 at Swatara Creek in central Pennsylvania.

When they reached the Allegheny Mountains, they found the snow prevented their wagons from moving. According to Rufus Putnam: "Our only resource was to build sleds and harness tandem, and in this manner with four sleds, and men marching in front, we set forward and reached the 'Yoh' the fourteenth of February." When they did arrive at the Youghiogheny River, they met up with Haffield White's group, which had been there since January 23.

Putnam discovered that much work was still needed—to build boats. Thirty-three-year-old Captain Jonathan Devol supervised the boat building,[7] which took nearly the entire months of February and March. The end result was a forty-five-foot long, twelve-foot-wide galley with a 50-ton capacity (which they named the *Mayflower*), a flat boat with a capacity of about three tons, and three canoes. The galley "had a covered deck, which was high enough for a man to walk under without stooping, and the sides were strong enough to resist the force of a bullet in case of an attack."[8]

On April 1, boat construction was completed at West Newton, Pennsylvania, and supplies were stowed away. The following day the entire party set off for Marietta. The settlers finally reached their new home on April 7, 1788. Of that day, Putnam in his Memoirs merely states "arrived there on the Seventh—Landing on the upper point where we pitched our Camp among the trees, and in a few days commenced the Survey of the Town of Marietta as well as the eight acre lots."[9] Ebenezer Sproat and John Mathews began laying out those first lots.

During the weeks the Putnam party had been traveling, back home, states were ratifying the new U.S. Constitution: Georgia on January 2, Connecticut on January 9, and Massachusetts on February 6. But the news was not all pleasant back in the "states" as a few days after Putnam arrived in Ohio, the new country's first riot took place in New York City.

Thousands took to the streets to protest medical students who had been robbing graves of recently interred corpses. Almost all the bodies had been obtained from the graveyards of African American and poor white residents.[10]

After a few days, the pioneers began to plot out city lots and streets of the new town of Marietta. Rufus Putnam was especially concerned with preparing the fortifications. He had researched the current treaties with the local Indian tribes and expected they "would not be peaceable very Long."[11] He ordered all men not engaged in surveying to labor at constructing defensive works. On May 5, Putnam let the settlers each plant two acres of crops. By fall, the Company had a total of about 130 acres of corn, which yielded an average of 30 bushels per acre.

Settler and shipwright Jonathan Devol supervised construction of the major fortification—the 180-by-180-foot-square stockade, Campus Martius. Named after a section of the Italian city of Rome,[12] it consisted of four wooden two-story-high block houses, each with a footprint 18 feet square. Two sides of the upper stories projected two feet out from the lower levels. Two of the block houses had two rooms on each floor; the other two had three rooms per floor.

Along the inside of the fort's walls, were private homes for about 60 families and government offices. In the center was a 144-foot by 144-foot open area, which could be used as a parade ground. In its center was an eighty-foot deep well that could provide drinking water in the event of a siege. Also, a large sundial was placed within the center of the fort to note "the march of time." On the west and south sides were fortified gateways.

Each of the block houses was equipped with a watch tower that could hold four men. The northwest watch tower also included a balcony with a cupola and spire. A room large enough to accommodate up to 300 people was planned for the lower floor of this block house. The northeast blockhouse was used for the offices of the Ohio Company, the southeast blockhouse was used for entertainment, and the northwest blockhouse was reserved for "public worship and the holding of courts." The southwest blockhouse was reserved for the residence of Governor St. Clair and his family. The southeast blockhouse was also "occupied by private families."[13] Work on Campus Martius was completed in 1791.

In 1842, Dr. Hildreth wrote in the journal *The American Pioneer*:

> The whole establishment formed a very strong work, and reflected great credit on the head that planned it. It was in a manner impregnable to the attacks of Indians, and none but a regular army with cannon could have reduced it. It is true, that the heights across the Muskingum commanded and looked down upon the defences of the fort; but there was no enemy in a condition to take possession of this advantage.[14]

Without a doubt the minute Rufus Putnam stepped ashore at the future site of Marietta, he took notice of the elevation of the land on the south shore of the river, as well any vulnerabilities from attack by water or from the forests to the north and west. After years as the Continental Army's Chief Engineer, constructing forts from Massachusetts to Rhode Island to Long Island. and up and down the Hudson, there was probably no one in North America better equipped to evaluate the natural terrain and potential enemy positions than Brigadier General Rufus Putnam.

The following month, additional settlers floated down the Ohio to Marietta. One, Col. John May, made notes of the end of the journey in his diary:

Six. Pioneer Leader 111

MAY 12th [1788], Monday. I am still in quarters opposite Pittsburg, living as cheaply as if I was at Muskingum. Am waiting for the boat to carry us all down.[15]

Wednesday, 21st. At 2 o'clock p. m. our boat—oh, be joyful!—hove in sight, coming around the point, and, in half an hour, was made fast at Pittsburg. She is forty-two feet long and twelve feet wide, with cover. She will carry a burden of forty-five tons, and draws only two and one half feet water....[16]

Saturday, 24th.... At 12½ o'clock cast off our fasts, and committed ourselves to the current of the Ohio. The scene was beautiful. Without wind or waves, we, insensibly almost, make more than five miles an hour....[17]

Monday, 26th.... Thus we moved on, constantly espying new wonders and beauties, till 3 o'clock, when we arrived safely on the banks of the delightful Muskingum.[18]

In less than two decades after Marietta's 1788 founding, the number of settlers traveling the Pennsylvania-Ohio River route west became so large that the United States Congress approved the construction of a road from Cumberland, Maryland, on the Potomac River to Wheeling on the Ohio River. Called the Cumberland Pike or the National Road, it was later extended to Zanesville.[19]

One man who remembered early Marietta well was Benjamin Franklin Stone. Born in Rutland, Massachusetts, a year after Rufus moved there, Stone at age eight accompanied the Rufus Putnam family to Marietta in 1790. In his autobiography, Stone mentions that his father Israel, a Revolutionary War veteran, was hit hard by the poor economy and traveled to Ohio in March 1789. Up to that time, the seven-year-old Benjamin had some good times—attending school with a cross-eyed teacher and children who were White, African American, and mixed race. He remembers fondly this family's dog Flora whose brass collar read: "The property of Israel Stone, He's my master, or I have none; My name is Flora, and I am true; Pray tell me now, whose dog are you?"[20]

Before his father departed Rutland, he left most of his children with local families. Benjamin was placed in the home of Christopher Burlingame and his wife Susanna, who was a daughter of Rufus Putnam. The Burlingames were married on December 13, 1787, in Rutland. Nineteen days later, Rufus Putnam was recorded as leaving Hartford, Connecticut, for Ohio.

When father Stone left, only two children were left with Mrs. Stone—two daughters. Life was not pleasant for Benjamin Franklin Stone at the Burlingame home; he could only look forward to a time that he would once again join his father. He remembers decades later:

Mr. Burlingame's was an unsuitable place for me or any child to live at. I was there about a year and a half before the family came to Ohio. They had but little for me to do. I was not sent to school, nor taught to read in the family. All that time was a blank, or worse than a blank, in my life. I sat on the dye tub in the corner most of the time.

Sometimes Mr. Burlingame set me to piling up his hat blocks in a regular row on the platform, then to tumble them down and put them up again.[21]

After years of living in Ohio, Stone looked back on his early life:

> While we lived in that garrison I read the Bible through. I was ten years old when I commenced it. I was quite ignorant of many things that I should have known if I had lived with my father and mother all the time. I did not know what was meant by the date of the year that I saw in books; 1790 was the first date that I noted, and I asked my father what it meant. He told me it was so long since our Saviour Jesus Christ came into the world. Nearly the same time, I found out that the earth was round, and turned over once in twenty-four hours—which seemed very strange to me. By reading Morse's geography, I got some idea of the different countries of the world; but geography was never taught in any school that I attended, till after I had taught school.[22]

This treatment by Rufus Putnam's son-in-law, who lived near the General, is very surprising since about 20 years later, Putnam wrote in his memoirs that his step-father, John Sadler (with whom he lived from ages nine through fourteen), denied him all opportunities to attend school. Rufus writes: "during the six year I lived with Capt Sadler, I never Saw the inside of a School house, except about three weeks, he was very illiterate himself, and took no care for the education of his family."[23] The septuagenarian Rufus added: "Oh! my Children beware you neglect not the education of any under your care as I was neglected."[24]

So, how was it possible that a man who felt this way did not notice how one of his sons-in-law was treating young Benjamin Stone? The answer can be found in the Putnam Memoirs. When young Stone went to live in the Burlingame home in March 1789, Rufus had already been in Marietta for eleven months, supervising land surveys, planning and supervising construction of the fort—Campus Martius—and attending to countless other tasks as the leader of the new settlement.

Also, perhaps Rufus Putnam was not totally comfortable with Christopher Burlingame. It is said that before Putnam would consent to his daughter's marriage, he required Burlingame to "pledge himself that he would go with him to Ohio."[25]

When Rufus set out to return to Rutland in July 1789 to retrieve his family, he stopped in New York City to see Manasseh Cutler "on the Company's business" and needed to stay there through the winter months. He finally left for Rutland again in June 1790 and returned to Ohio with his wife and children in November 1790. Thus, during Benjamin Stone's time with the Burlingames, Rufus was far from home, engaged in the busiest time of his life, or packing up his family for the Ohio move.

Once in Ohio, Benjamin went back to live at his father's house. Stone remembers that "Burlingame wished to keep me till I should be of age,

Six. Pioneer Leader   113

This drawing captures the arrival of Rufus Putnam and 47 other settlers at the location of what would become the town of Marietta, Ohio. The Muskingum River is in the foreground and the Ohio River is in the distance. Print from the 1920 *On the Trail of the Pioneers*.

and teach me the hatter's trade." However, his father chose to keep young Benjamin at home.[26]

It would be interesting to know Rufus Putnam's reaction if Stone had informed him of his treatment by Burlingame, given that Putnam had been a victim of child neglect himself, as well as a man who was sometimes noted for his temper.

Bringing Family West

Benjamin Franklin Stone left an account of the trip west in 1790 from Rutland to Marietta with the Rufus Putnam party.[27] Including this party, Jonas Reed estimates in his *A History of Rutland* that about 50 people emigrated from Rutland to Marietta and its surrounding communities.[28]

Stone describes Rufus Putnam's family who made the journey west as Rufus, his wife Persis, two sons and five unmarried daughters. The latter were: Elizabeth, Persis, Abigail, Patty, and Katherine. The sons were William Rufus and Edwin.

The Putnam party also consisted of two hired Rutland teamsters, William Brauning and Samuel Porter. Rufus's married daughter, Susanna, and her husband Christopher Burlingame, and their two children, Maria[29] and Susanna,[30] had their own wagon.

Benjamin Franklin Stone's mother brought along her family: Sardine, Matilda, Lydia, Israel, Augustus, Benjamin Franklin, Christopher Columbus, and Polly Buckley. A Rutland man, Samuel Bridge, and Col. John Mills' older brother Charles Mills also left for Ohio with the Putnam, Burlingame, and Stone families.

These 26 men, women, and children were transported on three ox-wagons with two yokes of oxen each, Rufus Putnam's two-horse carriage, and one saddle horse. Rufus had "three or four neat cattle, including a bull of a choice breed." Stone confesses that at age eight, he was "too young to remember much" about the eight-week-long trip. He does, however remember attending public worship services in Bethlehem, Pennsylvania, and that it was "a settlement of people of the Moravian church. Mr. Hakewelder (the missionary to the Delaware Indians), was then there."[31]

Stone also speaks of small problems that were magnified on the trail:

> Among other preparations for the journey, my mother and sister Lydia had knit up a large quantity of socks and stockings. They were packed in a bag, and that bag was used by the boys who lodged in the wagon, for a bolster. By some means the bag was lost out of the wagon or stolen. The boys missed it, of course, the first night. Next morning, Sardine went back the whole distance of the previous day's journey, inquired and advertised it, but without success. I do not remember how many pairs of stockings were in it, but from the size of the bag I judge there were at least one hundred. One pair to each of the family were saved, besides those we had on our feet, being laid aside in another place to be washed. It was a severe loss.[32]

The mountains of Pennsylvania were especially difficult for the travelers:

> I remember the steep rough roads in the mountains. Sometimes they would take the foremost pair of oxen and chain them to the hind end of the wagon, when going down a steep place, where they would naturally hold back, and so make it easier for the other pair to hold back. Once, when one of the wagons tipped and seemed on the point of oversetting,—when the teamster (Samuel Porter) cried out in despair, "It's going!" Charles Mills sprang to the off side, set his shoulder to the upper part of the wheel, and braced with all his strength and poised it back. It was a daring and a noble act. The road here was on the edge of a precipice. If the wagon had gone over, it would have been instant death to the team, and total destruction to the loading. At another place, one of Putnam's wagons did upset; but it was on comparatively level ground, and no injury was done to the team nor much damage to the loading.[33]

Six. Pioneer Leader 115

Benjamin Stone mentions that Rufus Putnam had "traveled the road three or four times before" and had a list of all the houses that he planned to sleep at. Almost every day he would go ahead of the party on horseback to make arrangements for the evening's lodging. Each morning he would tell the teamsters how many miles it would be to the next house. Stone remembers that except for two days, the party made it to the next stop "though sometimes it was at a late hour, owing to the badness of the roads on rainy days."[34]

Fortunately, they experienced little rain until they reached Simerill's Ferry on the Youghiogheny River. There they stayed at the home of a Mr. Carnahan until the boats were built. Rufus had arranged for their construction when he had passed through on the way to Massachusetts. At Carnahan's, Stone's father met up with his family after a separation of one-and-a-half years.

As they traveled along, the low water level resulted in the boats frequently running aground. Stone remembers: "It was slow, tedious work on the river, often getting aground, when all the men from both boats had to unite to shove the boat over the shoal place. Some of our party, writing to their friends in Rutland, informed them of our getting aground on the fish-dams, above Pittsburgh, but carelessly left out the word dams, so it read, 'got aground on the fish.' The answer came, 'You must have very large fish in the Ohio.'"[35]

Stone comments that Pittsburgh was "quite a town" and that there were "few houses, log houses only" at Buffalo (now Charleston) and Wheeling. They observed no settlements on the west side of the Ohio River between Pittsburgh and Marietta.

After arriving at Marietta, young Benjamin and his family continued on the same day to Belpre where he stopped at "the little log cabin" to see his sister Betsy and his brother Jasper. Betsy had been living with Captain Miles's family; Jasper was with their father. The latter's one-story cabin was only about fourteen feet square, and "not large enough for the whole family to lodge in conveniently."[36]

Until a new cabin could be built, some members of the family were sleeping in their boat. Stone goes on to explain: "This, our first residence in Ohio, was the southwest corner of what is now the Browning farm, then owned by General Putnam. All the settlers (as the inhabitants were generally denominated) gave us a hearty welcome. It can scarcely be realized now, by persons born and brought up here, with what feelings the first settlers welcomed every accession to their number."[37]

Stone notes that the settlers had "just passed through a time of scarcity of provisions," but it was November and the "Corn was now ripe; Providence had favored them with good crops; it was a time of peace, and they were full of hopes that soon they would be relieved from all the privations incident to a new settlement so far beyond the abodes of civilized man."[38]

Benjamin Stone often mentions small details of everyday life that give us a better idea of the lives of the pioneers. "The squirrels were very numerous that autumn and winter, and ate much of the corn before it was harvested," he relates. "They came into fields from the woods on the north, and after eating upon the corn a few days traveled on south and swam the Ohio River, and their place was filled by a new set from the north."[39]

> The woods in those times afforded good pasture for cattle and hogs all the spring, summer and fall, and the cattle would live through the winter in the woods with but little feeding at home. But many of my father's hogs became wild in the woods, and so were lost. One year, I remember, he took all his store hogs in a canoe up to Middle Island and put them on there and scattered some corn round in the woods for them, in hopes that they would stay on the island where he could feed them a little and keep them tame. But in a few days they swam off on to the mainland.[40]
>
> Stone also mentions that some people kept their cows on Blennerhasset's Island, and so had to go over in canoes to milk.[41]

Stone mentions that the war prevented the settlers from doing much hunting, and:

> The principal articles of food in the time of the war were Indian bread, pork, potatoes and other garden sauce, occasionally venison, bear meat, raccoons, opossums, squirrels and wild turkeys.... No apples, peaches, or other cultivated fruits till the trees had time to grow from the seed. Great use was made of pumpkin. We used to cut up and dry a great quantity of pumpkin. Corn in the milk was dried for use in the winter and spring. Pumpkins, melons and all garden vines grew more luxuriantly than in these times; they were not eaten by insects then, as now. But flies, the fleas, the gnats and the nettles were very annoying. Mosquitoes were not so numerous as in these times.[42]

In his autobiography, Benjamin Franklin Stone states that Jonas Davis, an unmarried man from Rutland, was the last resident of Belpre, Ohio, to be killed by Indians.[43] In 1795, before the signing of the Treaty of Greenville, Davis found a damaged skiff in the Ohio River. Borrowing a pair of pinchers from Stone's father, he went back to the boat to salvage its nails. As he was working, two Indians "tomahawked him, scalped him, took all his clothes except his drawers, and the tools."

When Davis didn't return in the evening, the Belpre settlers "suspected that he was killed." The next morning, they sent a party out to investigate. Before they returned, 13-year-old Benjamin Stone was approached by one of the party. Samuel Branch "came running in great fright. Davis is killed," he yelled, "and the Indians chased me! I snapped my gun at them several times, but it missed fire."

Stone asked where the rest of the Party was; Branch said he supposed they were killed. Branch proceeded to frighten the entire garrison until another of the party showed up to get a blanket to cover Jonas Davis' body. Stone viewed the body before it was covered and saw ravens had picked out the eyes.[44]

Throughout the time of great fear of Indian attack, Benjamin Stone describes the health of the early Ohio settlers as generally good with a low-grade fever the most common complaint. That changed in the fall of 1793 when "some boat people" landed at Marietta and infected the Belpre community with smallpox.

As a preventive measure against smallpox, Marietta-area doctors Jabez True and Samuel Barnes inoculated every family in Belpre and at Neal's Station (today's Parkersburg, West Virginia). Still, five people from these places died of smallpox. Stone explains that "most of the old men (the Revolutionary officers) had had it before."[45] Of the nearly 100 patients Dr. True inoculated, none died; two or three of Dr. Barnes patients died.[46]

Establishing Marietta

The first permanent settlement in the 260,000 square mile Northwest Territory by citizens of the newly independent United States of America began on April 7, 1788, when Rufus Putnam led a group of 46 pioneers to the juncture of the Muskingum and Ohio rivers. A 47th man, Return Jonathan Meigs, Sr., arrived on horseback five days later.[47] Counting Rufus Putnam, the party arriving that week consisted of 48 men ages 19 and older.

The settlement was a direct result of the passage of the Ordinance of 1787. In July 1788, the newly elected Governor of the Territory, General Arthur St. Clair, arrived and established a territorial government. At the time, General Rufus Putnam was in the process of directing the construction of the large fort named Campus Martius—large enough to accommodate virtually the entire population of the town in the case of a major Indian attack.

At 180 feet square with a two-story blockhouse and corner sentry towers, it was essential to Marietta's security for seven years—until the 1795 Treaty of Greenville marked the end of the Indian Wars. As there was no

Campus Martius at Marietta, Ohio, was designed by Rufus Putnam, who also supervised its construction. The strength of this fort was one of the main reasons that the Marietta settlement did not suffer from serious Indian attacks. Print from the 1903 *The Memoirs of Rufus Putnam and Certain Official Papers and Correspondence*, published by the National Society of the Colonial Dames of America in the State of Ohio.

man in the entire country with more experience in planning and constructing military fortifications than Rufus Putnam, Campus Martius surpassed all other frontier forts of its size.

On June 19, 1788, George Washington wrote to Richard Henderson[48]: "No Colony in America was ever settled under such favorable auspicies as that which has just commenced at the Muskingum. Information, property and strength will be its characteristics. I know many of the settlers personally & that there never were men better calculated to promote the wellfare of such a community."[49]

Shortly after Rufus had led the first settlers to Marietta, Major General Israel Putnam's son, Israel, Jr., joined them with his family.[50]

Some confusion has reigned over Major General Israel Putnam's burial place since a cemetery marker of Maj. L.J.P. [Lewis John Pope Putnam] Putnam in the Putnam Cemetery in Devola, Ohio, includes mention of L.J.P. Putnam's father, grandfather and great-grandfather. It reads:

To the Memory of
Israel Putnam.
Born at Salem Mass. Jan. 7, 1718.
Sen. Maj. Gen. of the Revolutionary War
A Friend and Confidential Advisor of Gen.
Washington. Died May 19, 1790. [It was May 29, 1790]

> Col. Israel Putnam, Son of
> Gen. I. Putnam. Died at Belpre, Ohio
> Mar. 7, 1812. Aged 72 Y.

> Israel Putnam
> Grand Son of Gen. I. Putnam.
> Died Mar 8, 1824. Aged 59 Y.

> This Monument Erected by
> Maj. L.J.P. Putnam,
> G. G. Son of Gen. I. Putnam, & Son of I. Putnam.

Major General Israel Putnam was actually buried in Brooklyn, Connecticut. L.J.P. Putnam's father Israel Putnam and grandfather Israel Putnam, Jr., are buried in the Devola cemetery. L.J.P. Putnam was 16 years old when Rufus Putnam died. He himself passed away in 1888 at age 80.

The new settlement at the mouth of the Muskingum River was first called Adelphia. In a December 3, 1787, letter to Rufus Putnam, Manasseh Cutler says:

> Saying so much about conveying letters reminds me of the necessity of a name for the place where you will reside. I doubt not you will early acquire the meaning of Muskingum; or you may meet with some other name that will be agreeable. At present, I must confess, I feel a partiality for the name proposed at Boston, and think it preferable to any that has yet been mentioned. I think that "Adelphia" will, upon the whole, be the most eligible. It strictly means brethren, and I wish it may ever be characteristic of the Ohio Company.[51]

Seven months later,[52] the settlers named it Marietta in honor of French queen Marie Antoinette. On July 9, the newly appointed governor General Arthur St. Clair arrived at Marietta. In 2010, 222 years after Adelphia was dropped as the town's name, it was picked up again—for the Adelphia Music Hall.

Also, the settlers named their county Washington. By 2019, 24 presidents have counties named after them, and 20 presidents do not. More counties are named after George Washington than any other president—31. Thomas Jefferson is second with 23 (or 26 if you consider counties named after something that was in turn named after Jefferson).

Of the presidents who have counties named after them, the last one to serve as president was Warren G. Harding. The twenty-ninth president of the United States, Harding served from 1921 to 1923. Harding County, New Mexico, was named after him when he became president. It had a population of 695 in the 2010 census.

While the Northwest Territories lands didn't see a permanent legal white settlement until Marietta in 1788, Kentucky (then part of the colony of Virginia) saw its first white village the year before the American Revolutionary War. Called Harrodstown, it was named after Pennsylvania-born hunter James Harrod.[53]

During the Revolutionary War an increasing number of settlers moved into Kentucky. The most famous settlement of the time was 1775's Fort Boonesborough, founded and named for legendary explorer Daniel Boone (1734–1820).

The new settlers to Ohio in many ways brought New England west with them. What George Bancroft said of New England towns could well apply to the new villages in eastern Ohio:

> Each town-meeting was a little legislature, and all inhabitants, the affluent and the more needy, the wise and the foolish, were members with equal franchises. There the taxes of the town were discussed and levied; there the village officers were chosen; there roads were laid out, and bridges voted; there the minister was elected, the representatives to the assembly were instructed. The debate was open to all.[54]

The new settlement held its first Fourth of July celebration three months after the first 48 settlers arrived. It was only 12 years since July 4, 1776, when the Declaration of Independence was signed, and less than five years since the treaty ending the Revolutionary War had stipulated that Ohio and the rest of the Northwest Territory would be transferred from British to American hands.

This 4th of July at Marietta, the thirteen-star flag of the United States "was hoisted in the forts, and the bastions and curtians decorated with standards."[55]

Colonel John May noted in his diary: "All labor comes to a pause today in memory of the Declaration of Independence. Our long bowery [a shelter made of tree boughs and/or vines] built on the east bank of the Muskingum; a table laid sixty feet long, in plain sight of the garrison, at one-quarter of a mile distance. At 1 o'clock General Harmer and his lady, Mrs. McCurders, and all the officers not on duty came over, and several other gentlemen."[56]

The day opened and closed with the firing of 13 cannon at nearby Fort Harmer. The dinner, set along the bank of the Muskingum River, featured "venison, bear meat, buffalo, and roasted pigs, procured from Williams's settlement, with a variety of fish."[57] However, the main attraction was a one-hundred-pound pike that was "suspended from a pole from the shoulders of two tall men, its tail dragged on the ground." According to historian Hildreth, it was the largest ever caught in the Muskingum River by white men.

Judge Varnum gave the main speech which began, "The memorable

Six. Pioneer Leader 121

Fourth of July will ever be celebrated with gratitude to the Supreme Being, for that revolution which caused tyranny and oppression to feed upon their own disappointment, and which crowned the exertions of patriotism with the noblest rewards of virtue."[58]

It was only 13 years since the Battle of Bunker Hill and few people present would have guessed that within less than 25 years there would be another war with Britain. To an audience that included many veterans of the war, Varnum said, "Our acknowledgments, therefore, are the more unreserved, as they flow from the most unequivocal feelings. Our friends—our country's friends—we embrace you as a band of brothers, connected by the most sacred ties! In the name of all who have fought, who have bled, who have died in the cause of freedom! In the name of all surviving patriots and heroes! In the name of a Washington! we declare that, in the honorable character of soldiers, you revere the sacred rights of citizens! Live then in this happy assemblage of superior minds! Whenever you may be called to the field of Mars, may you be crowned with unfading laurels! We know you fear not death—but, living or dying, may you receive the plaudits of grateful millions!"[59]

Rufus Putnam, leader and defender of the Marietta pioneers, was given the honor of proclaiming the toasts to celebrate the first Fourth of July celebration in the new settlement. He must have thought seriously about what he could toast on this special day. In fourteen toasts, he paid tribute to:

1. The United States
2. The Congress
3. His most Christian Majesty
4. The United Netherlands
5. The Friendly Powers throughout the world
6. The new Federal Constitution
7. His Excellency George Washington, and the Society of Cincinnati
8. His Excellency Governor St. Clair, and the Western Territory
9. The memory of those who have nobly fallen in defense of American freedom
10. Patriots, and Heroes
11. Captain Pipe, chief of the Delawares, and a happy treaty with the natives
12. Agriculture and Commerce, Arts and Sciences

13. The amiable partners of our delicate pleasures
14. The glorious Fourth of July[60]

Col. John May, who arrived in May 1788, describes well the steps he, as well as others, went through to create their homes in the wilderness. Some of his diary entries from May 31, 1788, through August 2, 1788, note some of the milestones reached in constructing a Marietta house.

> Saturday, May 31, 1788: All hands at work on my ten-acre lot. Took hold of it with spirit. There are six of us in all, and we completely cleared an acre and a half by sunset.[61]
>
> Tuesday, June 10, 1788: The people hewing timber for the house, which I am in hopes to raise in eight or ten days[62];
>
> Wednesday, June 11, 1788: I have enlarged my gang to-day, which I have divided into three squads: four men hewing timber; two clearing land; and two digging a cellar in the bank, near my boat. This conveniency is much wanted to keep the beer and other matters in. We have dug no wells as yet, and the river water is too warm to be pleasant....[63]
>
> Friday, July 11, 1788: A delightful day. All hands at work on the house. This an arduous undertaking, and will cost more than I intended. Am building from several motives. First, for the benefit of the settlement; second, from a prospect or hope of gain hereafter; third, for an asylum for myself and family, should we ever want it; fourth, as a place where 1 can leave my stores and baggage in safety; and lastly, to gratify a foolish ambition, I suppose it is. The house is thirty-six feet long, eighteen wide, and fifteen high; a good cellar under it, and drain; and is the first (of the kind) built in Marietta....[64]
>
> Monday, July 14, 1788: All hands at work on the house. Eat green peas today from my own garden, planted exactly five weeks ago. All this trusting to Providence but a little while. Things do grow amazingly!....[65]
>
> Friday, July 25, 1788: Yesterday employed in finishing the house.... Glazed the windows for the house to-day. I packed eighty quarries of glass at Boston, and found them all whole....[66]
>
> Friday and Saturday, August 1–2, 1788: We begin now to knock the boat to pieces, in order to obtain boards suitable for flooring the house.[67]

The westward expansion welcomed all people. Compared to elsewhere in the nation, there was relatively little prejudice—among the community every person needed to depend on each other. You were well-respected by your abilities. Many of the Ohio founders, especially Rufus Putnam, wanted no part of slavery to ever touch this new land.

Samuel Prescott Hildreth in his 1848 work on the history of the Ohio settlements,[68] mentions a key member of the early Marietta settlement—African American Kit Putnam. Kit had worked for General Israel Putnam in Pomfret, Connecticut, in the General's last years. He then lived with the General's son, Colonel Israel Putnam, Jr. (1739–1812). In the fall of 1789,

Israel, Jr., along with his son Aaron Waldo Putnam,[69] who was about 22 years old, and Kit Putnam, who was about 18 years old, traveled to the Marietta settlement. A year later, Israel Jr. returned to Connecticut to bring the rest of his family out to Ohio. His father, General Putnam had died the previous May.[70] In the winter of 1790-91, conflicts in Ohio between the settlers from New England and the local Native Americans prevented Israel Jr. from going back to Ohio with his family. They didn't leave until 1795.

Kit stayed at the settlement in Belpre, Ohio, where he was chosen as the leader of the young people:

> in all their athletic sports for his wonderful activity, and much beloved for his kind and cheerful disposition. When abroad in the fields cultivating or planting their crops, he was one of their best hands, either for work or to stand as a sentry. On these occasions he sometimes took his station in the lower branches of a tree, where he could have a wider range of vision, and give early notice of the approach of danger. Under the watchful vigilance of Kitt, all felt safe at their work.[71]

Benjamin Franklin Stone tells of the time Kit, also known to Stone as Christopher Malbone, almost drowned. Early in the spring of 1793, Kit, along with A.W. Putnam and Major Bradford of Farmer's Castle moved their cattle across the Ohio River where they could "run in the woods where they were less exposed to Indians." Stone explains:

> They took them over in a flat-boat. While they were on the river, the cattle took fright and crowded to one end and sunk the boat. The cattle swam away. Bradford, Putnam and Kit clung to the boat till it rose. They could not swim. They stood on the boat about up to their waists in water, calling for help. Two men went out to them in a very small canoe. It was not safe to take in more than one at a time. Kit, being shorter, stood deeper in the water and seemed more overcome. Bradford and Putnam both said, "Take Kit first." They did so, and brought him ashore at the garrison. He could not walk. He was helped up the bank into my father's house. One man only returned with the small canoe and took off Putnam and Bradford. Then the flat-boat was towed to shore and secured. This version of the story does more honor to Bradford and Putnam than Hildreth's "Pioneer." This is the true statement. I was an eyewitness.[72]

When Kit reached the age of 21, he worked for Captain Devol, on the Muskingum River, and "assisted in tending the floating mill, and clearing the land on the farm." Shortly before Kit's death, he voted in an election which was held to choose delegates for an Ohio Constitutional Convention. It is believed that he was the first African American to ever vote in Ohio.[73] When Kit Putnam died c. 1802, he was, in the words of Hildreth, "much lamented for his many personal good qualities and industrious habits."[74]

Marietta Earthworks

The value of Marietta's site at the confluence of the Muskingum and Ohio rivers was recognized many centuries earlier by the Hopewell, a pre–Columbian Native American people, who lived along rivers in the Northeastern and Midwestern United States from about 100 BCE to 500 CE. When Rufus Putnam originally surveyed city lots in 1788, he recognized the ancient ruins, and it was determined that the central mound would be respected and left undisturbed. He was instrumental in preserving it, and would later be buried in the Mound Cemetery, which surrounds the central mound.

Today, the Marietta Earthworks is the name given to a Hopewell archaeological site at Marietta, the parts of which were given Latin names by the 18th century American colonists. It includes the Sacra Via, with three walled enclosures, the Capitolium mound, the Quadranaou platform mound, and the Conus burial mound. The most intact of these is the burial mound. The thirty-foot-high hill Conus was originally used for ceremonies. When first seen by the settlers from New England, it had a circumference of 375 feet around its base, and a moat fifteen feet wide and five feet deep.

The mounds were the first of their kind in the country to be documented. They were first investigated in 1786 by Fort Harmar's commander Captain Jonathan Hart. Two years later, soon after the founding of Marietta, Rufus Putnam studied the works when he surveyed the city's lots.

On March 2, 1789, at a meeting of the agents of the Ohio Company, a committee of three members was formed to lease the public squares of Marietta. By that means, the "great Mound" was to be preserved. The minutes read: "The Committee are to point out the Mode of improvement for Ornament and in what manner the Ancient works shall be preserved & also to Ascertain the amount of what is to be given."[75]

In 1930, Henry Clyde Shetrone wrote *The Mound-Builders*. As director and archeologist for the Ohio State Archaeological and Historical Society, Shetrone investigated the builders of prehistoric earthworks and mounds throughout the United States. In his book, he singles out the importance of Rufus Putnam's efforts to study the mounds of Marietta:

> Of by far the greatest interest and importance among the early reports, however, is the rare old map of the Marietta works prepared by General Rufus Putnam for the Ohio Company in 1788. This venerable document, carefully preserved in the library of Marietta College, may be regarded as the genesis of the science of archaeology in the United States.[76]

Most of the area's mounds were damaged in the 19th century, but the establishment of Mound Cemetery in 1801 saved the Conus Mound from future damage. Mound Cemetery is believed by many to contain the graves of more Revolutionary War officers than any other cemetery in the United States.

In 1968, the Washington County Historical Society placed a plaque at Mound Cemetery, listing Revolutionary War veterans who are buried in the graveyard. Thirty-seven names are given, including these generals: Rufus Putnam, an Army brigadier general, Benjamin Tupper (1738–1792) a Continental Army brevetted brigadier general, Joseph Buell (1763–1812), a militia major general; and Gen. Joseph Willcox (1757–1817), a militia brigadier general.

The other 33 officers interred in Mound Cemetery are[77]:

Isaac Berry
Salah Bosworth
Nathaniel Dodge
Ephraim Emerson
Nathan Evans
Gershom Flagg
Ephraim Foster
Simeon Goodwin
John Green
Griffin Greene, Sr.
James Hatch
Samuel Hildreth, Sr.
John Holt
Matthew Kerr
Levi Lankton
Maj. Joseph Lincoln
Andrew McAllister
Capt. William Moulton, Jr.
Capt. Josiah Munro
Col. Ichabod Nye
Capt. Stanton Prentiss
Maj. Ezra Putnam
Capt. Joseph Rogers
Capt. Nathaniel Saltonstall
Col. Enoch Shepherd
Col. Ebenezer Sproat
Col. William Stacy, Sr.
Col. Robert Taylor
Jeremiah Thomas
Surgeon Jabez True
Maj. Anselm Tupper
Commodore Abraham Whipple
Judge Dudley Woodbridge

Marietta's location provided everything that a pioneer settlement could desire: a perfect location for traveling by two major rivers, primeval forests to furnish firewood and building materials, plentiful wild game, etc. However, as the people of Marietta would find in subsequent centuries, there was one major natural disadvantage—floods. It's been said that when construction of the settlement began, Native American onlookers were astonished that anyone would build so close to the water.

Today, on the south side of the Muskingum River from downtown

Marietta lies the 1796 Harmar Cemetery. A nearby historical marker states, "The earliest headstones have been destroyed by weather and floods."

Rufus Putnam's experience in many walks of life providentially came together with the Marietta settlement. With Indian hostiles an ever-present possibility, his vast experience in planning, designing, and constructing fortifications was invaluable. That the Marietta settlement was not attacked was due in large measure to the presence of his Campus Martius fort.

Putnam's prior occupation of millwright undoubted helped the settlement. Rufus was more than capable of planning and supervising the construction of everything from water mills to bridges to farm buildings.

For decades, Putnam had owned and managed his own farms in North Brookfield and Rutland, Massachusetts. When Marietta's settlers, some of whom had little farming experience, needed help with plantings, raising livestock, establishing orchards, etc., they always had Rufus Putnam available to consult.

In the early days of Marietta, Putnam supervised the surveying of private and public lands. If there were any questions or disputes in later years, it was not difficult to speak with an authority—eight years after Marietta's founding, Rufus Putnam was named surveyor general of the United States.

The bottom line: Putnam didn't just lead a group of pioneers into the wilderness and leave them to fend for themselves. He stayed for the rest of his life and guided his fellow citizens through the construction of their homes, businesses, boats, public buildings, etc. He was their rock and strength when they fretted about possible Indian attacks, or droughts, floods and other natural disasters. Putnam's role in Marietta might be summed up in one word—leader.

CHAPTER SEVEN

Father of Ohio

The First Court

The Northwest Ordinance of July 13, 1787, stated in its sections on judges:

> There shall also be appointed a court to consist of three judges, any two of whom to form a court, who shall have a common law jurisdiction, and reside in the district, and have each therein a freehold estate in five hundred acres of land, while in the exercise of their offices; and their commissions shall continue in force during good behavior.[1]

Along with the territorial governor, the judges had great power, as section 5 of the ordinance establishes:

> The governor and judges, or a majority of them, shall adopt and publish in the district such laws of the original states, criminal and civil, as may be necessary, and best suited to the circumstances of the district, and report them to congress from time to time, which laws shall be in force in the district, until the organization of the general assembly therein, unless disapproved of by congress; but afterwards the Legislature shall have authority to alter them as they shall think fit.[2]

In July 1788, three months after Rufus Putnam's party founded the first settlement in the Northwest Territory, government leaders arrived at the new village. They included Governor Arthur St. Clair, and territorial supreme court judges, Generals Samuel Holden Parsons and James Mitchell Varnum. These men initially were occupied with determining which statutes of the thirteen states of the new country would be appropriate in the frontier settlements.[3]

In 1788, the Northwest Territory's first common pleas court session was held in Marietta. Three judges had been appointed to the court: Rufus Putnam, General Benjamin Tupper, and Archibald Crary. However, Crary was "not much inclined to occupy public positions" and apparently left the court to Putnam and Tupper, since only two judges were needed for a quorum.[4]

On September 2, 1788, the court convened for the first time. The ceremony was impressive: a procession was formed, led by the high sheriff with his sword drawn. He was followed in order by the citizens of the settlement, the officers of the Fort Harmar garrison, members of the bar, the Supreme Judges, the governor and the minister, and the judges of the Court of Common Pleas—Rufus Putnam and Benjamin Tupper. They marched from the "point" where most of the homes were located to the Campus Martius stockade. The procession was witnessed by a large group of Indians from "the most powerful tribes," who had come for the purpose of making a treaty.[5]

At the site of the court, Judges Putnam and Tupper were seated, and the minister, the Rev. Manasseh Cutler (1742–1823), invoked the divine blessing. High Sheriff Ebenezer Sproat (1752–1805) proclaimed: "A Court is opened for the administration of even-handed justice to the poor and the rich, to the guilty and the innocent, without respect of persons, none to be punished without a trial by their Peers, and then in pursuance of the laws and evidence in the case."[6]

Excerpts from Col. John May's diary of 1788 give a good idea of the steps taken by Rufus Putnam and the other leader of early Marietta to establish a functioning community:

> Wednesday, May 28th.... The directors and agents present agreed to lease the ministerial lot to different persons, in lots of ten acres each, for a term not less than one hundred years, at the option of the lessee—to be without rent the first ten years, and then a fixed rent the remainder of the time. This was done to accommodate a number of proprietors present, whose eight-acre lots were drawn at a distance. Went this afternoon to survey the ten-acre lots, and drew for them in the evening....[7]
>
> Tuesday, [June] 10th 1788. Met this morning, according to adjournment, and after much debate and discussion, agreed to cut up our commons into three-acre lots, to be drawn for in July. This has appeased the minds of the people. We also appointed officers of police.[8]
>
> Tuesday, 17th.... This evening Judge Parsons' and General Varnum's commissions were read; also, regulations for the government of the people. In fact, by-laws were much wanted. Officers were named to command the militia; guards to be mounted every evening; all males more than fifteen years old to appear under arms every Sunday....[9]
>
> Wednesday, [July] 2d 1788.... Attended ... a meeting of directors and agents, according to order at Providence, 8th March. Chose a committee to make preparation for drawing the city lots. Entered into several debates, and at 2 o'clock adjourned until Monday, 7th inst., at 8 o'clock in the morning, for the purpose of drawing the city lots, and transacting such other business as may be thought necessary for the establishment of our infant settlement.[10]

> Wednesday, 9th.... This is, in a sense, the birthday of this Western World. Governor St. Clair arrived at the garrison. His landing was announced by the discharge of fourteen cannon; and all rejoiced at his coming....[11]
>
> Sunday, 20th.... At 11 o'clock to-day a religious service. Mr. Daniel Breck began the observances by singing, praying, and preaching. The place of worship was our bowery, on the bank directly over my ship.[12]
>
> Thursday, 31st. Last evening the governor sent the police officer to inform us that we must keep a good lookout, as there were three parties of Indian warriors out; some of them, he thought, intended against our settlement.[13]

In the days before jailhouses were practical, corporal punishment was common in 18th century Ohio. The territorial laws' punishments included ample use of stocks (with boards fastened around the ankles and wrists) and the pillory (where the head and hands were fastened to boards mounted to a pole).

On September 6, 1788, the first law was passed that prescribed whippings. The crimes that merited this punishment included rioting, breaking into houses, stores or shops in the night, perjury, refusing to be sworn to a fact, arson, drunkenness, failure to pay fines, larceny, idle, vain and obscene conversation, profanity, and irreverence to the Supreme Being.[14]

When Putnam was appointed surveyor general of the United States in 1796, he thought first of his responsibilities as a judge. In accepting the commission, he wrote to U.S. Secretary of State Timothy Pickering:

> But as I conceive my acceptance of this office will or may be supposed to vacate that of Judge, the interest of the Government requires that I should delay the matter a few days Because the General Court of the Territory ought to Set in this County next week which it cannot do without my attendance—but as Soon as this Court is over I Shall accept the appointment Shall take the oath of office required by Law & be ready to receive your further communication.[15]

Putnam Recommendations for His Successor

In his letter, accompanying Putnam's Surveyor General commission, Pickering asked Putnam whom he would recommend as his successor on the bench, as well as his "opinion of those who for their character, talents and integrity are entitled to a preference." Pickering "particularly" requested Putnam's opinion of Joseph Gilman.

Rufus Putnam's reply is interesting as it demonstrates the type of person the 59-year-old Putnam deemed to be of judicial temperament. In addition to the 58-year-old Gilman, he recommended 36-year-old Revolutionary War veteran Peregrine Foster, who was one of the 47 men who founded Marietta with Rufus in 1788[16]; and 49-year-old Connecticut-born Dudley

Woodbridge.[17] Also mentioned were 43-year-old Connecticut-native Thomas Ives, a Yale College–educated lawyer of Great Barrington, Massachusetts,[18] and 53-year-old William Judd, of Farmington, Connecticut.[19]

Joseph Gilman was appointed Rufus Putnam's successor.[20] One month younger than Rufus, New Hampshire–born Gilman had served as a state senator, and during the Revolution he had headed up the state committee responsible for supplying New Hampshire troops. With the onset of postwar economic problems, Gilman, his wife and son immigrated to Marietta, Ohio. Northwest Territory Governor Arthur St. Clair appointed him Judge of Probate, Judge of the Court of Quarter Sessions, and Judge of the Court of Common Pleas. Gilman served as Putnam's replacement as a U.S. territorial judge for seven years—up until Ohio became a state. He died at Marietta in 1806 at age 68.

Early Marietta

In 1842, Felix Renick writes of the early Ohio settlers:

> The pioneer's dress consisted principally of a tow linen shirt and pantaloons, manufactured by their wives, daughters and female friends. The remainder was nearly all of buckskin, killed with their guns and dressed by their own hands. Their moccasins fitted the foot neatly, and dry oak leaves mostly supplied the place of socks or stockings. Above these a pair of buckskin leggins, or gaiters, made to fit the leg and tie in at the ankle with the moccasins. These extended some distance above the knees, and a strap from the upper part extending up and buttoning to the hip of the pantaloons. These leggins were a defence against rattlesnakes, briars, nettles, &c. In cutting these leggins, or gaiters, there was a surplus left on the outside, at the outer seam. This surplus was left from one to two inches in width, which, after the seam was sewed, was cut into an, ornamental fringe.[21]

The men's hunting shirt also was made of dressed buckskin and "ornamented with the fringe down the outside of the arms, around the collar, cape, belt and tail, and sometimes down the seams under the arms, or even other parts." Renick comments: "ornaments on the buckskin hunting shirts were carried to excess by those among the pioneers whose tastes were less refined."[22]

Renick contends that so clothed, the frontier men would "attend church, go to a wedding, quilting, or visit their sweethearts, and even to get married." Although, "a new hunting shirt, leggins and moccasins had the same charms to draw forth the loving looks and the sweet smiles of the lassies then, as the long tailed blues, the dandy dress, or the glittering uniform now; and they were not a whit the less appreciated by the laddies, coming from rosy lassies in linsey wolsey, or perhaps partly in buckskin, than they are now after they have passed lines of silks, laces and artificials."[23]

On March 1, 1786, eight Massachusetts counties sent delegates to Boston to create the Ohio Company's Articles of Agreement. Several weeks later, surveyors were sent to the Northwest Territory. Again, General Tupper was sent instead of Putnam, who still had work to complete in Maine. Putnam, General Lincoln, and Judge Rice (of Wiscasset) were sent to negotiate with Maine's Penobscot Indians in late summer.

Rufus notes in his Memoirs that on November 23, 1787, the director of the Ohio Company appointed him "Superintendent of all the business, relating to the commencement of a Settlement of their Lands in the territory Northwest of the river Ohio." He was to be aided by four surveyors, 22 assistants to the surveyors, six boat builders, four carpenters, a blacksmith, and nine laborers with two wagons.[24]

The first party of settlers, under Major Haffield White, left Danvers, Massachusetts, on December 1. The other party met with Rufus at Harford, Connecticut, on January 1, 1788.

Next to Putnam, the most important man to the early Marietta settlement was probably Benjamin Tupper. A veteran of the French and Indian War, Tupper was a colonel during the Revolutionary War. At the end of the war, Tupper received the rank of brevetted brigadier general. Tupper lived the rest of his life in the Northwest.

Three months after their arrival at Marietta, the Ohio Company leaders were busy with creating a settlement. On July 2, 1788, the first meeting of the directors and agents of the Ohio Company held in Ohio was at the future site of the Town of Marietta. Present were directors Samuel Parsons, Rufus Putnam, and James Varnum, and eight agents for other shareholders.

At the meeting, three of the most important things covered were: to appoint a "Board of Police," to vote that the only valid votes of agents in the future be in cases where more than 500 shares are represented in the vote, and most noteworthy of all, to name their city "Marietta." It also gave Latin names to the public square (Campus Martius), prehistoric mounds within the city (Quadranaou, Capitolium and Cecelia), and the main road (Sacra Via).

At a Board of Directors meeting on July 21, 1788, it was ordered that: "...such Number of Carpenters and other Labourers as are necessary to complete the Block House now begun, with the greatest expedition be immediately furnished, and General Putnam is desired to engage them upon the best terms he can." The meeting's minutes also state: "Ordered That General Putnam be empowered to employ Teams as shall be found necessary for compleating the Block House and fixing the Landing place."[25]

The Ohio Company's land office in Marietta, Ohio. Rufus Putnam transacted much of the Ohio Company's business from this small structure. Today, it is the oldest surviving building in the state. Print from the 1903 *The Memoirs of Rufus Putnam and Certain Official Papers and Correspondence*, published by the National Society of the Colonial Dames of America in the State of Ohio.

Regarding land surveys, the Board ordered "that General Putnam continue in the pay and employment of the Company, such number of surveyors, under his direction, as are necessary to Survey the 8 acre, 3 acre, and City Lots already ordered to be laid out" and the surveyors were to receive two rations per day. The Board also "ordered that so many chain men and other persons necessary to a speedy completion of the surveys already mentioned in a foregoing Resolve be engaged by General Putnam."

They then set the wages of the carpenters at half-a-dollar per day and one ration. The other workers were to receive a maximum of seven dollars per month and one ration per day. A ration was described in the Board's minutes as:

- 1½ lbs. of bread or flour.
- 1 lb. of pork or beef, venison or other meat equivalent.
- 1 gill [about four ounces] of whiskey.
- Vegetables when to be procured.[26]

The later minutes include similar necessary projects. For example, on September 15, 1788, the Directors "Ordered That a Contract be proposed for finishing the Bridge and that the Highway Leading to Campus Martius and the Common in front be cleared as soon as possible by Contract. And Block that Cellers under Block Houses be dug by Contract."[27]

In this first year of the new settlement, security was a top priority. At a meeting on September 15, 1788, it was ordered:

> Whereas it is highly expedient that the Houses agreed to be built in Campus Martius should immediately be completed or that the lines connecting the Block Houses should be Stockaded. Therefore resolved that the persons who have engaged to erect Houses in those lines, do forthwith erect the outer walls of those Houses to the height of twelve feet, or, at their own expense erect a sufficient stockade in the lines connecting the Block Houses, and in case any persons shall neglect to build the outer wall of his House, or erect a stockade in the exterior line thereof, by a space of 14 fourteen Days his Right to build therein shall cease, and the Directors will grant the Right to other person; and the persons to whom the Licence to build is already granted, are called upon to inform the Directors whether they will comply with this order; and if any shall neglect to give such information within three Days, the Directors will consider such neglect as a determination not to build.[28]

Today, the only surviving part of the Campus Martius fortification is the c. 1788 Rufus Putnam House, which was used by the General as his residence and his office. In an effort to duplicate the best of New England carpentry, Putnam imported wrought iron nails for his new house. Most of Campus Martius' structure was recycled after the people of Marietta no longer feared Indian attacks; the lumber, hardware, and other building materials were used to construct new houses and barns. Rufus Putnam himself doubled the size of his house with wood from the adjacent Campus Martius blockhouse.

In the late 1920s, when the State of Ohio constructed the Campus Martius Museum on the site of the Campus Martius fort, it added exhibits on Native American clothing, tools, and culture, the early Marietta settlement, the Ohio River, and the Northwest Territory. Today, standing on its original foundation, the Rufus Putnam House is completely enclosed within the Campus Martius Museum, which was opened in 1928. On the grounds outside the museum, is the oldest office building still standing in the State of Ohio—the Ohio Company's 20-by-30-foot Land Office, which was built shortly after the first settlers arrived in Marietta in 1788. In that building as superintendent of the Ohio Company, Rufus Putnam oversaw the drawing of the first maps of the Northwest Territory and the recording of land sales.

In 1900, the Land Office was purchased by the Ohio Chapter of the Colonial Dames of America for use as a museum. In 1953, it was moved to the Campus Martius Museum, where today it is a major historic attraction.

Rufus Putnam described the growing of corn in the settlement's first season (1788):

> By May 5th, the necessary work in the woods for making the plan of the eight acre lots was completed, and I made a proposition to the people in the company's employ that as many as chose might clear the land, and plant on their own account, and make up the time after their present contract expired. To this proposition many of them agreed, and began the same day to prepare lands for planting by cutting away the small and girdling the larger trees.
>
> Putnam notes that a number of "adventurers" arrived, including Col. [John] May and Col. [William] Stacy. They went to work at clearing city land, despite knowing that if it was converted to private use at a later time, they might lose any rights to it. Putnam states that from early May to June 20th, "one hundred and thirty-two acres were planted with corn, besides a large quantity of potatoes, beans, &c." Of this, thirty-five acres of the corn land was plowed or harrowed so "as to be in tolerable good order for a crop" and the rest of the land was planted with hoes.
>
> Boston merchant Colonel John May was one of Marietta's early arrivals. An officer during the Revolutionary War, he first arrived in Marietta on May 26, 1788. He returned to Boston and came back to Marietta a second time—in 1789. He is credited with building the first framed house in the town.[29]

Putnam then relates a problem that caused some of the would-be farmers to neglect their crops:

> The great misfortune was that the leaves of the beech and poplar, or aspen, trees of which there are a considerable number, did not die with the girdling, by which means the corn was so shaded as to greatly lessen the crop. The prospect in the forepart of the season was so discouraging that some of the planters did not hoe their corn at all,

and some hoed but once and that very badly. Under all these circumstances there is a great deal of corn and forage raised.[30]

But there is obvious pride when Putnam relates the stories of the harvest:

> There is very little which will not yield from twenty to thirty bushels to the acre. A piece of interval on the bank of the Ohio, belonging to Mr. Cory has been gathered and measures 114 bushels of ears to the acre. Some of the ears have produced a pint and one-half of shelled corn, and it is very common for an ear to yield a pint. I made the following experiment upon corn gathered, braided and hung up in a room over a fire for three weeks until it was thoroughly dry. I took a pint, and on full trial both by scales and steelyard, I found the pint of corn *weighed fifteen ounces and a half*, which gives 62 pounds to the bushel. In short, the quality of the corn of this country is in all respects equal to any raised in New England, all excess in quantity therefore must be a balance in our favor.[31]

After all the pioneers' diligence in working the land in the new Northwest Territory settlements, their crops were still dependent on the mercy of the weather. The farmers could not fight nature, and their survival was not assured until they harvested their crops.

In 1789, early frosts ruined crops before harvest time. To make matters worse, the ever present possibility of an Indian attack made hunting a dangerous pursuit, and there was a general shortage of wild game in the immediate area. The settlers were reduced to eating nettle tops boiled with the little corn that they had.[32] Only an early squash crop in 1790 saved them from near starvation.[33]

The Marietta police force was a priority for citizenry that had "always been accustomed to law and good order." They were not "content to live without regulations, although they dwelt in the wilderness, and their city was yet covered by the trees of the forest." The first board of police included Rufus Putnam, Archibald Crary,[34] Griffin Greene,[35] Robert Oliver,[36] and Nathaniel Goodale.[37]

The first marriage in the Marietta settlement was between Winthrop Sargent, who was secretary of the Northwest Territory, and Rowena Tupper, the daughter of Benjamin Tupper. Joining the couple in matrimony on February 6, 1789, was the county's judge of the court of common pleas—Rufus Putnam.[38]

Later in 1788, New Jersey people began three other settlements near Cincinnati on the Ohio River. Before the end of the century, Connecticut men founded Cleveland, Ohio, and Virginia settlers came to live in Ohio's Scioto Valley.[39]

On December 20, 1790, weeks after bringing his family out to the Marietta settlement, Rufus Putnam wrote to President George Washington: "It was as late as the 5th of November before I arrived here with my family, since which I have been so busily engaged in preparing for the winter, that I have not been able to attend minutely to any other object, but in general I have observed that our crops have been very fine, that the spirit of industry and enterprise among the people is as great as ever, and the improvements and buildings which they have made are truly surprising."[40]

Rufus goes on to mention that fewer settlers had come from New England in 1790 than in 1789, but that about 500 French men, women and children had arrived to make the Marietta area their home. It was also a time when the settlers along the Ohio River were worried about Indian attacks. Putnam tells his old Commander-in-chief:

> "As to Indian matters we are fearful that the spring will open by a general attack of the frontiers unless prevented by Government carrying a war into the enemy's country. It is possible that the Shawanos &c. may be for peace but I consider it very doubtful."[41]

Putnam is concerned that formerly friendly Native Americans of the Delaware and other tribes are "keeping aloof." He writes: "From our first arrival here in April 1788 till the militia went down the river to join the expedition the Wyandots and Delawares were constantly among us, not a day, scarcely, passed but we saw more or less of them; but none have been in since, except two women."[42]

Putnam confides to Washington that he fears "mischief is concerting among" some of the tribes. He writes: "When or where it will fall God only knows: but I trust, Sir, that in the multiplicity of public concerns which claim your attention, our little colony will not be forgotten."[43]

Writing as someone hundreds of miles from the United States government, which indeed he was, he states: "I know that you consider the settlement of this Country of utility to the United States, and I believe you will not think me vain or presumptuous when I say that the inhabitants that compose this settlement have as great a claim to protection as any under the Federal Government."[44]

From this letter one can infer that the people of Marietta and its outlying settlements had been under great stress. Putnam reminds Washington that "A great proportion of us served our country through the war; our securities we received at par with which we purchased our lands, and in all other respects we have given unequivocal proof of our attachment to constitutional Government, and being good subjects in general." He states that if they are not provided with "necessary supplies" there may be "more ill consequences than some narrow-minded politicians may apprehend."[45]

Rufus Putnam's house, originally part of the southeast corner of Campus Martius, was his home until his death. It was then the home of Arius Nye until his death in 1865. Ownership passed to his daughter, Minerva T. Nye (1853–1926). In 1919, the State of Ohio purchased the site of Campus Martius from Minerva and Arius Nye's niece, Lucy Nye Davis (1849–1931), for a total of $16,000 and placed it under the control of the Ohio Archaeological and Historical Society.[46]

Rufus and his fellow settlers were very fond of names derived from ancient Rome. In addition to Campus Martius, they named a small steam that flowed through the southern part of Marietta the "Tiber." Today's Tiber Way is named for that stream. In the late 18th century, a 90-foot-long and 25-foot-high bridge was built over Marietta's "Tiber."[47]

Indian Wars

As David McCullough states in *The Pioneers*, Rufus Putnam "wanted always to be fair in his dealings with the native tribes, and he provided much needed, sound leadership through the dark time of the Indian Wars."[48]

Rufus and his party must have been well aware of the Gnadenhutten massacre, which occurred six years earlier, about 75 miles north of Marietta. In March 1782, Pennsylvania militiamen murdered and scalped 28 men, 29 women, and 39 children of the Delaware tribe at a Moravian Church mission. All of the victims were Christians.

After capturing the defenseless Indians, the militiamen voted on the way they would kill their captives. Tomahawking and scalping received more votes than burning them alive. According to the Moravian missionaries: "It may be easily conceived how great their terror was at hearing a sentence so unexpected. However, they soon recollected themselves, and patiently suffered the murderers to lead them into two houses, in one of which the brethren were confined and in the other the sisters and children."[49]

The Indians asked for "a short delay, that they might prepare themselves for death, which request was granted them. Then asking pardon for whatever offence they had given, or grief they had occasioned to each other, they knelt down, offering fervent prayers to God their Saviour and kissing one another. Under a flood of tears, fully resigned to his will, they sung praises unto him, in the joyful hope that they would soon be relieved from all pains and join their Redeemer in everlasting bliss."[50]

The murderers were impatient to begin in the men's house and one picked up a "cooper's mallet" and knocked down one after another of the Indians "until he counted fourteen that he had killed with his own hands.

He then handed the instrument to one of his fellow-murderers, saying: 'My arm fails me. Go on in the same way. I think I have done pretty well.'"[51]

In the second house, which contained the women, the children and a few men, there were only two survivors of the massacre—boys of about fourteen. One had been scalped, played dead, and escaped to the woods after dark. The other boy dropped through a trapdoor into the cellar. He hid there a full day while blood seeped down through the floor boards "in streams." At dark he escaped, found the other boy in the woods, and they fled to safety.

Two years before Rufus and the Ohio Company set out to establish their settlement at the junction of the Ohio and Muskingum rivers, farmer Abraham Lincoln was plowing a field on the Kentucky side of the Ohio River when he was shot to death by Indians. Twenty-three years later, his name would be given to a grandson who would also be shot to death.

In 1854, in a letter to relative Jesse Lincoln, the future U.S. President Abraham Lincoln stated: "I am the grandson of your uncle Abraham; and the story of his death by the Indians, and of Uncle Mordecai, then fourteen years old, killing one of the Indians, is the legend more strongly than all others imprinted upon my mind and memory."[52]

Since the first weeks of the Marietta settlement, Indian attacks were feared. On May 29, 1788, Col. John May noted in his diary:

> This evening, arrived two long boats from the Rapids, with officers and soldiers, the number about one hundred. On their passage up the river they were fired upon by a strong party of Indians, headed by a white man. They returned the fire, and had two men killed. They were obliged to drop down the river a piece, and come by the place in the night. There are various reports about the hostilities of the savages, but nothing to be depended on. The Indians are frequently in here, and seem to be on friendly terms. I have shaken hands with many of them. My people employed in clearing land. I have been, this afternoon, sowing garden-seeds....[53]

On July 23, 1788, Col. John May wrote:

> Henry Williams alarmed us a little this evening, when he returned from the Virginia shore: he brought information that our settlement was to be attacked this night by three strong parties of Chippewaw Indians—so said the report—to relieve the prisoners. We have sent this information over to the garrison. It proved false, however; but it made some trouble for us. We may always expect trouble while traveling through this life, which is nothing more than a wilderness world. We ought to make the best use we can of these matters, small and great. At Boston we have frequent alarms of fire, and inundations of the tides; here the Indians answer the same purpose.[54]

Benjamin Stone mentions that during the Indians Wars (1791 through 1794), Continental troops were stationed at Marietta and Farmer's Castle, which was the name of the fortification at Belpre, approximately 14 miles down the Ohio River from Marietta.

> Some of the inhabitants at each station in the Territory were enlisted and drew pay and rations during the war, though permitted to stay at home. Twice while we were at Farmer's Castle, Aaron Waldo Putnam and Nathaniel Little were fired upon and chased into the garrison. Some cattle were killed. A large pair of oxen of Captain Miles's were wounded, and came in,—one of them so badly that he was butchered and the meat divided among the people. The heads of families and all property owners entered into an association, agreeing that the loss of anyone by Indians should be the loss of the whole, and so each one should pay to the loser in proportion to the number of the individual livestock. Mr. Benoni Hurlburt, one of the spies, was killed by Indians near the mouth of Little Hocking—shot through the breast, scalped, and tomahawked. I remember seeing the wounds. It was a sorrowful sight to his wife and children.[55]

Stone continues:

> The people began to move out of Farmer's Castle in the fall of 1791 into the old cabins, each on his old clearing, hoping that they could live that way without being destroyed by Indians, depending upon the information which the spies would give of the approach of Indians near the settlements in time for the people to flee together back to Farmer's Castle or to build a new garrison nearer their fields. They hoped also to hear soon that Governor St. Clair, who had some months been marching his army up the Great Miami, would defeat and intimidate the Indians so that we should soon enjoy peace. But the event was the reverse of our hopes.[56]
>
> The way in which people had to cultivate their lands—by working in parties, changing work, going armed, and having sentinels, as you have heard me relate, was a hard way of living. And having to travel so far to their farms added to the trouble, so that the people of the upper and the lower settlements moved back in the fall of 1791 and built the upper and lower garrisons. The upper garrison was on the farm of Captain Jonathan Stone. The lower garrison was on Major Nathan Goodell's farm. The news of St. Clair's defeat by the Indians, after we had moved back to the upper settlement, spread terror through all the infant settlements. But we kept close in our garrisons, and the Indians never attacked a block house all the time of the war. They passed by us into Virginia, and killed many more there than in the Territory.[57]

At the suggestion of Rufus Putnam, the Ohio Company settlements early on employed "spies" and "rangers" in Ohio. As explained in *A History of Belpre, Washington County, Ohio*, the spies scoured

> the country every day the distance of eight or ten miles around the garrisons, making a circuit of twenty-five or thirty miles and accomplishing their task generally by three or four o'clock in the afternoon. They left the garrison at daylight, always two in company, traveling rapidly over the hills and stopping to examine more carefully such places as it was probable the Indians would pass over, in making their approach to the settlements, guided in this respect by the direction of the ridges or the water courses.[58]

The appearance of the spies was noteworthy. "Their dress in summer was similar to that worn by Indians. Their pay was five shillings, or eighty cents a day as appears from the old pay roll. They were amenable to the commanding officer of the station but under the direct control of Col. Sproat, who was employed by the United States. They had signs known to themselves, by which they recognized a ranger from an Indian even when painted like one."[59]

As E.C. Dawes states in his notes in Rufus's journal: "[Robert Rogers] battalion [of rangers] was the model from which Rufus Putnam organized the company of rangers which so effectively protected the Ohio Company settlements during the Indian war, 1791–1795."[60] Over three decades earlier, American guerrilla fighter Robert Rogers devised 28 "Rules of Ranging" for his soldiers in the French and Indian War. As a veteran ranger, Rufus Putnam knew those rules well.[61]

John Kilbourn in 1833 states:

> The inhabitants [of Washington county] are almost exclusively of New England descent, and numbered amongst the first settlers many officers and soldiers of the Revolution. It was doubtless owing to this circumstance, that the colony suffered so little from Indian depredation during the wars which attended the early settlement of the country.[62]

Mary Stockwell in her 2018 biography of Anthony Wayne, says Rufus Putnam brought settlers to Marietta from Massachusetts in 1788 "firmly believing that if he dealt fairly with the Indians, they would not attack his towns."[63]

At the end of 1788, the Marietta settlement was the only place in Ohio with white families. Judge Symmes went down the Ohio River with a few families during the summer, but they spent the winter of 1788–1789 in Kentucky.[64] The people of Marietta didn't have any problems with the local tribes in 1788, because, as Rufus relates they were hoping for a treaty soon.[65] One was to be signed at Fort Harmar on January 9, 1789.

Still the Marietta leaders were concerned about surprise attacks. Regulations were adopted that specified no new settlements should have less than 20 men who were able to bear arms, and that defensive works should be started.

In 1789, about 57 additional families settled on the Ohio Company lands. This included 152 men. In the spring, Indian trouble commenced with the killing of Captain Zebulon Ring at Belpre and four others in a wooded area below Gallipolis. The latter party included the surveyor Mr. Matthews and another man, both of whom escaped. A man named John Gardner was captured at Wolf Creek and also escaped.[66]

In 1790, about 131 families as well as some French settlers moved into the settlements. By the summer of 1790, detachments of militia, which were paid by the Ohio Company, were stationed at Marietta and its associated settlements.[67]

Under orders from Secretary of War Henry Knox to end Indian attacks, in 1790 Army commander Josiah Harmar marched from Fort Washington (now Cincinnati, Ohio) to attack a large Miami village near today's Fort Wayne, Indiana. With 320 regulars and about 1,100 poorly equipped Kentucky and Pennsylvania militiamen, Harmar's force was itself attacked.

One of Harmar's colonels, John Hardin, with several hundred soldiers (mostly militia) was ambushed in October 1790 by Miami chief Little Turtle. During the engagement, as well as another shortly afterward, Harmar's forces suffered 183 killed or missing. Although court-martialed, Harmar was exonerated and retired on January 1, 1792.

Harmar's actions only intensified the hatred between the native tribes and the white settlers. Congress then commissioned Arthur St. Clair a major general. He continued to serve as the Northwest Territory's governor.

On January 2, 1791, about 25 Wyandot and Delaware warriors attacked the Ohio Company's settlement at Big Bottom,[68] which was only 30 miles from Marietta. In the surprise attack, 12 settlers were killed and others were taken captive.

Benjamin Stone related that news of the Big Bottom massacre "came to Belpre at evening. Some of the family watched all night. My mother would let none of us undress for the night, saying, 'If any one escapes he will not be naked.' Morning came, and we were all alive, but fearful that we should not live much longer. In the course of the day a consultation of all the inhabitants of Belpre was held, and an agreement made to build, forthwith, a garrison about the centre, on the lands of Ebenezer Battelle, Nathaniel Cushing and Griffin Greene, Esquires. Within a few days (I think a week), the eleven block houses were so far constructed that the people moved into them."[69]

Benjamin Stone mentions that among the first settlers that went from Marietta to Big Bottom in 1790, was a son of Major Ezra Putnam. "Young Putnam was furnished by his parents with some cooking utensils to begin with, among which was a large iron dinner pot. When the appalling news of the massacre of the party by the Indians came to Marietta, the people all huddled round the messenger, Eleazer Buttard, to hear all the particulars of the awful catastrophe, when everyone trembled with fear of a like destruction soon. Old Major Putnam (who probably was then in his dotage), after listening to the sad story, broke out with the inquiry, 'Did you see or hear anything of my big pot?' General Rufus Putnam, losing all patience, turned his large wall eyes square upon him and said: 'Damn your big pot!'"[70]

Six days after the Big Bottom massacre, Rufus Putnam wrote to President George Washington: "The mischief which I feared, has overtaken us much sooner than I expected." Putnam states that the garrison at Fort Harmar, across the Muskingum River from Marietta, has "little more than twenty men," and "the governor and secretary both being absent; no assistance from Virginia or Pennsylvania can be had."

Putnam's count of men "capable of bearing arms" in Marietta and associated settlements is 287, with many of them "badly armed." Almost one-half of these men were "hired into the country, intending to settle by and by; these, under present circumstances, will probably leave us soon, unless prospects should brighten."

With his usual attention to detail, Putnam states that there are about 80 houses within a mile of Marietta, as well as scattered houses about three miles up the Ohio River. Down river at the settlement of Belpre are another 30 to 40 houses. Twenty-two miles up the Muskingum River are about 20 families, and two miles further on, another five families.

Not only are the Ohio people afraid of Indian attacks, but they are concerned, in the absence of outright hostilities, with the "destruction of their corn, forage, and cattle, by the enemy." Putnam reminds Washington that that in case of emergency there is no hope of "timely relief" from "any of our neighbors."

Putnam implores the government's protection "for myself and friends inhabiting these wilds of America," and states the "unless government speedily send a body of troops for our protection, we are a ruined people."[71]

Several weeks later, Putnam updated Washington on the situation in Ohio. Several men and women of the Wyandot tribe had traded at Fort Harmer. There were disconcerting stories of Indian parties passing through the area with captives and scalps. One soldier who was detained by Indians was questioned about the strength of forces at Fort Harmer, and the Marietta and Belpre settlements. Putnam argues that the "present Crisis appears to me important, not only as it respects the inhabitants of these frontiers but the United States in general." He insists that once it "Shall be known that Congress have given up the protection of the Country," the only purchasers of Northwest Territory land will be unscrupulous "private adventurers." Putnam closes with "All the Settlements in Virginia bordering on the Ohio in our neighborhood are erecting defenses." Unfortunately, the Ohio settlements did not have a state government which would lend them protection.[72]

A month later, on March 27, 1791, Henry Knox wrote to George Washington: "Judge Rufus Putnam informs me of a letter dated at Marietta, the 16th instant, that from the intelligence he had received it would appear, that the Wyandots and Delawares will join in the war against us and that appearances indicated a general Indian War."[73]

In September 1791, Arthur St. Clair headed up an expedition against Indians in western Ohio. In early November, most of his force was surrounded by about 1,000 native warriors near the headwaters of the Wabash River. He was defeated. "Of the 1,400 men under St. Clair, over 600 soldiers were killed and over 250 wounded." Many historians consider it the most compete victory ever won by Native Americans. President Washington forced St. Clair to resign from the army, but he stayed on as the Northwest Territory's governor.

In December 1791, Putnam updated President Washington on the situation in the Ohio settlements. For defense, four "stations" were established: two at Marietta, one at Belpre and one at Waterford.

In March 1792, warriors took a prisoner at Fort Harmer, killed a man near Marietta, and wounded a man at Waterford, which was 20 miles up the Muskingum River from Marietta. In April, one man was killed and a boy taken captive. In May, a boy was captured at Waterford. In June, only a horse theft was reported. In July, two Indians were killed within a few miles of Marietta, and one settler was killed near Marietta. Although August and September saw no casualties, in October one man was killed at Belpre and four others seven miles from Marietta. In his letter, Putnam insists: "unless we can be assured of governmental protection, self-preservation dictates the propriety of getting away as soon as possible."

At the end of the letter, Putnam relates that many people in the Ohio Company settlements think they "have very little to hope from Governor St Clair," as they see other settlements in the Ohio area receiving protection at their expense. He states: "This partiality in the distribution of troops to the several settlements both above and below, to the exclusion of those who were manifestly the most exposed has led the people generally to doubt the Governor's good disposition towards their settlements."

Putnam asks "To know therefore for certainty whether we may depend on Governmental protection or not, is a question very interesting; that on the one hand the people may be persuaded with patience to wait its arrival, and on the other hand to make their escape in time from the vengeance of an enraged enemy whom, if left to ourselves, we are by no means able to withstand."[74]

Historian Archer Butler Hulbert writes in his *Pilots of the Republic*:

> [Rufus Putnam was] now called upon by Washington to make the long journey, in the dark days of 1792 after St. Clair's terrible defeat, to represent the United States in a treaty with the Illinois Indians on the Wabash; again, with sweet earnestness settling a difficulty arising between a tippling clergyman and his church; now, with absolute fairness and generosity, criticising his brave but high-strung governor for actions which he regarded as too arbitrary, the character of Rufus Putnam appeals more and more as a remarkable example of that splendid simplicity which is the proof and crown of greatness.[75]

On September 29, 1792, Putnam spoke to the assembled tribes. Thirty-one Indian chiefs signed the treaty. "The witnesses were eight officers of the First American Legion, H. Vanderburgh, John Heckewelder, two interpreters, and the clerk. There were present at the Council 686 Indians—men, women, and children."[76]

In Marietta College's Special Collections is an August 1792 letter addressed to Rufus Putnam from a woman named Jean Shaw. She requests help in finding her husband and oldest son who were taken captive by Native Americans the previous May.

In 1792, Congress doubled the size of the army and appointed Rufus Putnam's old commander from the Battle of Stony Point, General Anthony Wayne, to succeed St. Clair as army commander.

In a confidential 1792 document, Washington expressed his opinions of many of the general officers of the Revolutionary War. Although his assessment of Wayne was primarily negative, it did not stop him from using his former subordinate to end what was called the Northwest Indian Wars. Washington wrote of Wayne: "More active & enterprizing than judicious & cautious. No economist it is feared. Open to flattery—vain—easily imposed upon—and liable to be drawn into scrapes. Too indulgent (the effect perhaps of some of the causes just mentioned) to his Officers & men. Whether sober—or a little addicted to the bottle, I know not."[77]

Over the next year, Wayne assembled and painstakingly trained a professional fighting force. He called it the Legion of the United States. In 1793, General Wayne ordered a fort to be constructed at the site of St. Clair's defeat. In order to convey the idea that the army could recover from that disaster, he named it Fort Recovery.[78]

In June between one and two thousand warriors attacked the fort, which had approximately 250 soldiers. After 10 days of fighting, the attackers were forced to retreat. The fact that they lacked the cannon necessary to successfully attack a fortified position, played a large part in their loss. That summer Wayne moved against the Indians with a force of about 3,000 troops. At a place named Fallen Timbers, which was very near British-controlled Fort Miami, the Native American forces made a stand.[79]

On August 20, 1794, at the Battle of Fallen Timbers, General Anthony Wayne's forces confronted a confederation of Ohio and Great Lakes Indian tribes led by Miami Chief Little Turtle (c. 1747–1812) and Shawnee war chief Blue Jacket (c. 1743–1810). A company of British soldiers assisted the warriors.

While General Wayne's infantry charged the fixed Native warrior positions with bayonets, his cavalry outflanked them. With their enemy pushed into the open, Wayne's men cut them down with musket fire. Wayne's casualties were about 35 killed and approximately 100 wounded. It's estimated that the Indian side suffered 200 killed and several hundred wounded.

The warriors sought protection at the British army's Fort Miami, but were refused admittance. Wayne relentlessly pursued the Indian survivors, burning villages and destroying their crops.

The loss demonstrated the power of the American armed forces, as well as the lack of support the Indian tribes could expect from the British. The result was the collapse of organized resistance of the Native American tribes to American colonial settlements.

On November 19, 1794, the United States and Great Britain signed Jay's Treaty. It addressed some areas of dispute between the two countries on trade matters, and dictated the British withdraw of its army units from Northwest Territory by June 1, 1796. In 1795, General Wayne negotiated the Treaty of Greenville with the tribes his troops had defeated at the Battle of Fallen Timbers. Leaders of 12 tribes—the Chippewa, Delaware, Eel-river, Kaskaskias, Kickapoos, Miami, Ottawa, Painkashaw, Potawatomi, Shawnee, Wea, and Wyandot—signed the Treaty of Greeneville on August 3, 1795, and gave up all of their land in Ohio except some in the northwestern corner of the state. The following year, the American army abandoned Fort Recovery.

Future U.S. President William Henry Harrison, an aide-de-camp to General Wayne, who also participated in the Battle of Fallen Timbers, was present as a witness at the Treaty of Greeneville signing.

The Treaty of Greeneville established the Greeneville Treaty Line which served as a dividing line between the newly designated Native American lands, and the lands the twelve tribes ceded to the United States government.

In 1797, in his capacity as U.S. surveyor general, Rufus Putnam hired Israel Ludlow, who had been surveying Ohio lands since 1786, to survey the line in the summer of 1797. The Greeneville Treaty Line was later superseded by other treaties that created Indian reservations.

With the Northwest Territory Indian Wars over, thousands of new settlers flooded in throughout Ohio from the East Coast. The town of Marietta provided a good example of how the end of hostilities affected the settlers. Whereas formerly the residents were gathered in and near the Campus Martius fortifications for protection, they now freely created settlements up the Muskingum River and far inland.

Gallipolis

One important Ohio settlement, Gallipolis, had problems at its onset, and Rufus Putnam had to intervene to assist its settlers. "As with any genuine opportunity to purchase a product, there are swindlers who deceive buyers to line-their-own pockets and gain illicit wealth, leaving the innocent investor defrauded." Such was the case with Gallipolis.

The name of the small Ohio city Gallipolis comes from the Latin word "Galli" for Gaul, i.e., France, and the Greek word "polis" or city. Nicknamed "The City of the Gauls," it is located on the west bank of the Ohio River about 70 miles, by land, southwest of Marietta.

The Scioto Company was a land speculation venture of a man who was nearly an American founding father—William Duer.[80] When investors learned of Duer's reputation, they were sure he could be trusted—he was a former Revolutionary War colonel, a delegate to the Second Continental Congress, and an assistant secretary of the United States Treasury Department. Duer and his associates encouraged people in France to purchase lands in Ohio, which was then part of the United States Northwest Territory. About 500 French citizens, later known as the "French 500," paid the Scioto Company for land and sailed to America. Sadly, they found that they had been swindled. Most traveled to Pittsburgh, Pennsylvania, and took flatboats down the Ohio River to Gallipolis; they arrived on October 17, 1790.

The Scioto Company did not own the land it had sold to the French; the Ohio Company of Associates was the legal owner. The would-be settlers asked the U.S. Congress and President George Washington for help; Washington asked the Ohio Company to lend aid to the new settlers.

Eventually, the French immigrants either needed to pay a second time for the land or else move to other land which was reserved for them by the United States government.

William Duer promised to pay the Ohio Company to construct cabins for the soon-to-arrive French immigrants. Rufus Putnam hired Major John Burnham[81] of Massachusetts to assemble 50 men in Massachusetts and travel to Gallipolis to clear land, build log cabins and, if necessary, protect the French in the event of an Indian raid.[82] As the French were mostly upper and middle-class city-dwellers with virtually no experience in clearing land, constructing buildings, and planting crops, the aid was a lifesaver. Once settled, the new settlers, through the hard work and determination, succeeded in making good use of the Ohio River for trade and transportation. Postal service was extended to Gallipolis in 1794 and in 1803, Gallipolis and its surrounding settlements became part of the newly created Gallia County.

In his Memoirs, Rufus Putnam states that he did not know how many French settlers arrived in 1790, but that on November 1, 1795, he found only 88 who were 18 years old and older. He needed a count at that time for the Secretary of the Treasury Department so that 24,000 acres of land that were granted to the French by the U.S. Congress could be surveyed and divided.[83] Estimates at the time put the total of men, women and children at over 300.

After the French settler swindle, the Scioto Company went into bankruptcy and in 1792, William Duer was sent to debtors' prison in New York City.[84] There he remained until a month before he died in 1799. When he passed away, Duer still owed the Ohio Company over $2800 for the cabins that Major Burnham's men had constructed at Gallipolis in 1790.[85]

Today, the city of Gallipolis is well-known for a unique historical celebration: each May, it marks the Marquis de Lafayette's visit of 1825. Also, each year Gallia County celebrates President Abraham Lincoln's 1863 signing of the Emancipation Proclamation. Countless other American municipalities also commemorate the Emancipation Proclamation, but Gallia has probably been doing it the longest—continuously since 1863.

Why the West Will Remain in the Union

In 1790, Rufus Putnam wrote a long letter to Fisher Ames (1758–1808), a Federalist member of the Massachusetts delegation to the U.S. Congress.[86]

Putnam reminded Ames of a question Ames posed to him months earlier: "Can we retain the western country [Northwest Territory] within the government of the United States? And if we can, of what use will it be to them?"[87]

Putnam admits that the western lands have a certain independence from the United States by virtue of their access to the Mississippi River. He states: "It is true that flour, hemp, tobacco, iron, potash, and such bulky articles will go down the Mississippi to New Orleans for market, and there be sold, or shipped to the Atlantic States, Europe, and West Indies; and it is also admitted that the countries west of the mountains and below or to the southward of the junction of the Ohio with the Mississippi may import goods from New Orleans."[88]

But Putnam insists that it is in the interest of the western country to maintain economic ties with the "Atlantic States." Trade is much less expensive with the rest of the United States than it is with New Orleans or Quebec. He points to "all the beef, pork, and mutton" that will be sent from the western lands to Virginia, Maryland and Pennsylvania, as well as the furs and skins received in trade with Native Americans that will be sent east. Looking to the future, Putnam points out that improvements in navigation should dramatically reduce expenses further still.[89]

Putnam insists that if the western lands seceded from the United States, it is possible that they would retain the advantages of trade with the United States, but it is "by no means probable," and "it is by no means reasonable to suppose that the legislature of the United States would pay the same attention to the subjects of a foreign power as to their own." In his opinion, "To be deprived of a commerce with the United States would be greatly to the injury, if not the ruin, of that country."[90]

Putnam sees no advantage in the western lands seeking to become part of British Canada or Spain. "I see nothing that is in the least degree worth their attention."[91]

To the question, "What about the western lands becoming a 'separate independent government'"? Putnam responds with thought-provoking questions of his own: "Will they not incur a great expense to support their new government beyond what their proportion to the old can possibly be?" and "Have these people considered that the United States are deeply interested in opposing such separation?" It is interesting that these questions were raised a full seven decades before the beginning of the American Civil War.[92]

Regarding those people of the western land who wanted free trade to the open sea, Putnam asks: "Do they know that the harbors of Pensacola and Havana are so situated that, a few cruisers from them sent into the Bay, not one vessel in a thousand going from or returning to the Mississippi would escape falling into their hands?" (Here we are reminded that Putnam 17 years earlier had been to the Caribbean Sea, navigated the Florida and Louisiana coasts, and explored the lower Mississippi River. He was a man who knew what he was talking about, as did few others in positions of authority.) Putnam insists that it is already in the interest of the United States that its western lands have access to freely navigate the Mississippi River.[93]

Playing devil's advocate, Putnam imagines a scenario where it would be advantageous for the western lands to break free from the United States:

> I allow that, should Congress give up her claim to the navigation of the Mississippi or cede it to the Spaniards, I believe the people in the Western quarter would separate themselves from the United States very soon. Such a measure, I have no doubt, would excite so much rage and dissatisfaction that the people would sooner put themselves under the despotic government of Spain than remain the indented servants of Congress; or should Congress by any means fail to give the inhabitants of that country such protection as their present infant state requires, connected with the interest and dignity of the United States; in that case such events may take place as will oblige the inhabitants of that country to put themselves under the protection of Great Britain or Spain.[94]

Here Rufus Putnam is speaking from self-interest in imagining a scenario in which Congress might "fail to give the inhabitants of that country such protection as their present infant state requires." His fledgling colony of Marietta was less than two years old at the time, and it continually faced the possibility of an Indian attack. The support of the United States government was considered essential to its security—especially until the end of the Indian Wars five years later.

Putnam wraps up the letter to Ames with thoughts about the advantages to the United States of retaining the western lands. He points out that if the country let the lands break away, they would likely be split up between Britain and Spain. It would cost the United States a great deal to protect itself from the presence of foreign-owned territory on its back doorstep. It would cost the U.S. more to protect its western frontier than it would to provide a defense for its wholly owned western lands.[95]

At every step in the settlement of Ohio, we find Rufus Putnam taking a leading role. It was Putnam who proposed that the lands of the west be provided to Revolutionary War veterans, it was Putnam who was the driving force behind the Ohio Company, and it was Putnam who personally led the first settlers to the Northwest Territory. Once in Ohio, Rufus Putnam used his surveying skills to plot out homesteads and public lands, and his military experience to protect Marietta and its associated settlements. He also brought his values and ideals west with him—including his uncompromising opposition to slavery.

Putnam's settlement was well-thought-out—with laws and regulations appropriate to the wilderness. As one of the first judges, he used his legendary common sense to settle disputes and plan for the future. Those people who personally knew Rufus Putnam, as well as future generations, rightfully considered him the "Father of Ohio."

Chapter Eight

A Legend in His Own Time

In a 1792 document in which George Washington expressed his opinions of general officers of the Revolutionary War, he wrote of Rufus Putnam: "Possesses a strong mind—and is a discreet man. No question has ever been made (that has come to my knowledge) of his want of firmness. In short, there is nothing conspicuous in his character—And he is but little known out of his own State, and a narrow circle."[1]

In her book *Unlikely General: "Mad" Anthony Wayne and the Battle for America*, historian Mary Stockwell interprets this as: "Yet Washington worried that Putnam, scholarly, squint-eyed, and not a young man to be sure [he was just shy of 53 years old], was little known outside of his native Connecticut. Like [Major General Benjamin] Lincoln, he might make a better negotiator than a general."[2]

On May 3, 1792, Washington nominated Putnam for promotion to brigadier general in a letter to the United States Senate.[3]

U.S. Surveyor General

On October 1, 1796, President Washington appointed Rufus Putnam the first surveyor general of the United States. Putnam had been the superintendent of surveys for the Ohio Company, and shortly before he had been appointed superintendent of the survey of Zane Trace, the most important road in Ohio. (Years later, the first federal interstate highway, the National Road, would be constructed across Ohio. It was authorized by Congress 1806 and begun in 1811. It wasn't until the year following Putnam's death [1825] that the Ohio portion was begun. Thirteen years later, that part was completed.)

In his memoirs, Rufus Putnam refers to the "last and best gift" he received from President Washington. (It would be just a little over three years before Washington's death.) Putnam received the following commission of surveyor general of the United States from U.S. Secretary of State Timothy Pickering.[4]

1. October 1796.

Sir,

The President of the United States desiring to avail the public of your services as Surveyor General, I have now the honor of enclosing the Commission, and of expressing to you the sentiments of the most perfect respect and esteem with which

I am, Sir,
Your most obt Servant
Timothy Pickering[5]

According to Lola Cazier in her *Surveys and Surveyors of the Public Domain, 1785–1975*, "Rufus Putnam's most enduring contribution to the public land surveys, lasting for more than a century, was the establishment of the terms under which deputy surveyors were to be employed."[6]

During his years as surveyor general of the United States, one of Putnam's main tasks was the surveying of the Greenville Treaty line. The Treaty of Greenville, signed on August 3, 1795, ended hostilities between the government of the United States and the Native Americans of the Northwest Territory. In it the latter ceded most of Ohio and parts of Illinois, Indiana, and Michigan. It was the duty of the surveyor general to survey and mark the boundary line specified in the treaty.

In a letter to Secretary of the Treasury Oliver Wolcott dated January 25, 1797, Putnam wrote, "It will be proper to have the boundary lines between these lands & the present Indian claims ascertained as soon as may be to prevent all danger of our encroaching on the Indian Lands."[7]

In another letter to Wolcott two years later (March 15, 1799), Putnam advocated the building of a "great road" as a way to give Native Americans "satisfaction & leave the white people without excuse with respect to their knowledge of the boundary line."[8]

An event occurred in the Spring of 1796 that introduced Rufus to a young man who would play an important part in his later life. The man showed up at Putnam's house in Marietta one morning carrying a "small grip sack" and an axe and asked if he could "give him some work." The 18-year-old man, Ebenezer Buckingham, had walked from Connecticut to Marietta and only had 12 cents in his pocket. Putnam replied that "he did not know that he needed any help." The man then said he would like to

Eight. A Legend in His Own Time

do the work to earn his breakfast. Putnam said, "I see you have an axe on your shoulder, and there is a pile of wood which you can chop up for firewood until breakfast time, and I will give you your breakfast."⁹

As he was chopping the wood, Putnam's daughter Catharine, who was looking out of the dining room window, asked her father, "Who is that good-looking young man out there chopping wood? He has now chopped more wood than that man you had yesterday all day." Sometime later, Putnam asked his daughter to call the man in for breakfast.¹⁰

Putnam later asked Buckingham if he knew how to drive oxen. When told he did, Putnam told him to yoke up the oxen, hitch them to a cart, and bring some clay up from the base of a hill. At noon, he said, they would eat and then "make it into mortar and chink and daub" a cabin adjacent to Putnam's house.¹¹

This portrait of Rufus Putnam was painted about the time President Washington appointed him Surveyor General of the United States. *Rufus Putnam* (1737–1824) by James Sharples Senior, from life, 1796–1797 (courtesy Independence National Historical Park).

At noon, Buckingham stopped hauling, sprinkled water on the clay and scattered some shelled corn over it, which he had grabbed from a nearby corn crib. Putnam walked over and asked what he was doing with the corn. Buckingham replied, "Do you see those hogs up there? While we are eating dinner they will come down here and rooting for that corn they will make the clay up into a nice pile of mortar." It "amused the General very much."¹²

Putnam and young Buckingham had much in common. Both had come from New England families, had very limited formal education, and had taught themselves mathematics and surveying from books.

James Buckingham, a nephew of Ebenezer Buckingham, wrote in his 1896 book *The Ancestors of Ebenezer Buckingham, who was Born in 1748, and of His Descendants*:

> The next day, the General went on a surveying trip on the west side of the river, taking him [Ebenezer] along as rodsman; and, on finding he was so adept and quick, he told him if he would stay with him, he would teach him surveying; in a few weeks time he was even a more expert surveyor than the General himself. At that period General Putnam had charge of surveying nearly all the south-east quarter of the State of Ohio. Whether the General was prepossessed by this circumstance or not, does not appear, but he was certainly kind and interested, and found a place for young Buckingham in a surveying party that started off in a day or two. In this trial trip he displayed such energy and skill as to quite win the heart of the General, who gave him other work, and admitted him to his family circle.[13]

Ebenezer Buckingham's early years were spent in both the Indian and White Man's societies. He learned the local tribe's language and "penetrat[ed] the interminable forest of the west," as well as graced the "refined circles, the judicial bench and the legislative hall."

According to his nephew James Buckingham, he "had no taste for farming," and in 1805 started up a trading post in a two-story log cabin at what is now Zanesville, Ohio.[14]

Buckingham helped Rufus Putnam survey the Muskingum River valley until 1805, and on November 27, 1805, he married Putnam's youngest daughter, Catharine (1780–1808). Only a little more than two years later, she died in childbirth. Once some of the local Indians stole some of Ebenezer Buckingham's horses and headed towards Lake Erie. He followed them alone through the wilderness to Sandusky and with the help of a local chief recovered the animals.[15]

Sometimes in his work, Rufus needed to work with famous and powerful individuals who lived hundreds of miles away. As an example, in 1792, he received a receipt from Alexander Hamilton, who received a deed for five shares of the land of the Ohio Company of Associates from directors Rufus Putnam, Manasseh Cutler, Robert Oliver, and Griffin Greene.

Four years later, Rufus wrote to Hamilton asking whether he would be agreeable to selling one of his eight-acre lots on the west bank of Muskingum river about two miles from where it emptied into the Ohio River. Hamilton's lot had soil "of the first quality," and "about 165 yards of frontage on the Muskingum," but "lacked a spring."[16]

The prospective buyer, 63-year-old Commodore Abraham Whipple, was a respected Continental Navy commander during the Revolutionary War. Rufus mentions to Hamilton that Whipple was "much reduced in his property (by the failure of public Credit: like most of us who Served their Country in the late War), has retired to this Country where he wishes to accommodate himself with a little farm." Whipple owned an adjacent lot on which he was building a house and making improvements to his land.[17]

When he was 78, Congress granted him a $30 monthly pension for his wartime service. Whipple died at age 85.

The Church

On December 6, 1796, Rufus Putnam is listed along with other original members of the First Congregational Church of Marietta. There is a notation that the church Putnam came from was the "2d Brookfield, Massachusetts." His wife Persis's prior church is marked as Westborough, Massachusetts.[18]

Originally there were 31 members in the congregation. Sixteen came from Connecticut, fourteen from Massachusetts, and one, James Pewtherer, was an immigrant from Linlithgow, Scotland.

On March 15, 1804, Marietta minister Daniel Story resigned his position.[19] An official letter was written to Yale College president Timothy Dwight, one of the most learned men in New England, asking if he knew of a replacement. This letter was accompanied by a personal one from Rufus.[20] In his letter, Putnam described Marietta:

> With respect to local circumstances, Marietta is beautiful for situation. The climate very fine and the inhabitants remarkably healthy. With respect to character we claim that of being a civil people in general. We have among us several gentlemen of literature and many respectable families, and I flatter myself the gentleman who comes forward will find agreeable society. With respect to improvement in buildings, etc. our houses are generally of wood, many of them large and well built. We have only one of brick. We have three rope walks. Ship building has been carried on for some years to a considerable extent Business is lively. Our population is not numerous, but rapidly increasing.[21]

Putnam goes on to state:

> I therefore beg leave to suggest that we hope he may be one who shall preach the pure gospel of Jesus Christ without teaching for doctrines the opinions of men. One of a liberal charity toward those who may differ from him in some points wherein some of the greatest divines have not been altogether agreed. One who for the sake of displaying his learning and talents will not entertain a common audience with meat which the strongest have not been fully able to digest. Yet we desire and hope he may be one of the first class for literature and science as well as popular talent.[22]

On June 26, 1804, Dwight wrote back that he knew of "a young gentleman of much merit" who was considering the position. However, a month later Dwight wrote Putnam that the young man's parents refused to approve his move to Marietta, and that he would be following their wishes. Dwight also stated that he knew of no other appropriate candidates.

In 1807, Putnam designed Marietta's Congregational church, helped finance it, and supervised its construction. In addition, he helped form a bible society and a Sunday school. The church's history states:

"In the autumn of 1812, Rev. Samuel J. Mills made a visit to Marietta in the interest of the American Bible Society. Mr. Robbins and the members of this church were greatly interested in this work, and October 22nd, 1812, the Washington County Bible Society was organized with Gen. Rufus Putnam as President."[23]

In the early 1800s, Sunday (Sabbath) schools were unheard of in Ohio. That was until 1816 when a Massachusetts teacher moved to Marietta. Having heard of the schools, Putnam asked the teacher to describe them. Later, Putnam had a dream in which he was standing by a window in a large public building watching a procession of children, which was accompanied by music. He asked a bystander what was happening, and the man replied, "These are the children of the Sabbath school."

After relating the dream, 78-year-old Putnam told the teacher that he thought it meant that he would live to see his dream fulfilled. In the spring of 1817, the first Sabbath school opened in the Muskingum Academy and the following year three of the schools opened in Marietta. Before the schools closed for the winter months, a procession of children formed and marched from the Academy to the Congregational Church. Shortly afterward the Massachusetts teacher visited Putnam at his house and found him standing by the window with tears in his eyes. He had just viewed the procession and now exclaimed, "Here is the fulfillment of my dream."[24]

Up until old age, Putnam had regularly attended church services in all kinds of weather. When his health made this impossible, he would stay home and read the "Assembly's Shorter Catechism." When a friend remarked in 1820 that 82-year-old Putnam must regret not being able to meet at the newly established revival meetings, the latter replied, "I do meet with you"—by which he meant that during the span of time the meetings were held, he was at home engaged in private prayer.[25]

In November 1820, 27-year-old Christian missionary Cyrus Byington was in Marietta to arrange for mission families to travel to a Choctaw Native American village. David Putnam explained that the river was iced up and wouldn't be navigable until spring.

The Reverend Byington was invited to deliver a sermon that afternoon for the people of Marietta. Later, Putnam's son took Byington to Rufus Putnam's house. Rufus was described by Byington as "infirm and advanced in life," but he approved of Byington's mission to the Choctaws, and Rufus even sent a one-hundred-dollar bill to missionary-to-the-Indians Cyrus Kingsbury (1786–1870). Rufus had a fatted ox butchered and sent to a family of missionaries who were preparing to travel to another Indian tribe.

The following spring, Byington established a mission at the Choctaws in Mississippi, and served them for the following forty-five years. (During that time, with the assistance of several local tribesmen he developed the first Choctaw language dictionary, speller book, and grammar book. When the Choctaws were forcefully moved to Oklahoma, Byington followed and in addition to establishing several churches, for many years he served the medical needs of the doctor-less tribe.)[26]

Ohio University

It was quite fitting that the foundations (both figurative and literal) of the first institution of higher education in the Northwest Territory were laid out by Rufus Putnam—a man who grew up deprived of a formal education, became a self-taught master of several highly skilled occupations, and placed great value on education throughout his long life.

In 1795, 57-year-old Rufus Putnam left with a surveying party to locate land for the new Ohio University. As Emilius Oviatt Randall (1850–1919) describes it in his *History of Ohio: The Rise and Progress of an American State*:

> In a fleet of canoes, propelled by the power of the setting-pole against the swift and narrow channel of the Great Hock-Hocking,[27] accompanied by armed men, guards against the lurking savage, and carrying with them pork, beans, and hard tack that made up their rude fare, the veterans of three wars proceeded to mark out the metes and bounds of the university lands. There was little polish or culture in the undertaking, but these old warriors were animated with a high purpose.[28]

In 1799, the territorial Legislature, by a resolution, requested Rufus Putnam and others "to lay off in one of the townships a town plat, to contain a square for the colleges, lots suitable for house lots, and gardens for a President, Professors, Tutors, etc., bordering on, or encircled by, spacious commons, and such a number of town lots adjoining said commons and outlots, as they should think will be for the advantage of the University."[29]

After completing his survey, and with the reduced chance of the Indian conflicts, Putnam encouraged settlement on the university lands. Once a settlement was established, funding could be solicited to start the school.

Rufus Putnam wrote to Manasseh Cutler, who was back in Massachusetts on February 3, 1799: "I hope you will give me your opinion, or rather a systematized plan [for Ohio's university] applied to our circumstances and the objects we have in view." In July, Cutler wrote back:

> I have attempted to throw my ideas on paper, but I have not been able to mature my mind sufficiently to satisfy myself and am sure I should not be able to satisfy others. So far as I had opportunity I have consulted the charters of public seminaries in Europe and America. Those in our own country are generally the most modern, and the best adapted to the purposes intended; but none appear to me to accord with a plan so liberal as I think ought to be the foundation of the constitution of this university.[30]

A few weeks later, Putnam again asked Cutler for his plan. It was obvious that Putnam's ability to be persistent on matters of great importance had not changed since the day back in 1775 that he had pressured General Heath to loan him the book on military engineering—a book which directly led to Washington forcing British troops from Boston, Massachusetts.

> This request I must again renew, and by a systematized plan I mean a bill in form of an act or law incorporating A. B., C. D., etc., and defining their powers, accompanied by such remarks as you may think proper to make. We are totally destitute of any copy of an incorporating act or charter of a college or even an academy; but this is not my principal reason for applying to you. It is a subject I know you have long thought of, therefore I request of you not only the form, but the substance.[31]

The following June, Cutler sent Putnam a "Charter of University." It was in a form "ready for adoption by the territorial legislature." The charter proposed a:

> "Board of Trustees of the American University" with eleven trustees, and "they were to be given the right of perpetual succession. The two townships of land were to be placed in the control of the board, and they were to be given power 'forever hereafter' to lease and rent the lands for the use of the university, the proceeds to be applied as the trustees might direct. They were also to have all powers of making rules and regulations for the university, selecting its president and faculty, and controlling the course of study."[32]

In 1801, the territorial legislature elected Rufus a trustee of Ohio University, in Athens. Ohio. That year, about nine hundred people lived on the lands set aside for the university. Ohio University history professor Clement Luther Martzolff wrote:

> the country was a wilderness. The campus was covered with poplar trees and flocks of wild turkeys were frequent. Dr. Eliphaz Perkins, at whose home the University trustees held their first meeting, took bear meat for his medical fees and he himself met bruin one day wandering over the campus inspecting the site of the proposed institution of higher learning.[33]

Eight. A Legend in His Own Time

In 1800, Manasseh Cutler proposed a charter for a university in Athens, Ohio. It would be the first institution of higher education in Ohio territory. On February 18, 1804, Ohio's General Assembly passed an act establishing the University. It stated:

> Be it enacted by the General Assembly of the State of Ohio, That there shall be an University instituted and established in the town of Athens, the ninth township of the fourteenth range of townships, within the limits of the tract of land purchased by the Ohio Company of Associates, by the name and style of the "Ohio University," for the instruction of youth in all the various branches of liberal arts and sciences, for the promotion of good education, virtue, religion and morality, and for conferring all the degrees and literary honors granted in similar institutions.[34]

The act included the names of the first trustees. Besides Rufus Putnam and four other men from Marietta (Elijah Backus, Dudley Woodbridge, the Rev. Daniel Story, and Griffin Greene, Sr.), they included the governor of Ohio. (Samuel H. Huntington was governor of Ohio when the University offered its first classes in 1809.) The yet-to-be-chosen university president was another member of the board of trustees. (Ohio University's first president, Jacob Lindley, served from 1809 to 1822.) The remaining trustees were Benjamin Tappan and Bazaleel Wells from Steubenville and one trustee each from Chillicothe, Cincinnati, Lancaster, West Union, and Worthington. (Chillicothe: Gen. Nathaniel Massie, Cincinnati: Daniel Symmes, Lancaster: Samuel Carpenter, West Union: Joseph Darlington, and Worthington: the Rev. James Kilbourn.)

When Rufus Putnam died in 1824, he was the last original member of Ohio University's board of trustees who was still serving. The Ohio State Senate and House of Representatives appointed the Rev. David Young to fill Putnam's seat.[35]

Of the over 46 trustees who served with Rufus Putnam on the Ohio University Board of Trustees between 1804 and 1824, the last remaining was Manasseh Cutler's son Ephraim, who served until the year he died, 1853.[36]

Ohio University opened in 1809 with one building, one professor and three students.[37] In 1815, its first graduate was Thomas Ewing, Sr., who had been taught to read by his sister, Sarah. Ewing's degree was the first conferred by a college in the area of the Northwest Territory. He went on to become a U.S. senator, Secretary of the Treasury, and Secretary of the Interior. Three of his sons became union army generals during the Civil War.[38]

Upon the celebration of Ohio University's centennial in 1904, alumni gathered on College Green under "Old Beech," a tree that was standing when Rufus Putnam surveyed the location in 1795. The tree died in 1921.

Today, Rufus Putnam is remembered on Ohio University's Athens campus by Putnam Hall. Built in 1926 to accommodate a school for training teachers, it is now the location of the School of Dance. However, the word Rufus is better remembered at the University today as the name of the athletic program's mascot.

In 1925, Ohio University adopted the bobcat as its official nickname. In 1960, the bobcat mascot made its first appearance at a football game. It wasn't until 2006 that a naming contest was held for the mascot. More than 500 people voted and the name "Rufus" was chosen. Some people voted for it to commemorate Rufus Putnam, who was instrumental in the founding and early success of the school; some chose it because the bobcat's scientific name is *Lynx rufus*. Probably some voters noticed the coincidence and voted for both reasons.

Ohio State Constitutional Convention

The United States Congress passed the Enabling Act of 1802, to "enable the people of the eastern division of the territory northwest of the river Ohio to form a constitution and State government and for the admission of such State into the Union on an equal footing with the original States, and for other purposes." President Thomas Jefferson signed it.

Ohio's Constitutional Convention was especially important since it was the first state to be created from Northwest Territory lands. Neighboring Indiana would not become a state until thirteen years after Ohio. The other three states of Illinois, Michigan, and Wisconsin would come along, respectively, 15, 34, 45 years after Ohio. Minnesota, the northeastern section of which was part of the Northwest Territory, would become a state 55 years after Ohio.

A majority of the delegates (26) at the Ohio Constitutional Convention were supporters of President Thomas Jefferson's Democratic-Republican Party, which favored a relatively weak national government. Seven, including Rufus Putnam, were Federalists who, like former U.S. presidents Washington and John Adams, supported a strong federal government. The remaining two delegates were independents.

Eight. A Legend in His Own Time   161

In 1802, Rufus Putnam was elected by Washington County to represent it at the Constitutional Convention. Perhaps the most important contribution of Putnam at the convention was his insistence that slavery not be legalized in the new constitution. When it came to a vote, Putnam and his anti-slavery forces succeeded by only one vote.

In 1898, U.S. Senator George F. Hoar noted that the two votes of Putnam and, at Putnam's urging, Manasseh Cutler's son, "saved [Ohio] from the imposition of slavery by its constitutional convention in 1802." He went on to pay Rufus Putnam a great tribute when he contended: "Now, in the light of this history, if Rufus Putnam be not entitled to the credit of the Ordinance of 1787, and of having saved this country from becoming a great slaveholding empire, then Wellington is not entitled to the credit of Waterloo, or Washington to the credit of Yorktown, or Grant to the credit of Appomattox."[39]

The opening of the convention was not without controversy. Territorial governor Arthur St. Clair, in an address to the delegates, asked them to ignore the Enabling Act and delay statehood. Jefferson immediately replaced him as governor.

The Convention delegates ultimately voted to pass the state constitution, with all Federalists, but one, voting for it. The only delegate of any party voting against it was Putnam's fellow Federalist, Ephraim Cutler. One account expressed it thus: "Judge Cutler, an indomitable Whig, of Washington County, voting in the negative, solitary and alone."[40]

Cutler later wrote "I said No, and found myself 'solitary and alone.'" He wrote to his father: "You have no doubt seen by the papers that the vote for accepting the law of Congress, and proceeding immediately to form a state government, passed by a majority of thirty-two to one; this one, sir, was simply me."[41]

The Constitution, which took effect in 1803, included a preamble which read:

> We, the people of the eastern division of the territory of the United States, northwest of the river Ohio, having the right of admission into the general government, as a member of the Union, consistent with the constitution of the United States, the ordinance of Congress of one thousand seven hundred and eighty-seven, and of the law of Congress, entitled, "An act to enable the people of the eastern division of the territory of the United States, northwest of the river Ohio, to form a constitution and State government, for the admission of such State into the Union, on an equal footing with the original States, and for other purposes," in order to establish justice, promote the welfare and secure the blessings of liberty to ourselves and our posterity, do ordain and establish the following constitution or form of government, and do mutually agree with each other to form ourselves into a free and independent State, by the name of the State of Ohio[42]:

The First Ohio Constitution

One of the most important provisions of the new Ohio constitution appeared in "Of Amendments to the Constitution." The full section reads (with bold print added):

> Sec 5. That after the year one thousand eight hundred and six, whenever two-thirds of the General Assembly shall think it necessary to amend or change this constitution, they shall recommend to the electors, at the next election for members to the General Assembly, to vote for or against a convention, and if it shall appear that a majority of the citizens of the State, voting for Representatives, have voted for a convention, the General Assembly shall, at their next session, call a convention, to consist of as many members as there shall be in the General Assembly; to be chosen in the same manner, at the same place, and by the same electors that choose the General Assembly; who shall meet within three months after the said election for the purpose of revising, amending or changing the constitution. **But no alteration of this constitution shall ever take place, so as to introduce slavery or involuntary servitude into this State.**

Even the United States Constitution does not go this far. The Thirteenth Amendment to the U.S. Constitution states:

> Neither slavery nor involuntary servitude, except as a punishment for crime whereof the party shall have been duly convicted, shall exist within the United States, or any place subject to their jurisdiction [and] Congress shall have power to enforce this article by appropriate legislation [Section 2].

However, according to the U.S. Constitution itself, this amendment can be changed in the future. Indeed, this was done with another amendment. In 1933, the Twenty-first Amendment repealed 1919's Eighteenth Amendment and reinstituted the legal "manufacture, sale, or transportation of intoxicating liquors."

In one of the first attempts in America to extend voting rights to African Americans, an Ohio Constitution Convention proposal read: "Provided, that all male negroes and mulattoes, now residing in this territory, shall be entitled to the right of suffrage, if they shall within twelve months make a record of their citizenship." This passed on a vote of 19 to 15, with Rufus Putnam and Ephraim Cutler voting for it. Later it was stricken out.[43]

Also important was the 1803 Ohio Constitution's guarantee of religious liberty and its protection of the rights of conscience:

> That all men have a natural and indefeasible right to worship Almighty God according to the dictates of conscience; that no human authority can, in any case whatever, control or interfere with the rights of conscience; that no man shall be compelled to attend, erect or support any place of worship, or to maintain any ministry, against his consent, and that no preference shall ever be given, by law, to any religious society or mode of worship, and no religious test shall be required as a qualification to any office of trust or profit. But religion, morality and knowledge being essentially necessary to

good government and the happiness of mankind, schools and the means of instructions shall forever be encouraged by legislative provision not inconsistent with the rights of conscience.[44]

The Ohio Constitution was signed at Chillicothe, Ohio, on November 29, 1802, by 35 men, representing the state's nine counties. Rufus Putnam, Ephraim Cutler, Benjamin Ives Gilman, and John McIntire represented Washington County.

The Ohio Constitution became effective on February 19, 1803.[45] In 1850 through 1851 a second Ohio constitutional convention was held and it passed the Constitution of 1851, which was still operating in the 21st century. Two other Ohio constitutional conventions were held—in 1873 to 1874 and in 1912—but they did not result in new state constitutions.

Today, outside the Ohio River Museum in Marietta a historical marker commemorates the Muskingum River Underground Railroad, which enabled the escape of fugitive slaves to freedom in Canada. It notes the history of slavery opposition of the people of Marietta and other places along the Muskingum River, highlighting Manasseh Cutler's role in formulating the Ordinance of 1787, which prohibited slavery in the Northwest Territory, and states "General Rufus Putnam, Captain Jonathan Stone, and other Ohio Land Company Revolutionary War veterans, founded Marietta at the mouth of the Muskingum River in 1788 bringing with them their anti-slavery sentiments." The marker includes the statement, "A proposal to legalize slavery in the proposed state of Ohio was vetoed largely due to the efforts of Marietta's Ephraim Cutler and General Putnam at the 1802 Ohio Constitutional Convention."[46]

Jefferson vs. Putnam

President George Washington appointed Rufus Putnam surveyor general of the United States in 1796. Seven years later, after having served in the Washington and Adams administrations, Putnam was dismissed by President Thomas Jefferson.

In his first inaugural address on March 4, 1801, Thomas Jefferson stated: "But every difference of opinion is not a difference of principle. We have called by different names brethren of the same principle. We are all Republicans, we are all Federalists." In practice, though, he proceeded to replace the Federalists who held offices in the national government with his own followers.

In a letter offering the position to Jared Mansfield (1759–1830), a mathematics instructor at West Point,[47] Jefferson unmercifully tore at Rufus Putnam[48]: "Mr. Putnam the present Surveyor General in the Northern quarter is totally incompetent to the office he holds ... the removal of the blunderer has been sorely and generally desired ... mr Ellicott has furnished us an accurate survey of the Mississippi from it's mouth to that of the Ohio,... but mr Putnam is incompetent & it would have been in vain to set him about it."[49]

It says more about Jefferson than about Putnam that the president of the United States would lash out at a man who played such an instrumental role in the helping win the country's freedom from Great Britain. Perhaps Putnam's anti-slavery positions over the years played a role in eliciting such an extreme reaction from Jefferson.

Mansfield accepted the position, although decades later his son Edward would write: "My father did not quite like the idea of such work, for he was a scholar and mathematician, fond of a quiet and retired life."[50]

After his termination, Putnam wrote: "In what manner I have fulfilled the duties of this office, I shall leave for those employed under me, and were best informed on the subject, to determine. Indeed, I might appeal to my correspondence with the secretaries of the treasury, or even to Mr. Gallatin personally, that no want of ability, integrity or industry was the cause of my removal from office. No! It was done because I did not subscribe to the measures of him whom I have called the arch-enemy of Washington's administration."[51] Putnam also stated, "I am happy in having my name enrolled with many, who have suffered the like political death, for adherence to those correct principles and measures, in the pursuance of which our country rose from a state of weakness, disgrace, and poverty, to strength, honor, and credit."[52]

Historian Andrew Cayton notes in his *The Frontier Republic: Ideology and Politics in the Ohio Country, 1780–1825* that "Putnam saw political office as something more than a hobby or way to make money; it was a public responsibility to be exercised by gentlemen." Cayton emphasizes that Rufus Putnam knew well that the young country's future depended upon power being "entrusted to the safe and sure hands of men of character in as regular and predicable fashion as possible."[53]

Though disgusted with Jefferson, Putnam was not the kind of man to take it out on his successor. Jared Mansfield's son, Edward Mansfield, writes in his memoirs:

> General Rufus Putnam, my father's predecessor as Surveyor-General, has been a Revolutionary officer and a Federalist, while his father was a Republican (now called a Democrat), and supposed to be a partisan of Jefferson. The political breeze, however,

Eight. A Legend in His Own Time

soon passed over. The people of Marietta were, in general, intelligent, upright people, and my father not one to quarrel without cause. The Putnams were polite, and my parents passed two years at Marietta pleasantly and happily.[54]

In 1804, newly appointed Surveyor General of the United States Jared Mansfield used the services of Putnam's assistant, Ebenezer Buckingham. He made Buckingham his deputy and assigned him to survey a part of the future state of Indiana, around Vincennes.

In 1805, Buckingham opened a trading post in a two-story log cabin in what is today Zanesville. In 1810, he built Buckingham Store & Warehouse, and six years later, went onto partnership with his brother Alvah and brother-in-law Solomon Sturges. The business was successful. Ebenezer also served in the Ohio state senate and he was a prominent proponent of the Ohio Canal. He built two bridges which crossed the Muskingum and Pataskala rivers at Zanesville. In 1832, as he was supervising the construction of the third Y-Bridge, a flood led to the collapse of the structure, and the 54-year-old Buckingham was killed. Today, he is buried next to his three wives, in Zanesville, Ohio.

The queue hairstyle, with hair in the back of the head pulled back in a single tail, was popular with many late 18th century American men. It is said that after Thomas Jefferson became president of the United States in 1801, he ordered members of his administration not to wear queues. He considered them old fashioned; Rufus Putnam did not and refused to remove his queue.[55]

In 1810, a Maine justice of the peace, Stephen Jones, Rufus's fellow soldier from the French and Indian War and a Federalist, wrote the following to Rufus:

> I noticed in the public prints, a few years since, that T. Jefferson had honored you by removing you from an office bestowed upon you by the great and virtuous Washington, the real father of his country. Your removal from office is full evidence of your adherence to the principles of the good old Washington school, of which I avow myself to be a true disciple; and the numerous removals of honest, capable men from office, and in many instances the vacancies so made by T. Jefferson filled again by him with d-d rascals, has excited my warmest indignation. I consider that heaven, in its wrath for the sins of our nation, permitted him to preside over our nation.[56]

Post–1800 Marietta

In 1803, the Northwest Territory, as well as the states of Kentucky and Tennessee, ceased to be the "far western United States" as President Thomas Jefferson's administration purchased a huge amount of land west of the Mississippi River. Napoleon's France, finding it difficult to defend its North American lands from the British, and in need of money to finance its European military ventures, sold the United States 828,000 square miles of land for between three and four cents per acre.

Known as the Louisiana Purchase, the purchased land would one day be carved up into the six states of Arkansas, Missouri, Iowa, Oklahoma, Kansas, and Nebraska, as well as parts of the nine states of Louisiana, Texas, New Mexico, Colorado, Wyoming, Montana, North Dakota, South Dakota, and Minnesota. It also included small parts of today's Canadian provinces of Alberta and Saskatchewan.

Nine years after the Louisiana Purchase, Louisiana would become the first state taken from its lands; one hundred years later (1912), New Mexico would become the last.

As the 27-year-old United States looked west as far as the Rocky Mountains, the Northwest Territory developed, prospered and matured economically, politically and socially.

In March 1803, Ohio became the first U.S. state to be taken from the Northwest Territory. The following month, the Louisiana Purchase Treaty was signed. By 1800, Ohio's population had risen from the 48 pioneers of 1788 to 42,159. By 1810, it was 230,760 and in 1820 it reached a population of 581,434 as more easterners moved westward.

During the end of the 18th century and beginning of the 19th century, Rufus Putnam was busy managing the land transactions of many veterans of the American Revolutionary War. Some were very important people, such as Alexander Hamilton, George Washington's war secretary Jonathan Trumbull, Jr., and even Washington himself.

Former United States Secretary of the Treasury Alexander Hamilton owned shares in the Ohio Company. In an October 1802 letter to Oliver Wolcott, Jr., who had succeeded him as Secretary of the Treasury,[57] Hamilton states that he would like to exchange the Ohio land for "settled farms" in Connecticut. Hamilton includes a "tariff of values" [official valuation] in the letter totaling 2,293 dollars, writing that "This tariff was formed by Judge [Rufus] Putnam, who appears to have thought it not exaggerated."[58] Later, Hamilton estimated the value of his Ohio holdings at $6,000. He never had a chance to trade the lands—21 months later he was killed by Vice President Aaron Burr in the most famous duel in American history.

Jonathan Trumbull, Jr., was another important American leader that Rufus Putnam represented on Ohio land matters. In 1740, Trumbull was born in the family village of Lebanon, Connecticut, which is located about 30 miles southwest of Major General Israel Putnam's home in Pomfret,

Eight. A Legend in His Own Time 167

Connecticut. His father, Jonathan Trumbull, Sr., was the only royal governor to join the Patriot side at the beginning of the American Revolution; his brother John Trumbull was the most famous painter of American Revolutionary War people and events. During the War, Jonathan Trumbull, Jr., served as secretary and aide-de-camp to George Washington. After the war, he was elected to the U.S. House of Representatives, where he rose to the position of speaker. Subsequently, he became a U.S. senator, and a long-time governor of Connecticut.

During correspondence extending over the last nine years of Jonathan Trumbull, Jr.'s life, Trumbull asks Rufus Putnam to sell a mill and some land he owns in Ohio (1801) and gave Putnam power of attorney to act for him in the Northwest Territory (1801). Acting in this capacity, Putnam sold Trumbull's land to Ebenezer and William Barrows. In 1802, Putnam sent Barrows' first payment to Trumbull. Complaining of high taxes in Ohio, Trumbull asked Putnam to help him sell two 160-acre lots (1802). As of 1805, Trumbull still owned land in Ohio's Washington, Gallia, and Athens counties, but Putnam informed him that the market was saturated and he did not expect to sell more of his land in the near future.

In 1808, Trumbull wrote to Putnam, stating that he was at an age that he would like to sell all of his land "on very easy terms for the purchaser." The following month, Putnam wrote back that he envisioned no further sales in the foreseeable future. At the end of 1808, Trumbull sent Putnam $15.00 for the management of his land sales, taxes, etc., for two years.

In August 1809, Jonathan Trumbull, Jr., died, and three months later Putnam received a letter from his nephew, Jonathan George Washington Trumbull, stating that he had inherited his uncle's Ohio lands and asking Putnam to continue their management. In 1811, he informed Putnam that he had traded his Ohio land for land in Massachusetts.

In 1798, former president George Washington sent Rufus Putnam a copy of a letter he had just mailed to Winthrop Sargent, the governor of the Northwest Territory.[59] It related to a rumor he heard that his claim to three parcels of land (totaling 3,051 acres) in the Northwest Territory was in jeopardy. Two of the parcels were along the Little Miami River, while the third was near the Ohio River. Washington asked Putnam if in his capacity as surveyor general of the Territory he had any further information on the matter.

Putnam replied to Washington that he had heard that the man spreading the rumor, Joseph Massey, had been surveying for several years in the Virginia Military Tract, but he did not have any further information.[60]

In 1808, Ohio freemasons elected Rufus Putnam to the office of Grand Master of Ohio, but he needed to decline on account of his age and infirmities. An Ohio historical marker at Chillicothe states:

> Grand Lodge of Free and Accepted Masons of Ohio
>
> On this site, on January 4–7, 1808, the six Masonic lodges then existent in the state met and formed the Grand Lodge of Ohio. General Rufus Putnam of Marietta was elected the first Grand Master. Because of advanced age and failing health, he declined the honor and Governor Samuel Huntington was named in his stead.[61]

Historian Archer Butler Hulbert writes of Rufus Putnam:

> As manager for the Ohio Company, a thousand affairs of both great and trifling moment were a part of his tiresome routine. Yet the heart of the colony's leader was warm to the lowliest servant. Many a poor tired voyager descending the Ohio had cause to know that the founder of Marietta was as good as a whole nation knew he was brave. In matters concerning the founding of the "Old Two-Horn," the first church in the Old Northwest,—and in the organizing of the little academy in the block-house of the fort, to which Marietta College proudly traces her founding, the private formative influence of Putnam is seen to clear advantage. Noble in a great crisis, he was noble still in the lesser wearing duties of that pioneer colony of which he was the hope and mainstay.[62]

In Rufus Putnam's time, the Muskingum River at Marietta could only be crossed by boat. A ferry transported passengers to and from Harmar on the western bank. Nine years after Putnam's death, an article described the ferry across the Muskingum River in Marietta:

> [It] is managed by a boat attached to a strong rope, stretched from bank to bank, in such a way as to be propelled by the current, acting on a "lee board," in the same manner as the breeze acts on the sails of a ship when she is "sailing on a wind." The motion is easy, rapid, and pleasant. It was first constructed, thirty years ago, after the model of one across the river Seine at Paris, under the direction of Monsieur Francis Thiery, one of the early emigrants from France, who formed the settlement at Gallipolis. It is a beautiful specimen of the ingenuity of man in turning to his own benefit the operations of nature.[63]

In 1807, the Ohio state legislature allowed a lottery to be held to raise money for a bridge across the Muskingum River connecting Marietta with Harmar. Some tickets were sold, but the project "was abandoned as premature, and in advance of the means of the country."[64]

In 1880, over a half-century after Putnam's death, the first bridge was built across the Muskingum River between Marietta, and Fort Harmar. Appropriately, it was named after its eastern end—Putnam Street, which in turn had been named after Rufus Putnam. It had two swing spans and was Marietta's first free bridge. After it was destroyed in an 1884 flood, a replacement was built on the same piers. In 1900, due to increased traffic, a replacement bridge was needed. It was built on four new piers. That one was swept away in a 1913 flood. In 1914 another replacement bridge opened. It was made four feet higher to prevent future flood damage. In 2000, it was replaced with a fourth replacement bridge. Costing 11.4 million dollars, the 700-foot-long, four-lane structure has a modern curved design. In 1953, Marietta opened its second bridge, which connected Washington Street with the west side of the Muskingum.

Putnam's Relatives

Sometimes there is confusion among the early Ohio pioneers of the Putnam family. The most famous Putnam, Major General Israel Putnam (1718–1790), never settled in Ohio or anywhere else in the Northwest Territory. When his cousin Rufus Putnam left to found the Marietta settlement, Israel was 70 years old and still laboring under the effects of the paralytic stroke he had suffered eight years earlier. Massachusetts was Israel's home until his early 20s, and then Connecticut became his home for the rest of his life.

Although little has been written about it, Rufus Putnam's leadership in the Ohio Company and the move of his immediate family to Marietta encouraged other members of the Putnam family in Connecticut and Massachusetts to move to the Ohio territory. Here we will cover two of Rufus's cousins: Major General Israel Putnam's son and grandson, both of whom bore his name. As they traveled to Southeastern Ohio early in the life of the Marietta settlement, the details of their journey and their observations of the people and events of the time shed additional light on what Rufus experienced.

Israel Putnam, Jr. (1738–1812), often known as Colonel Israel Putnam, was one of the first pioneers of Ohio. Shortly after Rufus had led the first settlers to Marietta, Israel Jr. joined them with some of his family.[65] His son Israel Putnam III (1766–1824) was born in Connecticut, but also came west to Ohio.

Born in Danvers, Massachusetts, to Israel Putnam, Sr., and Hannah Pope Putnam, Israel Putnam, Jr., moved to the village of Pomfret, Connecticut, with his parents while an infant. At about age 25, he married local woman Sarah Waldo and established his own farm. They had five sons and three daughters.

When the American Revolution broke out with the British firing on American militia in Lexington and Concord, Massachusetts, Israel Jr. raised a company of militia volunteers and led them to Cambridge, Massachusetts, as their captain. After his father's appointment as one of George Washington's major generals, Israel Jr. became one of his father's military aides. Stationed primarily in New York State, Israel Jr. rose to the rank of colonel and served for three years in the Continental Army.

Dr. Samuel Prescott Hildreth, who was only present in Marietta for two years before Israel, Jr.'s wife Sarah died, spoke with her many family and friends and wrote of her: "While [Israel Jr. was] absent from his home, his wife took charge of the family of six children. She was a woman of great spirit, and as firm a patriot as the general himself … supplying [American soldiers] with food and clothing to the extent of her abilities. In the winter of 1779, when the patriot troops suffered so much from the want of warm garments, she had spun and wove in her own house, a number of blankets made of the finest wool in the flock, and sent on for their relief. Numerous pairs of stockings were also manufactured by her own hands, and contributed in the same way."[66]

An early member of the Ohio Company, Israel, Jr., traveled west with two of his sons to establish a farm. He returned for his wife and the rest of their children the following year, but the Indian Wars prevented their return to Ohio until 1795. Israel Jr. was best known for his love of farming and his notable work breeding cattle and cultivating fruit trees (including introducing the Roxbury Russet apple to Ohio). With the benefit of more education than most of his generation, Israel Jr. also assembled a large library of books during his life. In the late 1790s, his collection became part of the first public library in Ohio—and probably the entire Northwest Territory.[67] Sarah Putnam passed away in 1808; Israel, Jr., died in Belpre, Ohio, in 1812.

In the years following the original Rufus Putnam party of 1788, thousands of new settlers floated down the Ohio River to Marietta and other Ohio settlements. Some were poor people who spent every penny they owned to finance their trip; others were people of means who were ambitious enough to leave a relatively easy life in New England, or another state, to travel westward either for adventure or to own some of the western lands that had been touted as having incredibly rich soil overflowing with wildlife.

In the late 18th century, Ohio was considered as far away from New England as China or India. Many people traveling from Massachusetts or Connecticut to Marietta and its surrounding settlements gave up all hope of again seeing the family they left back home. Others, usually younger adventurers, would travel the route to Ohio to see family, friends and the land, and then return within a few months. Such was the case with a man who possessed one of the most famous names of 18th century America—Israel Putnam III—the grandson of the legendary general Israel Putnam of Connecticut.

Israel Putnam III chronicled his 1794 journey, when at age 27 he traveled from Brooklyn, Connecticut (where his grandfather had established a tavern in the late 1760s) to Marietta.[68] His journal is especially important because it provides many details missing from other accounts of the New England to Ohio migration of the late 1700s. Israel Putnam III's experience traveling to Marietta would be similar to Rufus Putnam's trips of 1788 and 1790.

Back in the fall of 1789, Israel Putnam III's parents, Israel Putnam, Jr. (1740–1812), and Sarah Waldo Putnam (1740–1808), along with their other son, Aaron Waldo Putnam (1767–1822), traveled to Ohio. The following year, Israel Putnam, Jr., returned to Connecticut to take other members of his family west. The Indian Wars delayed their return trip for about five years. In the meantime, Israel Putnam III and his first cousin Benjamin Dana left Brooklyn on March 31, 1794 on horseback to visit the "much talked of & famed Ohio."[69]

Passing through the state of Connecticut, Israel Putnam III and his cousin Benjamin purchased mulberry seeds, accepted letters from a doctor friend for folks in Marietta, and took in the sights. It took them about four days to travel through Connecticut, which included crossing the Connecticut River, which was flowing at a high level, and riding through a series of Long Island Sound towns to the New York border. Soon after arriving in New York State, Israel received a smallpox inoculation. After a week on the road, he and his cousin reached New Jersey.

Finally, Israel Putnam III reached the Ohio River. When Israel Putnam III traveled down the river for Marietta, he paid for his trip by his labor: "upon the condition only that we would work our passage with the rest of the men & take our watch with them & find our provision and take our chance for a berth. Hard as the conditions were I agreed to them rather than take the chance of waiting for another upon uncertainty altogether."[70]

As Putnam passed down the river, he was "hourly passing little contented cottages distributed almost all along the fertile banks" of the "beautiful river," Israel III also considered that "it almost grieves one to see so much good land lying idle."[71] As a native of Eastern Connecticut where the soil is relatively poor, Israel III lamented that in the "old country" he saw so much poor land where "people strive for a living and just barely subsist" despite their "indefatigable industry & frugality."

Arriving at Marietta on May 1, 1795, at about four o'clock in the afternoon, Israel III and his cousin Benjamin Dana stored their baggage and were immediately taken to Campus Martius to meet Rufus Putnam. Israel remarks that Judge Putnam "appeared to be glad to see us.... He took us to his house and introduced us to his family, who appeared to be exceeding glad to see us, & we think they received us with the most genuine cordiality & true plain Putnam friendship. After spending an agreeable evening we retired to rest."[72]

The next day after breakfast, Rufus Putnam's son William Rufus, then only 22 years old, showed Israel III Campus Martius and the "Grand Mound." As Israel writes in his journal, "It Has been and still is the wonder of the world and Antiquity. Seems to be the only thing to be seen, and antiquarians left to conjecture as to the cause of it—it being a regular square and fortified. The mound is elevated above the plain about thirty feet, in the form of a cone, surrounded by a parapet or fosse & the grand square contains between 10 & 20 acres."[73]

Upon returning to Rufus Putnam's house, Israel Putnam III had dinner with the General, later writing in his journal:

> The Gen'l seems to be the most sage good old man that I have seen. After dinner I had some conversation with the Gen'l at his land office alone, & he showed me the plots & plans of the whole of the land of the Ohio Company's Purchase. I could not look upon the Gen'l but with veneration, and love for his philanthropy; for seeing him upset in hiving a swarm of bees & the softness, tenderness and kindness he expressed in hiving the pretty creatures & the sorrow he expressed for a few poor bees that happened to be killed in the hiving made me prepossessed in his favor, so that I shall always love him for his tenderness to the bees.[74]

At the time, Israel Putnam III wrote in his journal: "I feel myself exceedingly delighted with the country by what I have seen of it & much more so by what I hear from Gen'l Putnam."[75] Rufus Putnam certainly knew what he was talking about—it had been six years since he had led 47 other men to found the Marietta settlement, and he had since traveled extensively up and down the Muskingum and Ohio Rivers on surveying work and on trips during the Indian conflicts.

The next day Israel III headed toward the settlement of Belpre to see his brother. Entering the latter's house, he found him in bed. Israel describes their meeting:

> I went to him and took him by the hand, but he did not know me at the first sight, but thought it must be some friend by the liberty I took coming to his bed without any ceremony. But after a short interval I called him brother, but could say but a few other words before I lost my utterance entirely, & I was so much overcome that I could not help it. After a few minutes indulgence in a plentiful flood of tears, I began

Eight. A Legend in His Own Time

to have the liberty & use of speech, which to recite will be too lengthy & to little or no effect. Found him and his family well, &c.—his wife, & a fine woman she is, & a son & Daughter. Spent the evening and lodged there.[76]

In December 1794, Israel Putnam III traveled by foot from Ohio back to Connecticut. He stopped at various taverns and inns, some better than others. He described one innkeeper as "a proud, imperious man, and his wife was more so than himself" in a house that "looked too much inclined to dirt." Putnam was given three pints of "poor" milk and half a pint of whiskey. "For this and a spot on the floor to sleep he was charged a half dollar."[77]

At another place he found "a dirty room and stove, a cross woman, a dirty house, and poor breakfast." However, these were in the minority; most lodging places were excellent or at least acceptable. On the way to Bedford, Pennsylvania, Israel III wrote in his journal:

> I had a most delightful Landscape that ever I beheld; from the top of a high mountain I looked down into a vast valley—so beheld the beautiful meadows, fields, hills, vallies, the beautiful purling stream of Juniata meandering through meadows & lawns covered with the feeding herd, interspersed with gentle hills, abrupt precipices, sharp ridges, beautiful well cultivated fields, barren hills, tremendous precipices under our feet. And to complete the whole scenery yonder toward the Allegheny "the lord of the Earth," with his towering height above the clouds, whose sides were covered with snow, & we poor feeble men looking up the mountains scarcely able to comprehend what we saw. In short, the one comprehensive view was the most picturesque that my eyes ever beheld.[78]

Israel III quotes Col. Thomas Forrest's march through the Allegheny Mountains in October 1794. For several days, Forrest (and by implication Putnam) only saw "Stupendous hills without inhabitants, narrow valleys badly cultivated, huge rocks where naught but moss has ever ventured, giddy precipices which the most daring approach with dread, headlong streams murmuring loudly at the roughness of their beds, and sickly vegetables contracted in size by the bleakness of their situation, and by deficiency of nutriment, are in continual succession. We have, however, at length arrived and are now encamped at a place where the enterprise and industry of man has reared more memorable monuments."[79]

Israel Putnam III's 1794–1795 round-trip from Brooklyn, Connecticut, to Marietta took about nine and a half months. He had left Brooklyn on March 31, 1794, and arrived at Marietta on May 1—a total of 31 days on the road. He left Ohio for Connecticut on December 15, 1794, and got as far back as New Jersey, when his journal ends. Assuming that he took the same number of days to travel between New Jersey to Connecticut (about six on the way west), then he probably arrived back in Brooklyn around

January 13, 1795. Israel Putnam III would soon return to Ohio with his family.[80] Israel Putnam III died in Marietta in 1824 at age 58.[81]

In writing of Washington County, Ohio, in 1833, John Kilbourn mentions something for which Israel Putnam III was well-known:

> Orchards of the finest fruit were planted at an early day by the first settlers; particularly so by the late Hon. Paul Fearing, and Mr. Israel Putnam, grandson of the celebrated general of that name. Mr. Putnam visited personally no less than thirteen different states for the express purpose of selecting the choicest varieties of fruits then known. From his extensive nurseries this county and several of the adjoining ones, have been enabled to fill their orchards with a great variety of the most delicious fruits.[82]

The Steamboat

On Friday, January 9, 1824, a large crowd gathered on the banks of the Muskingum River, in Marietta to watch the departure of the steamboat *Rufus Putnam* on its maiden voyage. It would be the first steamboat to travel on the Muskingum River from Marietta to Zanesville, which lies about 80 miles to the north.[83]

Invented in the late 1700s, steamboats gained popularity in Europe and North America throughout the 1700s and 1800s. Inventor Robert Fulton introduced the first commercially viable steamboat—in 1807, his *Clermont* traveled the Hudson River at the speed of about five miles an hour.

Before steam-powered boats, the speed of river boats depended on a river's current. It was common for settlers to travel down a river, disassemble their boats at their destination, and use the wood in the construction of permanent houses, barns and outbuildings.

Built by Caleb Bastow months earlier for John Green and Oliver Dodge, the *Rufus Putnam* cost between $10,000 and $12,000 to construct. Its engine was built at Steubenville, Ohio, while its other iron work was completed at Marietta.

The *Rufus Putnam* was 75 feet long by 18 feet wide with a 75-ton capacity. The cabin was built on the deck, with bunks fastened to the sides and made private with curtains. The freight was carried in the hold.[84]

It's been said that on this maiden trip the ship was piloted by Captain Daniel Green, who had "a deep base [sic] voice of tremendous carrying power." According to one account, "sometimes when his steamer was rounding a bend out of sight, the people, from the sound of Green's voice in conversation reaching them, knew it was the *Rufus Putnam* that was coming."[85]

The words "Rufus Putnam" were on everyone's lips the day of its launch. But that was not unusual. For the past 36 years, it was the name

Eight. A Legend in His Own Time

of the man who had been the founder, the patriarch, the heart of the community. He was as much a legend for the citizens of Marietta—indeed for anyone in the state of Ohio—as any person then living. Only one other general of the Revolutionary War's Continental Army was still living— the Marquis de Lafayette.[86]

So, as the bell of the steamboat rang,[87] that sound carried to the home of Rufus Putnam, which was only about 700 feet away. Although it's possible that Putnam did not hear the bell—since he was now "quite deaf"—it has been said he was watching that day as his namesake steamboat left the dock.

Was Rufus Putnam remembering how the flat boats he and his fellow soldiers navigated down the rivers and streams of the wilderness in upper New York State in the French and Indian War 65 years earlier; or the whale boat that he and his cousin, later promoted to the rank major general in the Continental Army, Israel Putnam, had used to explore the lower Mississippi River over 50 years before; or the riverboat *Mayflower* on which 36 years earlier he had led four dozen other pioneers to establish Marietta the first permanent settlement in the Northwest Territory.

As soon as the steamer *Rufus Putnam* was out of sight, how likely was it that almost everyone present turned their heads to look toward Rufus Putnam's house and strive to catch a glimpse of the town's beloved 85-year-old founder? About a year earlier, he had been described as "feeble with age," but "a very fine looking man" and "very erect in his carriage and dignified in manner."[88]

An article in the *Zanesville Messenger* on January 13, 1824, reported the arrival of the *Rufus Putnam* in Zanesville: "Last Saturday night, about nine o'clock, our town was alarmed by several reports of cannon which appeared to come up the river." A crowd formed on the riverbank to view the first steamboat "that has ever visited this place." The steamboat was "vomiting fire and smoke" before it released over 100 passengers from Marietta. It later took local residents on two of short trips down the river before it left for Louisville.[89]

Putnam's Death

In the last census (1820) before Rufus Putnam's death, Ohio is credited with a population of 581,434, which was only exceeded among the then 23 states by the four states of New York, Pennsylvania, Virginia, and North Carolina. However, the largest city in Ohio—Cincinnati—only had a population of 9,642.

The year of the census, Rufus's wife, Persis (Rice) Putnam passed away at age 82.[90] Rufus and Persis had been married for 55 years. Their main homes had been in North Brookfield, Massachusetts (about 16 years), Rutland, Massachusetts (about nine years), and Marietta, Ohio (about 30 years). Rufus's military service, explorations and work had separated them on a number of occasions: during most of the American Revolutionary War; between December 10, 1772, and August 13, 1773, when Rufus explored the Mississippi River; in the mid–1780s when he surveyed lands in Maine; and during the approximately two-and-one-half years Rufus led the settlers to Ohio, established and fortified Marietta, and traveled back to Massachusetts to bring Persis and their children to Ohio.

Rufus Putnam died on May 4, 1824, in Marietta at age 86. He was the last surviving American-born Continental Army general of the American Revolutionary War.[91] It would be James Monroe's eighth and last year as president of the United States.[92] Putnam lived a long and fruitful life; he was a man of good character who did much good—especially for the benefit of the people of Ohio.

Rufus's grandson, Colonel W.R. Putnam, erected a granite monument over the grave of Rufus and Persis Putnam with the inscription:

> Gen. Rufus Putnam
> A Revolutionary Officer
> And the Leader of the
> Colony Which Made the
> First Settlement in the
> Territory of the Northwest
> At Marietta, April 7, 1788.
> Born April 9, 1738.
> Died May 4, 1824.

> Persis Rice.
> Wife of
> Rufus Putnam.
> Born Nov. 19, 1737.
> Died Sept. 6, 1820.

Below their names on the monument appears a verse from the Bible's Book of Proverbs (10:7) "The Memory of the Just Is Blessed."

The last will and testament of Rufus Putnam included the lines: "First, I give my soul to a holy, sovereign God Who gave it in humble hope of a blessed immortality through the atonement and righteousness of Jesus Christ and the sanctifying grace of the Holy Spirit. My body I commit to the earth to be buried in a decent Christian manner. I fully believe that this body shall, by the mighty power of God, be raised to life at the last day; 'for this corruptable [*sic*] must put on incorruption and this mortal must put on immortality.'"[93] This last line is from I Corinthians 15:53.

Decades later, Eben Putnam, in his *A History of the Putnam Family in England and America*, wrote:

> [Rufus Putnam] was laid to rest in the Mound Cemetery, so called from the ancient mound, the preservation of which is due him who rests so near it. Even in that early day, when American archaeology was as yet unheard of, he manifested a keen appreciation of the relics of the people who had once inhabited that fruitful region. He was nearly the first to realize the importance of preserving the memorials of a bygone race if we would know aught concerning them.[94]

The *Boston Patriot* published this extract from a May 6, 1824, letter from Marietta:

> The venerable and highly distinguished General, RUFUS PUTNAM, died at his seat in this town, on the 4th instant, aged 86. This distinguished champion of the war of the revolution, and the fast friend of Washington, gathered a small band of tried souls, and at the close of the war, in 1783, made arrangements and settled on the west bank of the Ohio in 1787 [*sic*], at this place, then a savage wilderness. He has here lived to see the state of Ohio the fourth in the union, in point of population, having 14 representatives in congress, while Massachusetts, his native state, has but 13. General Rufus Putnam is acknowledged the father of the western country, and lived to the day when Ohio can number 800,000 souls. This is worthy of note. His soul was pure and unsullied; a christian that carried the mantle of charity; liberal, generous, hospitable; with a large share of philanthropy. He did honor to human nature.[95]

In quoting a version of this letter, the *Gettysburg Compiler* in its June 9, 1824, issue added: "Lafayette is now the only surviving general officer of the revolutionary army."[96]

One year after Rufus Putnam died, the Marquis de Lafayette briefly visited Marietta as he traveled the Ohio River. On May 22, 1825, he stopped at the French settlement of Gallipolis, Ohio, and sailed north to visit Marietta on Monday, May 23.[97] He then proceeded to stop at Wheeling, Virginia (in 1863, it became part of West Virginia), on May 24.[98]

CHAPTER NINE

Legacy

On the one hundred and twenty-fifth anniversary of the British troops leaving Boston in the second year of the Revolutionary War, U.S. Senator George F. Hoar delivered the speech, "Evacuation Day Memorial, City of Boston." In it he said: "I shall take no laurel leaf from the pure chaplet of Washington's fame if I give due honor in this transaction to a son of Massachusetts whose great military and civil service, surpassed in my opinion, by those of no other man, save Washington and Lincoln alone, has not yet received its due credit from history. I speak of Rufus Putnam."[1]

As Marietta matured, its residents were very proud of their past. Dr. Hildreth expressed the sentiment in 1842:

> While many of the early settlements in the West were made up from the ignorant, the vulgar, and the rude, the colony at Marietta, like those of some of the ancient Greeks, carried with it the sciences and the arts; and although placed on the frontiers, amidst a howling and savage wilderness, exposed to many dangers and privations, there ran in the veins of its little community some of the best blood of the country. It enrolled many men of highly cultivated minds and exalted intellect: several of them claimed the halls of old Cambridge as their Alma Mater. 1842.[2]

Hildreth recognizes the contribution of the American military veterans:

> The army of the revolution furnished a number of officers who had distinguished themselves for their good conduct as well as for their bravery. To this latter circumstance is probably to be attributed the fact of the settlement's passing through a four years' war with the most cunning and bold enemy the world ever produced with so few losses.[3]

It might seem a bit much to compare Marietta with ancient Greece, but it was true that a number of the settlement's leaders had received classical educations at New England colleges. Probably more important is the large number of Revolutionary War officers who settled in Marietta. After all, the reason for the town's existence was to provide veterans with land for themselves and their families.

It's also noteworthy that Dr. Hildreth describes the British military of the late 18th century as "the most cunning and bold enemy the world ever produced." Interestingly, at the Battle of Long Island, the American forces faced what has been called by many historians the largest naval force in the history of the world. Along with 400 ships, the British brought to bear 1,200 guns and 32,000 British, Scottish and Hessian troops. In the months leading up to the battle, Rufus Putnam planned and supervised the construction of fortifications. Later, Putnam would use his skills and knowledge to protect western pioneers in the same way.

Last of the 48 Marietta Pioneers

According to Ephraim Cutler's daughter, Julia Perkins Cutler, the last seven survivors of the original 48 Marietta pioneers were:

Peletiah White, 1766?–1832
Benjamin Shaw, of Washington County Ohio, 1753–1838
Hezekiah Flint, Jr., of Cincinnati, Ohio, 1771–1843
Jervis Cutler, of Nashville, Tennessee, 1768–1844
Allen Devol, of Washington County Ohio, 1768–1845
Phineas Coburn, of Washington County Ohio, 1766–1848
Amos Porter, Jr., 1769–1861[4]

The last survivor of the original 48 Marietta pioneers was Amos Porter, Jr., who was nineteen years old when he arrived at the new settlement, which is now called Marietta. Porter was born in Danvers, Massachusetts, on February 20, 1769. Two years after coming to Ohio, he returned to Massachusetts on foot. He then married Sabra Tolman (1777–1812) of Chelsea, Massachusetts. In 1795, he returned with his father and his mother, Annie Bradstreet Porter. They and their sons moved to farms in Salem Township. Between 1802 and 1810, they had several children. After Sabra died, Amos married Sally Perkins Sutton (–1850).

In 1858 (the year Rufus Putnam would have turned 120 years old), last survivor Amos, Jr., attended Marietta's 70th anniversary celebration of the settlement's founding. He drove "slowly into the city, in an ancient looking vehicle…. He was dressed in an old drab cloak of the style of ancient days. His long silvery locks hung closely over a ruddy brow, from which still peer forth sharp and piercing eyes; although ninety years of age on the 20th of February, 1858, his form is still as manly and erect as when contending with the savage foeman of the olden time. He still retains a clear and distinct recollection of the early history of the Buckeye state, and it is refreshing to hear from his own lips the relation of those events which have long since became matters of history in the archives."[5]

During his trip to Marietta the old man complained about "houses with closely sealed rooms" and stated his love for houses where "on a winter's morning, he could, shake the snows from the bed covering when he arose."[6]

At the celebration, Porter was given the seat of honor as former Ohio Senator Thomas Ewing "turned to Mr. Porter and delivered an eloquent tribute to his life and work, as one of the pioneers of the Northwest Territory." At the end of Ewing's remarks, as Amos "slowly made his way down the aisle the vast audience arose, moved by a spontaneous outburst of enthusiasm and stood to let him pass and do him reverence."[7]

An elder in the Presbyterian Church, Porter died on November 28, 1861, at age ninety-two. His grave marker in the family cemetery in Washington County, Ohio, has the inscription, "The Last of the Pioneers Who Landed at Marietta Apr. 7, 1788."[8]

Amos Porter's sister Nancy married fellow Danvers resident and ship carpenter Allen Putnam and moved to a farm in Stanleyville, Ohio, in 1797. When the *Mayflower* pulled up to shore at Marietta in April 1788, Allen was the first man to jump to shore. Two years later, he and Amos Porter walked back to Danvers to bring out their families. Because of the Indian Wars, they stayed in Pennsylvania two years, not arriving at Marietta until 1795. Allen died in 1807 when he fell through a hatchway at work.[9]

In looking back on Rufus Putnam's life, historian David McCullough writes: "No one had played so important a role in the creation of the settlement or shown such leadership, perseverance, and strength of character without fail."[10]

In 1888, writer and educator William Henry Venable (1836–1920) published this poem in his book, *Footprints of the Pioneers in the Ohio Valley*:

FIRST ENGLISH SETTLEMENT IN OHIO
The footsteps of a hundred years
Have echoed since o'er Braddock's Road,
Bold Putnam and the Pioneers
Led History the way they strode

On wild Monongahela's stream
They launched the Mayflower of the West,
A perfect State their civic dream,
A new New World their pilgrim quest.

> When April robed the Buckeye trees,
> Muskingum's bosky shore they trod;
> They pitched their tent, and to the breeze
> Flung freedom's star-flag, thanking God.
>
> As glides the Oyo's solemn flood,
> Their generation fleeted on:
> Our veins are thrilling with their blood,
> But they, the Pioneers, are gone.
>
> Though storied tombs may not enshrine
> The dust of our illustrious sires,
> Behold, where monumental shine
> Proud Marietta's votive spires.
>
> Ohio carves and consecrates
> In her own heart their every name;
> The Founders of majestic States—
> Their epitaph: immortal fame.[11]

George F. Hoar, who served as a U.S. senator from Massachusetts for 27 years (1877–1904), wrote of Rufus Putnam:

> To be a great engineer is to be a great soldier. To be a great engineer with only such advantages of education as Rufus Putnam enjoyed is to be a man of consummate genius. But to have been the trusted friend of Washington, to have conceived as by a flash of inspiration the works with which an inferior force compelled England to evacuate a fortified town and to quit Massachusetts forever, to have constructed the very fortress and citadel of our strength and defence in the war of the Revolution, to have been in Lord Bacon's front rank of sovereign honor,[12] to have founded a mighty State, herself the mother of mighty States, to have planned, constructed, and made impregnable the very citadel and fortress of liberty on this continent, to have turned the mighty stream of current and empire from the channel of slavery into the channel of freedom, there to flow forever and forever,—if this be not greatness, then there is no greatness among the living or the dead.[13]

At the end of the 19th century—over three decades after the Civil War ended—the Rev. Sidney Crawford stated in regards to Rufus Putnam:

> Had it not been for his providential leadership.... "The United States of America would now be a great slaveholding empire." He was the originator of the colony to make the first settlement in the territory northwest of the Ohio River when it was yet a wilderness, and that settlement carried with it the famous Ordinance of 1787, by which slavery was forever to be excluded from all that region. Now that section is occupied by the great States of Ohio, Indiana, Illinois, Wisconsin and Michigan. Had slavery once crossed the river, it is not difficult to see what would have been its bearing upon our national destiny.[14]

After traveling to North America in the years 1831 through 1832, French political scientist Alexis de Tocqueville wrote one of the classic books of the 19th century: *Democracy in America*, which was published in two parts in 1835 and 1840. In his discussion of American slavery, he compared the free state of Ohio with the slave state of Kentucky.

Tocqueville observes that on the left bank of the Ohio River is Kentucky, while on the right is the state of Ohio. "These two States only differ in a single respect; Kentucky has admitted slavery, but the State of Ohio has prohibited the existence of slaves within its borders."

> Thus the traveller who floats down the current of the Ohio to the spot where that river falls into the Mississippi, may be said to sail between liberty and servitude; and a transient inspection of the surrounding objects will convince him as to which of the two is most favorable to mankind. Upon the left bank of the stream the population is rare; from time to time one descries a troop of slaves loitering in the half-desert fields; the primaeval forest recurs at every turn; society seems to be asleep, man to be idle, and nature alone offers a scene of activity and of life. From the right bank, on the contrary, a confused hum is heard which proclaims the presence of industry; the fields are covered with abundant harvests, the elegance of the dwellings announces the taste and activity of the laborer, and man appears to be in the enjoyment of that wealth and contentment which is the reward of labor.[15]

The story of Rufus Putnam and the founding of Marietta was popular in schools through the 19th century and into the 20th century.

In 1912, prolific children's book writer James Otis Kaler (1848–1912) released *Benjamin of Ohio: A Story of the Settlement of Marietta*, which told the story of Rufus Putnam and the pioneers in the early days of Marietta through the words of a fictional thirteen-year-old named Benjamin.[16]

Rutland, Massachusetts, has always taken great pride in a title given to it long ago—the "Cradle of Ohio." In 1907, the Rufus Putnam Memorial Association arranged a celebration which included a re-creation of the departure of Putnam's party for the Northwest Territory. The reenactors used three ox teams, each with two yokes of oxen, one two-horse carriage, four cows, one bull, and "Putnam's saddle horse." They passed through the town, with a stop at the church.[17]

In 2013, street signs in Rutland and Marietta recognized their relationship. Rutland's signs, placed at the town lines stated:

> Sister City
> Marietta, Ohio
> "This Rutland on the hill
> is the cradle of Ohio,
> the cradle of the West"

One newspaper article discussing the signs, and Rufus Putnam, commented: "Rutland residents can enjoy the pride of their native son's accomplishment every time they leave Rutland and come back again."[18]

Timothy Flint, who knew Rufus Putnam personally, wrote of him in 1828:

> He was probably the member of the Ohio Company who had the greatest influence in imparting confidence to emigration from New England to Ohio. When he moved there it was one compact and boundless forest. He saw that forest fall on all sides under the axe; and, in the progress of improvement, comfortable and then splendid dwellings rise around him. He saw his favorite settlement survive the accumulated horrors of an Indian war. He saw its exhaustless fertility and its natural advantages triumph over all. He saw Marietta making advance toward an union of interest with the Gulf of Mexico by floating down to its bosom a number of sea vessels built at that place. He saw such a prodigious increase of navigation on the Ohio as to number a hundred large boats passing his dwelling within a few hours. He heard the first tumult of the steamboats as they began to be borne down between the forests. He had surrounded his republican mansion with orchards bending with fruit. In the midst of rural abundance and endeared friends who had grown up around him; far from the display of wealth, the bustle of ambition and intrigue, the father of the colony, hospitable and kind without ostentation and without effort, he displayed in these remote regions the grandeur, real and intrinsic, of those immortal men who achieved our revolution. He has passed away. But the memory of really great and good men, like Gen. Putnam, will remain as long as plenty, independence, and comfort shall prevail on the shores of the Ohio.[19]

In 1888, on the 100th anniversary of Ohio's founding at Marietta, an exhibit of artifacts was opened at the town. It included a 100-year-old candlestick once owned by Rufus Putnam, as well as a plate, teapot, cup and teaspoon that he had used. Other Ohio Company figures were represented: Manahash Cutler's 1788 traveling trunk, Return Jonathan Meigs, Jr's chair, Abraham Whipple's tongs, and militia general Joseph Buell's wine chest.

From beyond Ohio, in terms of location and history, the show featured shoes worn by Nathan Hale's fiancée, part of George Washington's saddle, and two pieces of Miles Standish's wife's wedding dress, which had traveled on the original *Mayflower* in 1620.[20]

Commemorative Stamps

The American who has been featured on the greatest number of U.S. postage stamps is, without question, George Washington. The number two spot goes to fellow Founding Father Benjamin Franklin, who was the first Postmaster General appointed by the Continental Congress. A survey of United States stamps since the 18th century shows that only eleven of the 75 Continental Army generals have been prominently featured on official U.S. postal stamps.[21] They are:

- Commander-in-Chief George Washington.
- Major General John Sullivan, who was featured on a 1929 two-cent stamp marking the Sullivan Expedition in New York State during the Revolutionary War.
- General Anthony Wayne, who was featured on a 1929 two-cent stamp marking the 135th anniversary of the Battle of Fallen Timbers.
- General Von Steuben, who was featured on a 1930 two-cent stamp, the Von Steuben issue.
- General Casimir Pulaski, who was featured on a 1931 two-cent stamp marking the 150th anniversary of Pulaski's death.
- General Kosciuszko, who was featured on a 1933 five-cent stamp marking the 150th anniversary of Kosciuszko receiving U.S. citizenship.
- General Nathanael Greene, whose portrait appeared along with Washington's on a 1936–1937 stamp honoring the U.S. Army.
- General Rufus Putnam, whose portrait appeared along with Manasseh Cutler's on a 1937 three-cent stamp marking the 150th anniversary of the adoption of the Ordinance of 1787 and the creation of the Northwest Territories.
- General Lafayette, whose portrait appeared on three stamps: a 1952 three-cent stamp marking the 175th anniversary of his arrival in the American colonies, a 1957 three-cent stamp marking the 200th anniversary of his birth, and a 1977 thirteen-cent stamp.
- General Henry Knox, whose portrait appeared on a 1980 eight-cent stamp of a Great Americans Issue.
- Benjamin Lincoln (1976)

In addition to these stamps, Continental Army generals have appeared on a couple of stamps featuring group scenes. On the one-dollar 1994 Surrender of General Burgoyne Stamp, we find generals John Stark of New Hampshire; Philip Schuyler of New York; Horatio Gates and Daniel Morgan of Virginia; and John Greaton, John Glover, and Rufus Putnam of Massachusetts.

On the Declaration of Independence stamp, we see General George Clinton.

Thus, only three Continental Army generals have appeared prominently on more than one postage stamp in the history of the United States: Washington, Lafayette and Rufus Putnam.

Nine. Legacy

The 1937 U.S. postage stamp marking the 150th anniversary of the adoption of the Ordinance of 1787 and the creation of the Northwest Territories. Rufus Putnam appears on the right; Manasseh Cutler on the left. Putnam also appeared on a 1994 stamp which marked the surrender of General Burgoyne at Saratoga (courtesy U.S. Post Office/U.S. Postal Service).

For five days in July 1889, relics were exhibited at the Centennial Celebration of the Establishment of Civil Government at Marietta, Ohio. They included Rufus Putnam's army chest, sword, military sash and epaulette, commissary chest, teapot, china, mahogany stand table, antique clock, and other items.[22]

Perhaps Rufus Putnam's most famous grandchild was Union Army general Catharinus Putnam Buckingham (1808–1888). Sixteen years old at the time of Rufus Putnam's death, Buckingham became a cadet at the United States Military Academy at West Point in the late 1820s. There, he practiced military drills under the watchful presence of the famous fort that his grandfather had built one-half century earlier.

After graduation, Buckingham followed in his famous grandfather's footsteps by serving as a surveyor in the U.S. Army's Topographical Corps. Careers as a college professor and a businessman followed. At the beginning of the Civil War, he was appointed Adjutant General of Ohio. Buckingham later was promoted to brigadier general of U.S. Volunteers, and an assistant to the U.S. Secretary of War, Edwin M. Stanton.

In 1862, when President Lincoln chose to remove Gen. George McClellan from command of the Army of the Potomac, it was Catharinus Putnam Buckingham who was selected to catch up with the moving army and notify McClellan.[23]

In his memoirs, General McClellan describes the scene:

> Late at night I was sitting alone in my tent, writing to my wife. All the staff were asleep. Suddenly some one knocked upon the tent-pole, and, upon my invitation to enter, there appeared Burnside and Buckingham, both looking very solemn. I received them kindly and commenced conversation upon general subjects in the most unconcerned manner possible. After a few moments Buckingham said to Burnside: "Well, general, I think we had better tell Gen. McClellan the object of our visit." I very pleasantly said that I should be glad to learn it. Whereupon Buckingham handed me the two orders of which he was the bearer.[24]

One was a message from General H.W. Halleck stating: "On receipt of the order of the President, sent herewith, you will immediately turn over your command to Maj.-Gen. Burnside"[25]

The other, signed by Assistant Adjutant General Edward Townsend, stated: "By direction of the President of the United States, it is ordered that Maj.-Gen. McClellan be relieved from the command of the Army of the Potomac, and that Maj.-Gen. Burnside take the command of that army."[26] I saw that both—especially Buckingham—were watching me most intently while I opened and read the orders. I read the papers with a smile, immediately turned to Burnside, and said: "Well, Burnside, I turn the command over to you."[27]

In November 1843, on a trip to Ohio to lay the corner stone of the Cincinnati Observatory, former U.S. president John Quincy Adams stopped at Marietta. From the wharf, he proceeded to the Congregational church surrounded by the "whole town." In a half-hour extemporaneous address from the pulpit, Adams spoke of the settlement of Ohio and in particular stated that "he had known Rufus Putnam, what part he had borne in the Revolutionary War, and what had been the leading influence he exerted in founding the colony and in raising it through the hardships of its first decade. He paid a noble tribute to the memory of this man so dear to the Marietta people."[28]

Adams went on to speak of the other founders of Ohio's first settlement, including Abraham Whipple, Benjamin Tupper, Return Jonathan Meigs, James Varnum, the Derols, the Greens, the Putnams, the Fearings, Samuel Holden Parsons, and Manasseh Cutler.[29]

In attendance that day were Deacon William Rufus Putnam and his son William Rufus, the son and grandson of Rufus Putnam, as well as the children, grandchildren and great-grandchildren of many of the other founders. After Adams' speech, they came up to shake his hand.[30]

Many of Ohio's counties are named for leaders of the American Revolution: Franklin and Hamilton Counties honor Benjamin Franklin and Alexander Hamilton. Other counties are named after military leaders Nathanael Greene, Daniel Morgan, Henry Knox, and John Stark. The first five U.S. presidents/founding fathers have counties named for them: Washington, Adams, Jefferson, Madison, and Monroe. Given Rufus Putnam's legendary status as the "Father of Ohio" it might be assumed that Putnam County is named for him. However, it was named for Rufus's cousin, Major General Israel Putnam.

At the dedication of Fayerweather Hall and the Library at Marietta College in 1906, Ralph Cole, a member of the U.S. House of Representatives from Ohio, spoke on Rufus Putnam as the "Father of Ohio." Cole's remarks were appropriately prefaced with lines from James Russell Lowell's poem "The Bridge."

> "Thou skilled by Freedom and by great events
> To pitch new States as Old World men pitch tents."

An Ohio historical marker that was installed on the campus of Marietta College in 2003 by the Ohio Bicentennial Commission states:

> "Muskingum Academy, 1797—Birth of Higher Education in Ohio"
>
> In April 1797, a committee of Marietta citizens, led by General Rufus Putnam, met to establish an academy suitable for preparatory instruction for their youth. Muskingum Academy, completed late that year, became the first institution of its kind in the Northwest Territory, providing "classical instruction ... in the higher branches of an English education." Almost one-third of the monies raised to found the Academy were donated by Rufus Putnam himself.
>
> Its first instructor was David Putnam, a 1793 Yale graduate and grandson of Rufus Putnam's famous cousin Israel Putnam. One of his duties was to teach Latin and Greek. The building also served as the home of the Congregationalist Church until 1808. Growing and expanding with Ohio's first city, the academy served Marietta's educational needs for more than thirty years as the forerunner of Marietta College. It's building on Marietta's Front Street was used until 1832.

Rufus Putnam's Descendants

Henry Howe in his 1891 edition of *Historical Collections of Ohio* mentions that Rufus Putnam Burlingame was still alive.

"There lives in Chillicothe to-day an aged man who is the last grandchild of Rufus Putnam, who led the first colony of settlers to Ohio in 1788. The grandson bears the full name of his distinguished ancestor, Gen. Rufus Putnam, and he has in his possession a great many relics of historical interest and a large part of his grandfather's correspondence and private papers and manuscripts. Gen. Putnam is president of the Northwest Pioneer Association, and has a lively interest in all matters bearing upon the early history of the Northwest Territory."[31]

Born in 1805, when his grandfather was 67 years old, Burlingame died in 1898 and is buried in Springfield, Ohio.

Marietta never grew into a large metropolis, but it was always successful. About a half-century after Putnam's death (1871), Marietta had eight churches, two academies, a college, two public libraries, two printing offices, a bank and factories. Its population was 5,500. Across the Muskingum River, Harmar was home to about 1,600 people and a greater manufacturing presence than Marietta, with several mills, factories and steamboat construction.[32]

One 21st century Putnam descendant, Lisa Welte Herzig, states:

> From the fortification of Boston's Dorchester Heights to the construction of other major fortifications, Rufus did whatever was needed to keep General George Washington's troops out of harm's way. After the Revolution, he continued his survey work up and down the East Coast—in fact, he landed at a place in Maine, where his 8th great-grandson resides today. His surveying took him as far south as Cuba and 400 miles up the Mississippi. In 1788, he led a company of people out to Ohio to settle that territory. Rufus Putnam's accomplishments were many, and his character exemplary.

Conclusion

A constant thread throughout Rufus Putnam's life was his ability to teach himself something new and then merge that knowledge with his experiences to solve problems. The origin of this is clear: in childhood he was deprived of a formal education (and in the years he lived with his stepfather, he was even denied free time to teach himself). When he finally did get an opportunity to learn a trade—as a millwright—he wholeheartedly applied himself to the task.

His application of experience is even more remarkable. The skills he learned as a millwright apprentice in his teenage years were applied to building of fortifications and other structures during the French and Indian War. These refined skills achieved their greatest importance during the American Revolutionary War when George Washington named him Chief Engineer of the Continental Army and trusted him with the most important military engineering projects.

While living in North Brookfield, Massachusetts, during his twenties,

Nine. Legacy

Rufus learned land surveying. This skill not only enabled him to supplement his living, but it was the main reason why his cousin Israel Putnam selected him to be a part of the Mississippi River expedition of 1772–1773. He not only surveyed but he documented his observations of this uncharted territory. In the 1780s, Rufus Putnam, then in his forties, was employed to survey the eastern part of what was to become the State of Maine. His next endeavor was to lead Massachusetts settlers west and to establish the first permanent settlement in the Northwest Territories. Putnam was busy planning Ohio land surveys, hiring surveyors and performing surveys himself, as was the case when he surveyed land for the campus of Ohio University. His surveying career reached its pinnacle in 1796 when President George Washington appointed him surveyor general of the United States.

Also, in regard to the Mississippi expedition, it is easy to see the application of Rufus' knowledge of navigation—a knowledge he acquired through books. As the expedition headed down the Eastern Seaboard, into the Caribbean Sea, through the Gulf of Mexico, and up the Mississippi River, Rufus Putnam proved himself a valuable member of the party of "adventurers."

Farming was another of Rufus Putnam's areas of expertise. For over 20 years he owned and operated a farm in North Brookfield, Massachusetts, and then he moved to Rutland, Massachusetts, where he managed his family farm for about eight years. In North Brookfield, he served in the town government and was a member of the local Committee of Correspondence; in Rutland, he also held important state and town offices. This made Rufus Putnam well qualified to assume the main government duties of the new settlements in Ohio. He planned land allocations, settled disputes, and advised his fellow citizens on a multitude of subjects, including farm-related issues.

History records that Putnam's most notable occupation was being a military officer. It is easy to trace the progression of his military career: a nineteen-year-old private in the French and Indian War, a colonel in the American Revolution, a brevetted brigadier general near the war's end, a full United States brigadier general during the Ohio Indian Wars of the early 1790s.

Significantly, his Revolutionary War service to General Washington began with the application of "book knowledge." Rufus Putnam provided the commander-in-Chief a way to drive the British from Boston forever—after having spent only minutes with a military engineering book! Rufus Putnam's skill as an engineer led to Washington assigning him the most critical military engineering projects during the Revolution. Included were the fortification of West Point and other military locations on the Hudson River that prevented the British from merging their Canadian and New York forces.

These military engineering skills came into play when Rufus Putnam came to Ohio; he designed and supervised (in record time) the construction of the Campus Martius fortification at Marietta. It is said that his work was the reason that this settlement, unlike its neighbors, never experienced an Indian attack.

It is a testament to Rufus Putnam's character that he shared his skills, time and money for the improvement of Marietta. His dedication to his community was shown by the fact that he called Marietta home for the rest of his life. In fact, one of the many private residences built into the Campus Martius fort was Putnam's own home—a building that he lived in for 35 years.

Always interested in the welfare of his country and his home, Putnam had the foresight to see how important it was to the Northwest Territory to have antislavery laws that could never be repealed or amended. His stamp on history earned him the title of "Father of Ohio."

Millwright, surveyor, farmer, explorer, soldier, military engineer, pioneer leader, and judge were some of the careers of Rufus Putnam. The fact that he mastered each of them was remarkable; the fact that he was highly successful at all of them was incredible.

Chapter Notes

Preface

1. Cone, Mary. *Life of Rufus Putnam: With Extracts from His Journal, and An Account of the First Settlement in Ohio.* Cleveland: William W. Williams, 1886. Cone's parents moved to Marietta, Ohio, in 1806. Mary, the third of their ten children, was born on March 17, 1813. At that time, fellow Marietta resident Rufus Putnam was approaching his 75th birthday. When he died, his future biographer Mary Cone was eleven years old. Mary passed away in 1898 at age 84. The lack of professional biographies is offset by the availability of many other materials—especially Rufus Putnam's diaries during the French and Indian War, his Memoirs, which were written in his later years, and numerous letters between Rufus Putnam and key people of his time. Much of this material is included in this 2020 biography with only obvious spelling corrections.

Introduction

1. In 1860, the states that stayed with the Union had a population of a little over 22 million people, while the Confederate states had only about 9 million. However, if the Northwest Territory states had sided with the Confederacy, those numbers would have changed significantly: the Confederacy would have numbered 16 million people, while the Union would have had 15 million.

2. When Lincoln was born in 1809 in Springfield, Illinois, Putnam's Marietta settlement was already 21 years old. Union Army generals Grant and Sherman were natives of Ohio. Grant was born on April 27, 1822, in Point Pleasant, Ohio, and Sherman was born on February 8, 1820, in Lancaster, Ohio.

3. "George Washington to the Board of War, 29 July 1776," Founders Online, National Archives, accessed April 11, 2019, https://founders.archives.gov/documents/Adams/06-04-02-0188.

4. Hoar, George F. "Rufus Putnam. An Address by Hon. George F. Hoar, at Rutland, Mass., Sept. 17, 1898." Eighth Annual Report of the Trustees of Public Reservations, Boston: Geo. H. Ellis, 1899. 38.

5. Roy, Patricia. "Acclaimed Historian Visits Rutland Home." *The Landmark*, The Landmark, 2 Nov. 2017, www.thelandmark.com/articles/acclaimed-historian-visits-rutland-home/.

Chapter One

1. Putnam, *Memoirs of Rufus Putnam* 63–64.

2. Benedict, William A., and Hiram A. Tracy. *History of the Town of Sutton, Massachusetts, from 1704 to 1876: Including Grafton until 1735; Millbury until 1813; and Parts of Northbridge, Upton and Auburn.* Worcester: Sanford & Company, 1878.

3. Salem Village is today named Danvers.

4. *Ibid.,* 57.
5. *Ibid.*
6. The Rev. Hall (1704–1789) kept a dairy from 1740 to 1789. He served as pastor of the First Congregational Church of Sutton, Massachusetts, from 1729 (nine years before Rufus was born) to 1789 (when 51-year-old Rufus Putnam was building up the Marietta settlement).
7. Benedict, *History of the Town of Sutton* 68.
8. *Ibid.* Fifteen-year-old Princess Sophie of Russia observed the comet when she was travelling to Russia to be betrothed. Years later, she was crowned Catherine, Empress of Russia.
9. It would be another 138 years (1882) before a brighter comet would be visible from the Earth.
10. Sutton Reconnaissance Report. Massachusetts Department of Conservation and Recreation, 2007. APPENDIX A, Archaeology section, page ii, Sutton Reconnaissance Report, Blackstone Valley / Quinebaug-Shetucket Landscape Inventory of the Massachusetts Heritage Landscape Inventory Program. The 2007 Sutton Reconnaissance Report by the Massachusetts Department of Conservation and Recreation, the John H. Chafee Blackstone River Valley National Heritage Corridor, and the Quinebaug and Shetucket Rivers Valley National Heritage Corridor stated that the Gen. Rufus Putnam house site with memorial marker on Boston Road is on the site of the Gen. Rufus Putnam house and there are "no remains of building left."
11. Rufus is not the only famous person commemorated by a grave marker mentioning his relationship to George Washington. General Nathanael Greene's marker in Georgia is inscribed: "The Friend of Washington." The slab above Revolutionary War painter John Trumbull's grave at Yale University in New Haven, Connecticut, includes only one line of biographical information: "Patriot and Artist, Friend and Aid of Washington." David Humphreys, an aide de camp to George Washington during the Revolutionary War, and later the first minister appointed to a foreign country (Portugal) under the U.S. Constitution, has an obelisk above his New Haven grave with the words: "During the war he was an aide to Washington and a member of his household." Interestingly, Humphreys was the first American citizen in the new republic to publish a biography of a fellow American. In 1788, he wrote *An Essay on the Life of the Honourable Major-General Israel Putnam*—a biography of Rufus Putnam's famous cousin.
12. Hoar, *Rufus Putnam. An Address* 42.
13. Putnam, *Memoirs of Rufus Putnam* 9.
14. Upton was incorporated less than three years before Rufus's birth, and during his early life it was perhaps best known for its shoe and boot makers. Its name is probably taken from a town in England. Interestingly, Upton, England is about 13 miles south of Worcester, England, while Upton, Massachusetts, is about 13 miles south of Worcester, Massachusetts.
15. Livingston, William Farrand. *Israel Putnam: Pioneer, Ranger and Major General, 1718–1790.* G.P. Putnam's Sons, 1901. 56.
16. Putnam, *Memoirs of Rufus Putnam* 10.
17. *Ibid.*
18. Temple, J. H., and Charles Adams. *History of North Brookfield, Massachusetts: Preceded by an Account of old Quabaug, Indian and English Occupation, 1647–1676; Brookfield Records, 1686–1783.* North Brookfield: The Town of North Brookfield, 1887. 681. Huldah was born on May 25, 1734; Daniel Matthews was born on October 28, 1725, and died in 1805.
19. Mill privilege referred to the right to dam a stream so there would be enough waterpower to turn a mill wheel.
20. Putnam, *Memoirs of Rufus Putnam* 10.
21. *Ibid.,* 10–11. Rufus would later be joined in the history books by such other self-educated American leaders as Abraham Lincoln, who had only about one year of formal education, and President Andrew Johnson who had no formal education. In regard to spelling, even Albert Einstein had problems with it. In a 1944 letter to physicist Max Born, Einstein writes: "I cannot write in English, because of the treacherous spelling. When I am

reading, I only hear it and am unable to remember what the written word looks like." *Born-Einstein Letters, 1916–1955: Friendship, Politics and Physics in Uncertain Times.* Palgrave Macmillan. 2004. 145.

22. Hoar, *Rufus Putnam. An Address* 29.

23. After Putnam finally returned from the War, in March 1761, he would take up the millwright occupation again.

24. Thomas Putnam (1614–1686) was Israel Putnam's grandfather and Rufus Putnam's great-grandfather. Thomas's first wife, Mary Veren, was Israel Putnam's grandmother, while Thomas's second wife, Ann Holyoke, was Rufus Putnam's great-grandmother.

Chapter Two

1. Putnam, Rufus. *Journal of Gen. Rufus Putnam Kept in Northern New York During Four Campaigns of the Old French and Indian War, 1757 1760: The Whole Copiously Ill.* Albany: Joel Munsell's Sons, 1886. 26.
2. Putnam, *Memoirs of Rufus Putnam* 11.
3. Putnam, *Journal of Gen. Rufus Putnam* 27.
4. *Ibid.*
5. *Ibid.*, 23–24. Frye at this time was about 48 years old. About two decades later, during the Revolution, Massachusetts appointed him a major general of the militia. In 1776, the Continental Congress appointed him a brigadier general in the Continental Army. He resigned shortly thereafter for health reasons.
6. Putnam, *Memoirs of Rufus Putnam* 11.
7. Putnam, *Journal of Gen. Rufus Putnam* 29.
8. Putnam, *Memoirs of Rufus Putnam* 11–12.
9. *Ibid.*, 12.
10. *Ibid.*, 12–13.
11. Putnam, *Journal of Gen. Rufus Putnam* 33.
12. *Ibid.*
13. *Ibid.*, 34–35.
14. *Ibid.*, 37.
15. *Ibid.*
16. *Ibid.*, 39.
17. *Ibid.*, 38–39.
18. *Ibid.*, 39.
19. Putnam, *Memoirs of Rufus Putnam* 13.
20. *Ibid.*
21. *Ibid.*, 14.
22. Although General Webb served in the British Army for years, participating in the battles of Battle of Dettingen (1743) and the Battle of Fontenoy (1745), he is best known as the general who in 1757 refused to send aid to Fort William Henry. His action condemned the garrison and the camp followers to be captured and murdered. However, his inaction did not prevent him from being promoted to lieutenant general in 1761. Webb died in November 1773—a year and a half before the American Revolution began.
23. Putnam, *Journal of Gen. Rufus Putnam* 40.
24. *Ibid.*, 41.
25. Putnam, *Memoirs of Rufus Putnam* 14.
26. *Ibid.*, 14–15.
27. *Ibid.*, 15.
28. Putnam, *Journal of Gen. Rufus Putnam* 45.
29. Putnam, *Memoirs of Rufus Putnam* 15.
30. Putnam, *Journal of Gen. Rufus Putnam* 50. Candlemas is a Christian festival, traditionally held on February 2, commemorating the presentation of Jesus Christ in the temple.
31. Putnam, *Memoirs of Rufus Putnam* 16.
32. *Ibid.* After a career in the British army, which included being wounded at the Battle of Culloden in Scotland and in the attack on Ticonderoga in 1758, Philip Skene was credited with preventing the French blowing up Fort Carillon's gunpowder magazine in 1759. He also played a prominent role in the capture of Havana from the Spanish at the end of the French and Indian War. He founded Skenesboro, New York, after receiving fifty thousand acres of land grants on Lake Champlain. With his vast holdings in New York State, Skene stayed loyal to Britain during the American Revolutionary War, served as one of General Burgoyne's main advisers, and with the victory of the Continental

Army, had his New York property confiscated. Skenesboro was renamed Whitehall, and Skene died in England in 1810 at age 85.

33. Putnam, *Memoirs of Rufus Putnam* 16.
34. *Ibid.*, 16–17.
35. *Ibid.*, 17.
36. *Ibid.*, 17–18.
37. Putnam, *Journal of Gen. Rufus Putnam* 52.
38. Putnam, *Memoirs of Rufus Putnam* 18.
39. *Ibid.*, 18–19.
40. *Ibid.*, 19.
41. *Ibid.*, 19–20.
42. *Ibid.*, 20.
43. *Ibid.*, 20–21.
44. Sprague, John Francis. "Stephen Jones, the First Justice of the Peace East of the Penobscot." *Sprague's Journal of Maine History*, April 1913, pp. 187–191. Twenty years earlier, Jones had been appointed chief justice of the court of common pleas and judge of probate for Washington County, Maine.
45. Putnam, *Memoirs of Rufus Putnam* 21.
46. Putnam, *Journal of Gen. Rufus Putnam* 57.
47. Putnam, *Memoirs of Rufus Putnam* 21.
48. *Ibid.*
49. *Ibid.*, 22.
50. *Ibid.* Born in 1728 in Framingham, Massachusetts, Learned later became an early supporter of American independence, and marched to Cambridge, Massachusetts, after the battles of Lexington and Concord. He was commissioned a colonel of the 3rd Continental Infantry Regiment the first day of 1776. Two months later, he commanded forces on Dorchester Heights that compelled the British troops to leave Boston, and when they did, Learned was the first to enter the city. Learned was praised for his part in the Battle of Saratoga and spent the following winter (1777-1778) with Washington at Valley Forge. In March 1778, just before his 50th birthday, he asked to resign because of poor health. On March 5, 1778, General Washington wrote to Learned, noting General Heath "mentioned your desire to resign as you found no probability of recovery at least so far as to bear the fatigues of a Campaign. I wrote him word that I thought you might under such Circumstances quit the service with honor having worn yourself out in the Cause of your Country." "From George Washington to Brigadier General Ebenezer Learned, 5 March 1778," *Founders Online*, National Archives, accessed April 11, 2019, https://founders.archives.gov/documents/Washington/03-14-02-0052.
51. Cutter, William Richard. *New England Families, Genealogical and Memorial: A Record of the Achievements of Her People in the Making of Commonwealths and the Founding of a Nation.* Vol. 4, Lewis Historical Publishing Company, 1914. 2097. About 58 years old when Rufus joined his company, Joseph Whitcomb was a native of Lancaster, Massachusetts. After his service in the war, he moved to Swanzey, New Hampshire, where he became a prominent land and mill owner. Although his sons served with distinction during the Revolutionary War, Whitcomb was too old—he was 75 at the beginning of the war. He died in 1792.
52. Putnam, *Memoirs of Rufus Putnam* 22.
53. *Ibid.*, 22.
54. Putnam, *Journal of Gen. Rufus Putnam* 63.
55. Putnam, *Memoirs of Rufus Putnam* 22–23.
56. *Ibid.*, 23.
57. *Ibid.*
58. *Ibid.*
59. *Ibid.*
60. Humphreys, David, Col., *An Essay on the Life of the Honourable Major-General Israel Putnam, addressed to the State Society of the Cincinnati in Connecticut.* Hartford: Hudson and Goodwin, 1788. 55–56.
61. *Ibid.*, 58.
62. *Ibid.*
63. Putnam, *Memoirs of Rufus Putnam* 23. A common thread throughout military history is the person who faces fear for the first time. The Duke of Wellington—the man who defeated Napoleon—once said: "The only thing I am afraid of is fear. I told Lord Grey at Windsor that I was quite sure if three or four hundred Notables were to

leave London for fear of it, they would be followed by three or four hundred thousand, and that then this country would be plunged into greater confusion than had been known for hundreds of years." *Notes of Conversations with the Duke of Wellington*. Philip Henry. John Murray, 1888. 13.
    64. Putnam, *Memoirs of Rufus Putnam* 24.
    65. *Ibid.*, 25.
    66. *Ibid.*
    67. *Ibid.*
    68. Putnam, *Journal of Gen. Rufus Putnam* 77. Born in Sutton on July 22, 1730, Amos Putnam was almost eight years older than Rufus. Amos died in Sutton in 1811 at age 81.
    69. Putnam, *Memoirs of Rufus Putnam* 25.
    70. *Ibid.*
    71. *Ibid.*, 88.
    72. *Ibid.*, 89.
    73. *Ibid.*, 27.
    74. *Ibid.*
    75. *Ibid.*, 27–28.
    76. *Ibid.*
    77. *Ibid.*, 28–29.
    78. *Ibid.*, 28. Jacobs, whose Indian name was Nawnawapateoonks, was the captain of a company of Native Americans.
    79. *Ibid.*, 29.
    80. Putnam, *Journal of Gen. Rufus Putnam* 93.
    81. Putnam, *Memoirs of Rufus Putnam* 29–30.
    82. *Ibid.*, 30.
    83. Putnam, *Journal of Gen. Rufus Putnam* 94.
    84. Putnam, *Memoirs of Rufus Putnam* 31.
    85. *Ibid.*, 31–32.
    86. The thirty-six-year-old Paige had risen from lieutenant in 1755 to captain in 1758. After government service during the American Revolution, he died at age 66 in 1790. His wife Mercy Aikens Paige outlived him by 33 years, passing away at age 102. She was the oldest person ever buried in Old Hardwick [Massachusetts] Cemetery.
    87. Putnam, *Memoirs of Rufus Putnam* 32.
    88. *Ibid.*, 33.
    89. Born in 1724, Abijah Willard participated in the expulsion of the Acadian people from Canada, and in 1760 was with the British forces as they captured Montreal. In 1775, after the battles of Lexington and Concord, he joined the loyalist forces in Massachusetts. After the Revolutionary War, Britain granted him an annual pension and an important government position in New Brunswick, where he died in 1789.
    90. Putnam, *Memoirs of Rufus Putnam* 32–33. An ensign was the army's lowest-ranking commissioned officer.
    91. *Ibid.*, 34.
    92. *Ibid.*, 34–35.

Chapter Three

    1. Temple, J. H. *History of North Brookfield* 715.
    2. Putnam, *Memoirs of Rufus Putnam* 35.
    3. Fairbairn, William. *Treatise on Mills and Millwork: On the Principles of Mechanism and on Prime Movers. Treatise on Mills and Millwork*. Longman, Green, Longman, Roberts, & Green, 1864. v–vi.
    4. *Ibid.*, vi.
    5. *Ibid.*
    6. Fairbairn, *Treatise on Mills*.
    7. Putnam, *Memoirs of Rufus Putnam* 35.
    8. *Ibid.*
    9. Putnam, *Memoirs of Rufus Putnam* 35.
    10. *Ibid.*, 35–36.
    11. Temple, J. H, *History of North Brookfield* 450. That house lasted until 1885.
    12. Putnam, *Memoirs of Rufus Putnam* 36. Rufus's new father-in-law, Zebulon Rice, was born about 1712 and died in 1777. The Rice family were prominent Massachusetts citizens. The Campus Martius Museum collection at Marietta includes a set of silver spoons, dated ca. 1770–1790, engraved with the initials of Persis Rice and bearing the mark of silversmith Paul Revere. Also in the collection are a hat, a sabre, and a circa 1775 campaign chest that belonged to Rufus Putnam.
    13. Temple, J. H, *History of North Brookfield*.
    14. Committees of Correspondences were unofficial government bodies organ-

ized by colonial leaders who opposed British policies.

15. Cone, *Life of Rufus Putnam* 53.

16. Putnam, Rufus. *Connecticut Courant* (1791–1837); Hartford, Conn. [Hartford, Conn] 30 Apr 1816: 2.

17. Born in Durham, Connecticut, Yale College-educated Lyman was a major general of British provincial troops during the French and Indian War, including about 5,000 Connecticut troops. He commanded with distinction at the Battle of Lake George and the Capture of Crown Point. A key commander in the 1760 capture of Fort Ticonderoga from the French, he also was part of the 1762 capture of Havana, Cuba, from the Spanish.

18. *History of Durham, Connecticut: From the First Grant of Land in 1662 to 1866*. William Chauncey Fowler, Hartford: Press of Wiley, Waterman & Eaton, 1866. 109.

19. Today, Port Gibson, Mississippi, is near the river at 32 degrees latitude, and Rosedale, Mississippi, is about 10 miles south of 34 degrees latitude.

20. Putnam, Rufus. *Connecticut Courant* (1791–1837); Hartford, Conn. [Hartford, Conn] 30 Apr 1816: 2.

21. Daniel Putnam would later play a role at key moments in his father Israel's life. Two years later, when a messenger informed Israel that colonial militia were fired on by British troops at Lexington, Massachusetts, he was plowing a field near his home with Daniel, who was then fifteen. He handed the oxen reins to his son and took off on an 18-hour horseback ride to Massachusetts. Also, before the Battle of Bunker Hill, the wife of an absentee Tory expressed to Israel Putnam her fears concerning the numerous militia troops who were camped on her property, which she shared with her nieces. In addition to posting extra guards, Israel arranged for Daniel to stay every night for weeks at her house. Daniel later wrote: "Young as I was, the family confided much in the protection afforded by General Putnam's son" (Livingston, *Israel Putnam* 386). During the Revolution Daniel went on to serve (along with future Washington aide David Humphreys and future U.S. Vice President Aaron Burr) as one of his father's military aides. Even after Israel died, Daniel supported his father. Twenty-eight years after Israel's passing, a former general, Henry Dearborn, attacked the famed general's reputation—something that never occurred during Putnam's life—and Daniel was the chief defender of his father's legacy, eliciting support from John and Abigail Adams, as well as numerous veterans of the Revolutionary War.

22. Putnam, Israel, and Rufus Putnam. *The Two Putnams: Israel and Rufus in the Havana Expedition 1762 and in the Mississippi River Exploration 1772–73, Etc.* Hartford, Connecticut Historical Society, 1931.

23. *Ibid.*, 143–146.

24. *Ibid.*, 145.

25. Connecticut-born farmer Roger Enos (1729—October 6, 1808) was an officer in Israel Putnam's regiment during the expedition to help the British army capture Havana, Cuba, at the end of the French and Indian War. In 1775, he again served under Israel in opposing the British at the Battle of Bunker Hill, and a few years later while stationed in New York's Hudson Highlands. In 1780, at about age 50, Enos moved to Vermont where he was commissioned a colonel in that state's militia. He retired as a major general in the militia and passed away in 1808.

26. Putnam, *Two Putnams* 146.

27. *Ibid.* This was an age of discovery. While Rufus, ill with seasickness, was headed down the east coast of the 13 colonies, bound for the Caribbean Sea, British Captain James Cook's *Resolution* became the first ship to travel south of the Antarctic Circle (on January 17, 1773).

28. This is today's Môle-Saint-Nicolas. Christopher Columbus landed here on December 6, 1492, during his first voyage.

29. Putnam, *Memoirs of Rufus Putnam* 37. On this day, back in the Virginia colony, William Henry Harrison was born. A quarter of a century later, he would be appointed secretary of the Northwest Territory, which was first settled by Rufus Putnam, and serve as a delegate from the Northwest Territory to the Sixth Congress from 1799 to 1800. In 1841, Harrison would become the ninth President of the United States—the last president who was born as a British subject.

30. Chester served as governor of West Florida from 1770 until Spain took over Pensacola in May 1781.
31. Putnam, *Memoirs of Rufus Putnam* 37–38.
32. *Ibid.*, 38–39.
33. "British Colonial Office West Florida Records." *David Library of the American Revolution*, www.dlar.org/pdf/CO5%20West%20Florida—PDF.pdf.
34. Putnam, *Memoirs of Rufus Putnam* 39–40.
35. *Ibid.*, 40.
36. *Ibid.*, 41.
37. *Ibid.*
38. *Ibid.*, 42.
39. *Ibid.*, 42–44.
40. *Ibid.*, 44.
41. *Ibid.*, 44–46.
42. *Ibid.*, 48. Big Black River is a 330-mile-long tributary of the Mississippi River. Flowing entirely through the present state of Mississippi, in May 1863 it was the site of the Battle of Big Black River Bridge.
43. Putnam, *Memoirs of Rufus Putnam* 47.
44. *Ibid.*, 47–48.
45. *Ibid.*, 48.
46. *Ibid.*, 49.
47. *Ibid.*
48. *Ibid.*, 49–50.
49. *Ibid.*, 50.
50. *Ibid.*
51. "British Colonial Office West Florida Records." *David Library of the American Revolution*, www.dlar.org/pdf/CO5%20West%20Florida—PDF.pdf.
52. "Old Soldiers Lands." *Connecticut Courant*. 30 Apr 1816: 2.
53. Putnam, *Two Putnams* 260.
54. "Old Soldiers Lands." 2.
55. Putnam, *Memoirs of Rufus Putnam* 53–54.
56. "Old Soldiers Lands." 2.
57. Putnam, *Two Putnams* 261–262.
58. "Old Soldiers Lands." 2.
59. Hildreth, Samuel Prescott, and Ephraim Cutler. *Biographical and Historical Memoirs of the Early Pioneer Settlers of Ohio with Narratives of Incidents and Occurrences in 1775*. Cincinnati: H. W. Derby, 1852.
60. Ross, Charles, and Charles Cornwallis. Cornwallis. *Correspondence of Charles, First Marquis Cornwallis*. London: John Murray, 1859. 3. One of the leading British generals of the Revolution shared an eye injury with Rufus Putnam. "During his Eton career [General Cornwallis] received, while playing at hockey, a blow on the eye, which produced a slight but permanent obliquity of vision. The boy who accidentally caused this injury was Shute Barrington, afterwards the highly esteemed Bishop of Durham."
61. "Rufus Putnam." *National Parks Service*, U.S. Department of the Interior, www.nps.gov/museum/exhibits/revwar/image_gal/indeimg/putnam.html.
62. Hildreth, *Biographical and Historical* 118–119.
63. McCullough, *The Pioneers* 92.
64. Hoar, *Rufus Putnam. An Address* 25.
65. Dickinson, C. E., and John W. Simpson. *A History of the First Congregational Church of Marietta, Ohio*. E.R. Alderman, 1896.
66. *Ibid.*
67. Reed, Jonas. *A History of Rutland: Worcester County, Massachusetts, from Its Earliest Settlement, with a Biography of Its First Settlers*. Tyler & Seagrove, 1879. 165.
68. Campbell was nominated by newly elected U.S. President Andrew Jackson in 1829 and served on the bench until his death in 1833.
69. Campbell, John Wilson. *Biographical Sketches: With Other Literary Remains of the Late John W. Campbell*. Columbus, Ohio Scott & Gallagher, 1838.
70. Cone, *Life of Rufus Putnam* 72–73.
71. Gibbon, Peter. "Reflections on a Man of Undeniable Character." *Baltimore Sun*. 16 Feb 1998.
72. Dallek, Robert. *Franklin D. Roosevelt: A Political Life*. Penguin Books, 2018. 24.

Chapter 4

1. Heitman, Francis B. *Historical Register of Officers of the Continental Army during the War of the Revolution, April, 1775 to December, 1783*. Washington, D.C.: The Rare Book Shop Publishing Company, 1914. 32.
2. A Massachusetts medical doctor,

Thomas (1724–1776) had served with distinction as an officer in the French and Indian War.

3. Heitman, *Historical Register* 32.

4. Putnam, *Memoirs of Rufus Putnam* 54. Putnam was following in the path of many military leaders who when young had experience in previous wars. Most notable for Rufus was his cousin Israel, who volunteered as a private in the French and Indian War and rose to the rank of major. In future years, many top American generals would parlay their experience in one war to an advanced rank in a second war. For example, some of the veterans of the Mexican American War were Civil War Union Army generals Ulysses S. Grant, George B. McClellan, George G. Meade, and William Tecumseh Sherman, and Confederate Army generals Robert E. Lee, "Stonewall" Jackson, and James Longstreet. World War II commanders who fought in the First World War included Douglas MacArthur, George S. Patton, and William F. Halsey, Jr.

5. Massachusetts soldiers and sailors of the Revolutionary War: A compilation from the archives, prepared and published by the Secretary of the Commonwealth in accordance with chapter 100, resolves of 1891, Volume 12.

6. About 52 years old at this time, Brigadier General Thomas had been educated as a medical doctor and served with distinction in the French and Indian War. In early 1776, Thomas would command troops that fortified Dorchester Heights and forced the expulsion of the British Army from Boston. Shortly afterward, the Continental Congress commissioned him a major general. In June 1776, he died of smallpox while on an attempted invasion of Canada.

7. Putnam, *Memoirs of Rufus Putnam* 54.

8. Richard Gridley was the Continental Army's Chief Engineer from June 1775 to April 1776, at which time Rufus Putnam acquired the title. Putnam held it until December 1776.

9. Cone, *Life of Rufus Putnam* 44.

10. *Ibid.* A farming town south of Boston at the time, Roxbury was annexed to the City of Boston in 1868. In the 21st century it was a home to Boston's African American culture.

11. *Ibid.*

12. *Ibid.*

13. *Ibid.*

14. "General Orders, 23 October 1775," *Founders Online,* National Archives, accessed April 11, 2019, https://founders.archives.gov/documents/Washington/03-02-02-0194.

15. *Ibid.,* 55–56.

16. Knox, a former Boston bookstore owner, at age 19 had been a key witness in the infamous Boston Massacre. He fought at the Battle of Bunker Hill, as well as at Trenton, Brandywine, and Yorktown. During Washington's presidency, Knox served as his Secretary of War.

17. Putnam, *Memoirs of Rufus Putnam* 56.

18. *Ibid.,* 57.

19. *Ibid.*

20. Walker, Paul K. *Engineers of Independence: A Documentary History of the Army Engineers in the American Revolution, 1775–1783.* University Press of the Pacific, 2002. Rufus designed "chandeliers" for the breastworks, which were temporary fortifications (usually breast-high), often made of earth to protect defending soldiers.

21. The March 17, 1776, departure of the British from Boston has been celebrated in Suffolk County, Massachusetts, since 1901 as "Evacuation Day." Boston and the surrounding county towns close schools and government offices on that day.

22. https://www.loc.gov/collections/george-washington-papers/articles-and-essays/george-washington-survey-and-mapmaker/tracing-the-maps-in-george-washingtons-life/. In addition to Washington, fellow presidents Thomas Jefferson and Abraham Lincoln had surveying experience. Other Americans who worked as surveyors sometime during their lives include Kentucky pioneer Daniel Boone and writer Henry David Thoreau.

23. George Washington wasn't the only U.S. president whose spelling left much to be desired. John Quincy Adams once referred to President Andrew Jackson as "a savage who can scarcely spell his own name."

24. Roy, "Acclaimed Historian Visits Rut-

land Home." *The Landmark*, The Landmark, 2 Nov. 2017, www.thelandmark.com/articles/acclaimed-historian-visits-rutland-home/.

25. Putnam, *Memoirs of Rufus Putnam* 58–59.

26. "From George Washington to John Hancock, 10 July 1776," *Founders Online*, National Archives, accessed April 11, 2019, https://founders.archives.gov/documents/Washington/03-05-02-0188. Continental Army Brigadier General Hugh Mercer (1726–1777) was a Scotland-born medical doctor who, as a 21-year-old supporter of the Stuarts to the English throne, had served at the Battle of Culloden in 1746. George Washington knew Mercer well: they had both fought in the French and Indian War, and Mercer had purchased Washington's boyhood home when Washington's mother relocated to Fredericksburg, Virginia. In a 1776 letter of introduction for Mercer, Washington had stated "in his Experience & Judgment you may repose great Confidence." "From George Washington to Brigadier General William Livingston, 6 July 1776," *Founders Online*, National Archives, accessed April 11, 2019, https://founders.archives.gov/documents/Washington/03-05-02-0156. Mercer was killed by British soldiers at the Battle of Princeton in 1777 when his horse was shot from under him and he was repeatedly bayoneted. He was a great-great-great grandfather of World War II's General George S. Patton.

27. "George Washington to the Board of War, 29 July 1776," *Founders Online*, National Archives, accessed April 11, 2019, https://founders.archives.gov/documents/Adams/06-04-02-0188. Washington concluded this letter with: "If this appointment should take place then, It makes a vacancy in Wyllys's Regiment which I understand he is desirous of having filled by Majr. Henley an active and Spirited Officer, now a Brigade Major to Genl. Heath."

28. "From George Washington to Colonel Rufus Putnam, 11 August 1776," *Founders Online*, National Archives, accessed April 11, 2019, https://founders.archives.gov/documents/Washington/03-05-02-0508.

29. Putnam, *Memoirs of Rufus Putnam* 60–61.

30. "From George Washington to John Hancock, 5 October 1776," *Founders Online*, National Archives, accessed April 11, 2019, https://founders.archives.gov/documents/Washington/03-06-02-0366.

31. Putnam, *Memoirs of Rufus Putnam* 60. General Thomas Mifflin (1744–1800), a Pennsylvania businessman, served as the Continental Army's Quartermaster General. Like fellow American major general, Nathanael Greene, Mifflin was raised in a Quaker family. At the conclusion of the Revolutionary War, Mifflin was elected president of the Continental Congress. Later, he became the first governor of the state of Pennsylvania.

32. "From George Washington to Colonel Rufus Putnam, 5 November 1776," *Founders Online*, National Archives, accessed April 11, 2019, https://founders.archives.gov/documents/Washington/03-07-02-0062.

33. Putnam, *Memoirs of Rufus Putnam* 66.

34. "From George Washington to John Hancock, 20 December 1776," *Founders Online*, National Archives, accessed April 11, 2019, https://founders.archives.gov/documents/Washington/03-07-02-0305.

35. Cone, *Life of Rufus Putnam* 51.

36. This fort was named for General William Alexander (1727–1783), who also claimed the title Lord Stirling. A highly rated Continental Army leader, he fought in many key battles, including Brooklyn, Princeton and Brandywine. At one point, he was captured by the British and exchanged.

37. Named for General Nathanael Greene.

38. Named for Major Daniel Box, a former British soldier who joined the Patriot cause.

39. Later, during the War of 1812, Fort Putnam was renamed Fort Greene and ultimately became the site of Fort Greene Park, which contains the Prison Ship Martyrs' Monument. Beneath it are the remains of many of the over 11,000 American prisoners who died under horrible conditions aboard British prison ships during the American Revolutionary War.

40. Today, a marble marker sits on the site reads:

> This Memorial Marks the Site of Fort Washington Constructed by the Continental Troops in the Summer of 1776 Taken by the British After a Heroic Defense November 16, 1776 Repossessed by the Americans Upon Their Triumphal Entry Into the City of New York November 25, 1783.

41. Daughan, George C. *Revolution on the Hudson: New York City and the Hudson River Valley in the American War of Independence*. W.W. Norton & Company, 2017.
42. "Remains of Revolutionary Forts." *New York Times*. 12 Mar 1901: 8.
43. "America: Extracts from Letters." *The Scots Magazine*. A. Murray and J. Cochran. Jan. 1776. 716.
44. Ibid.
45. Glover (1732–1797), a fisherman and merchant in civilian life, was best known at this time for having led his regiment of Massachusetts troops in transporting thousands of Continental Army troops to the safety of Manhattan Island after the Battle of Long Island in August 1776. Glover and his men would play another critical role in the war when they moved Washington and his army across the Delaware River in December 1776 so they could successfully attack the Hessian garrison at Trenton, New Jersey.
46. Putnam, *Memoirs of Rufus Putnam* 61–62.
47. Ibid., 62.
48. Ibid.
49. Ibid.
50. Ibid., 62–63.
51. Hoffman, Renoda. *The Battle of White Plains*. Battle of White Plains Monument Committee. 1776. 7.
52. Putnam, *Memoirs of Rufus Putnam* 63.
53. George Clinton served as governor of New York from 1777 to 1795, and from 1801 to 1804, as well as vice president of the United States from 1805 until 1812.
54. Putnam, *Memoirs of Rufus Putnam* 63.
55. Ibid., 63–64.
56. Ibid., 63–64.
57. Ibid., 64.
58. A Delaware Presbyterian minister, Haslett was killed at the Battle of Princeton ten weeks later.
59. Memoirs of the War in the Southern Department of the United States, Henry Lee, P. Force, 1827. Green received a shoulder wound in the fighting. Five months later, he was promoted to lieutenant colonel. In his memoirs, Light Horse Harry Lee called Green "one of the bravest of brave soldiers."
60. Putnam, *Memoirs of Rufus Putnam* 64–65.
61. McDougall (1732–1786) was promoted to brigadier general in the Continental Army on August 9, 1776, and to major general on October 20, 1777. He served until the end of the war. In 1780, after Benedict Arnold's traitorous action, McDougall replaced him as the commander at West Point. Born on the Scottish island of Islay in 1731, McDougall came to America in 1740. At age 25, the New Yorker "commanded two privateers" during the French and Indian War. An early advocate of American independence, he was the author of "Revolutionary pamphlets" for which he was sent to prison. McDougall also served as a delegate to the Continental Congress.
62. Putnam, *Memoirs of Rufus Putnam* 64.
63. Ibid.
64. December 5, 1776 issue of the *Maryland Gazette* in Annapolis and the *Military and Naval Magazine of the United States*, Volume 5. Thompson and Homans, 1835.
65. Putnam, *Memoirs of Rufus Putnam* 65.
66. Wright's Mills, named for a mill on the Bronx River, was located about four miles north of White Plains.
67. Peekskill is located about 25 miles north of White Plains.
68. John Lasher (1724–1806) was a New York militia colonel during the seven years of the Revolutionary War.
69. Putnam, *Memoirs of Rufus Putnam* 65.
70. In 1776, writer and activist Thomas Paine was serving in Washington's army on the banks of the Hudson. He watched

from Fort Lee as New York's Fort Washington was conquered by the British. It was then that he began his pamphlet, *The American Crisis*. It included one of the most famous lines in America history: "These are the times that try men's souls. The summer soldier and the sunshine patriot will, in this crisis, shrink from the service of their country; but he that stands by it now, deserves the love and thanks of man and woman." Paine, Thomas. *The American Crisis*. James Watson, 1835. 3.

71. Putnam, *Memoirs of Rufus Putnam* 65.

72. Then 41 years old, Morgan would go on to prove himself one of the most competent American commanders—especially with his brilliant victory at the Battle of Cowpens in 1781.

73. Major General Benjamin Lincoln, 44 years old at the time of the Battles of Saratoga, was born in Massachusetts and distinguished himself throughout the Revolutionary War. After the Battle of Bemis Heights, a British musket ball shattered his ankle leaving that leg two inches shorter than the other (https://www.nps.gov/people/benjamin-lincoln.htm). Lincoln was also one of the few officers present at all three of the most important surrenders of the war: Saratoga (1777), Charleston (1780), and Yorktown (1781).

74. A native-born Massachusetts man, 50-year-old John Nixon was a veteran of the first battles of the war—Lexington, Concord, Bunker Hill, as well as the New York campaign. At the Battle of Bemis Heights a cannonball came so close to his head that his eyesight and hearing were damaged for the rest of his lie. He died at age 88 in 1815.

75. Putnam, *Memoirs of Rufus Putnam* 68. A year earlier, Massachusetts-born Continental Army brigadier general John Glover (1732–1797) was instrumental in saving the army commanded by George Washington and Rufus Putnam's cousin Israel Putnam after it lost the Battle of Long Island.

76. United States Department of the Interior, National Park Service, National Register of Historic Places, Inventory-Nomination Form, General Rufus Putnam House. Washington: GPO, 1972.

77. Griswold, William A., and Donald W. Linebaugh. *The Saratoga Campaign: Uncovering an Embattled Landscape*. University Press of New England, 2016.

78. A little over three years after the Battle of Saratoga, Morgan would be credited with one of the great American victories of the war—the Battle at Cowpens.

79. "A Fragment—Putnam's Rock." *The American Journal of Science and Arts*, vol. 5, 1822. S. Converse, 37.

80. *Ibid.*, 38.

81. *Ibid.*, 38.

82. *Ibid.*, 38.

83. *Ibid.*, 38.

84. Livingston, *Israel Putnam* 262. Rufus's cousin, General Israel Putnam, performed a similar ceremony nearly three years earlier. In the fall of 1775, Americans captured a British ship, *Nancy*. On board was a one-and-a-half ton, 13-inch brass mortar. It was brought to Cambridge Common where Israel Putnam celebrated its acquisition. He mounted the cannon with a bottle of rum in his hand, while he and quartermaster general Thomas Mifflin named it "Congress."

85. Vandewater, Robert J. *The Tourist, or Pocket Manual for Travellers on the Hudson River, the Western and Northern Canals and Railroads: the Stage Routes to Niagara Falls; and down Lake Ontario and the St. Lawrence to Montreal and Quebec*. New York: Harper & Brothers, 1841. 24. A tourist booklet in 1841 mentioned that a man named Newbold was planning on establishing three cities on the top of Butter Hill with the names Faith, Hope, and Charity. He also proposed constructing a railway from the river to the cities to supply their inhabitants. In 1868, a similar railway was built on New Hampshire's Mount Washington. That "Cog Railway" has been continuously run ever since, with the exception of the years of World Wars I and II.

86. *The Centennial of the United States Military Academy at West Point, New York. 1802–1902*. U.S. Government Printing Office, 1904. 161–162.

87. Romans died at sea in 1783 or 1784 while returning to the colonies after three years as a British prisoner.

88. Educated in Poland and France, Thaddeus Kosciuszko volunteered to aid

the American colonies in their fight to break free of Great Britain. In 1776, he was appointed a colonel of engineers in Washington's army. Kosciuszko played an important role in the American success at Saratoga, worked tirelessly to strengthen West Point defenses, and served as one of General Nathanael Greene's top officers in North Carolina. At war's end, he was promoted to brigadier general in the U.S. Army. After the war, Kosciuszko returned to Poland to spend the rest of his life fighting for the independence of Poland. He died in 1817 at age 71.

89. Small, usually temporary, fortifications outside of main forts.

90. De La Radiere was killed at West Point in 1779.

91. Barbour, Lucius Barnes. *Families of Early Hartford, Connecticut.* Genealogical Publishing Company, 1977. 699.

92. Born in Rhode Island in 1748, Sherborne died in 1824.

93. "The Backwoodsman. A Poem." By J. K. Paulding. M. Thomas. 1818. 31. Paulding was born in Pleasant Valley, New York (about 50 miles upriver of West Point) in the month Rufus's men completed Fort Putnam (August, 1778). In later life, he was appointed secretary of the Navy in the Martin Van Buren administration and died in 1860 at age 81.

94. Constitution Island was captured by the British in 1777 but retaken by Colonial forces in 1778. Today, Constitution Island is the only part of the U.S. Military Academy Reservation on the east side of the river.

95. Arnold had taken over command of the fortifications at West Point a few weeks earlier—on August 3.

96. *The Centennial of the United States Military Academy at West Point, New York. 1802–1902.* U.S. Government Printing Office, 1904. 181. By the time this letter was written, Arnold had already made arrangements to hand over West Point to the British.

97. "Old Forts Along the Hudson: Built During The Years Of The Revolutionary War. Picturesque Reins Now, but Once Formidable Defenses Against British Invasion—Fort Montgomery Was the First Erected, a Few Miles South of West Point—Kosciusko, the Famous Polish General Planned Most of These Fortifications." *New York Times.* 11 Nov 1894: 20.

98. Situated outside the city walls of Quebec, Canada, the Heights of Abraham, also known as the Plains of Abraham, was the location in 1759 of a key battle of the French and Indian War. The British forces under General James Wolfe defeated the French troops led by the Marquis de Montcalm.

99. Bruce, Wallace. *The Hudson: Three Centuries of History, Romance and Invention.* Bryant Union Co., 1907. 92.

100. *Ibid.*, 95.

101. Cone, *Life of Rufus Putnam* 52–53.

102. "From George Washington to Colonel Rufus Putnam, 9 October 1778," *Founders Online,* National Archives, accessed April 11, 2019, https://founders.archives.gov/documents/Washington/03-17-02-0343.

103. In 1780, they would try to gain West Point by deception when they persuaded American general Benedict Arnold to turn traitor.

104. As the British approached, Israel Putnam sent his 150 men east to the town of Stamford and waited alone until the enemy horsemen arrived. The 61-year-old Putnam stayed behind. When the enemy reached him, Putnam, on horseback, plunged down the hill. The British fired at his back. By the time they took paths around the hill, Putnam was a safe distance away. Subsequently, he rallied the few troops he had and captured several British stragglers.

105. Hufeland, Otto. *Westchester County during the American Revolution: 1775–1783.* Published for Westchester County by the Westchester County Historical Society, 1926.

106. *Ibid.*, 283.

107. "Anthony Wayne." *Wayne County NY,* web.co.wayne.ny.us/index.php/office-of-the-county-historian/anthony-wayne/.

108. Putnam, *Memoirs of Rufus Putnam* 80.

109. Continental Village was a military post and supply depot. Established in 1776 as the location of a barracks for three Connecticut brigades, it was occupied by American troops through 1783. It had been

burned by the British in October 1777. Today, Continental Village is part of the town of Philipstown, New York.

110. Putnam, *Memoirs of Rufus Putnam* 81.

111. *Ibid.*, 80–81.

112. *Ibid.*, 82.

113. Alden, Henry Mills. "The Storming of Stony Point." *Harper's New Monthly Magazine*, vol. 59, 1879, p. 240. Henry P. Johnston (1842–1923) was a professor of history in the College of the City of New York.

114. Hazard, Samuel. *Hazard's Register of Pennsylvania: Devoted to the Preservation of Facts and Documents, and Every ... Kind of Useful Information Respecting the State Of.* Vol. 4, Samuel Hazard, 1829. 54.

115. "From George Washington to John Jay, 21 July 1779," *Founders Online*, National Archives, accessed April 11, 2019, https://founders.archives.gov/documents/Washington/03-21-02-0492.

116. For all his personal faults, Lee was arguably the best educated man in the Continental Army, as well as the one with the most varied military experience, having fought as a British officer in the French and Indian War, been a military advisor to the King of Poland, and served as a lieutenant colonel in the Portuguese army.

117. Hazard, Samuel. *Hazard's Register of Pennsylvania: Devoted to the Preservation of Facts and Documents, and Every ... Kind of Useful Information Respecting the State Of.* Vol. 3, Samuel Hazard, 1829. 390.

Chapter Five

1. Putnam, Rufus, and Rowena Buell. *The Memoirs of Rufus Putnam and Certain Official Papers and Correspondence*, Published by the National Society of the Colonial Dames of America in the State of Ohio. Boston and New York: Houghton, Mifflin, 1903. 54.

2. Reed, Jonas. *A History of Rutland* 65.

3. *Ibid.*

4. Son Franklin Putnam had died in 1776.

5. Today a large maple tree on Central Tree Road marks the site of the state's center. Sometime in the past it replaced an elm tree at the same location.

6. United States Department of the Interior, National Park Service, National Register of Historic Places, Inventory-Nomination Form, General Rufus Putnam House, https://npgallery.nps.gov/GetAsset/cc34111c-0bab-44ca-bfbb-479cfcad8f46, 1972.

7. Reed, Jonas. *A History of Rutland* 165.

8. Even though he was to become the richest person in Newport, Rhode Island, Lopez was rejected when he attempted to become a naturalized citizen of the colony. So Lopez temporarily made his home in Massachusetts, became a citizen there, and then moved back to Rhode Island. He did not live to see the opening of Leicester Academy; in 1782, he drowned in a Smithfield, Rhode Island, pond while watering his horse.

9. Reed, Jonas. *A History of Rutland* 165.

10. The Evening Star, July 17, 1911, 8.

11. *The Rutland Home of Major General Rufus Putnam*, Stephen Carpenter Earle, Ezra Ripley, Press of G. G. Davis, 1901. From 1896 to 1950 the house served as a museum. Afterwards it became a private residence, and today is a bread and breakfast.

12. United States Department of the Interior National Park Service, National Register of Historic Places, Inventory-Nomination Form, General Rufus Putnam House, https://npgallery.nps.gov/GetAsset/cc34111c-0bab-44ca-bfbb-479cfcad8f46, 1972.

13. *The Rutland Home of Major General Rufus Putnam*, Stephen Carpenter Earle, Ezra Ripley, Press of G. G. Davis, 1901.

14. "From George Washington to Rufus Putnam, 2 December 1782," *Founders Online*, National Archives, accessed April 11, 2019, https://founders.archives.gov/documents/Washington/99-01-02-10095.

15. Shepard would go on to serve in the Massachusetts legislature (1785–1786), and in 1786, as major general of in the Massachusetts Militia, led forces defending the Springfield Arsenal during Shays' Rebellion. He also served as a U.S. congressman from 1797 through 1803.

16. After a distinguished career during the Revolutionary War, Paterson was commander of the Massachusetts troops during Shays' Rebellion, and he served one term in the U.S. Congress (1803–1805).

17. "From George Washington to Rufus Putnam, 2 December 1782," *Founders Online*, National Archives, accessed April 11, 2019, https://founders.archives.gov/documents/Washington/99-01-02-10095.

18. "To George Washington from Rufus Putnam, 17 December 1782," *Founders Online*, National Archives, accessed April 11, 2019, https://founders.archives.gov/documents/Washington/99-01-02-10228.

19. *Ibid.*

20. Putnam, *Memoirs of Rufus Putnam* 99.

21. *Ibid.*

22. *Ibid.*, 100.

23. *Ibid.*

24. Heitman, *Historical Register of Officers*.

25. "Petition of Officers in the Continental Line of the Army." The Ohio State Archaeological and Historical Society, vol. 1. Fred J. Heer. 1887. 38.

26. "From George Washington to Officers of the Army, 15 March 1783," *Founders Online*, National Archives, accessed April 11, 2019, https://founders.archives.gov/documents/Washington/99-01-02-10840.

27. Washington, George. *The Writings of George Washington*, Volume 10. New York: G.P. Putnam's Sons, Vol. X. 1891. 170.

28. "To George Washington from Rufus Putnam, 25 April 1783," *Founders Online*, National Archives, accessed April 11, 2019, https://founders.archives.gov/documents/Washington/99-01-02-11171.

29. *Ibid.*

30. Located in Northern Michigan, between Lakes Huron and Michigan, Fort Michilimackinac was built by the French in the early 1700s, and turned over to the British after the French and Indian War.

31. Located on the Ohio River in Massac County, Illinois, Fort Massac was built in 1757 by the French and decommissioned in 1814, which was four years before Illinois became a state.

32. Located at the confluence of the Monongahela and Allegheny rivers, Fort Pitt was built by the British during the French and Indian War. Today, the City of Pittsburgh occupies the site.

33. Located in northeastern Ohio, the Cuyahoga river empties into Lake Erie.

34. "To George Washington from Rufus Putnam, 16 June 1783," *Founders Online*, National Archives, accessed April 11, 2019, https://founders.archives.gov/documents/Washington/99-01-02-11466.

35. *Ibid.*

36. "From George Washington to the United States Senate and House of Representatives, 7 August 1789," *Founders Online*, National Archives, accessed April 11, 2019, https://founders.archives.gov/documents/Washington/05-03-02-

37. *Ibid.*

38. "A Short History of the Society of the Cincinnati." *The Society of The Cincinnati*, 2019, www.societyofthecincinnati.org/about/history. Cincinnatus was a former Roman consul who was called by the leaders of the Roman Republic to lead them against invaders. According to legend, he left his plow in a field and rallied Roman citizens to successfully battle and defeat the foe. He then retired to a quiet life on his farm. George Washington has been compared to Cincinnatus—both left their farms when their countries were in peril, led their soldiers to victory, and returned to their farms after their service. Rufus Putnam's cousin Major General Israel Putnam also has been compared to Cincinnatus. Both men literally were plowing their field when they heard that their countries needed their leadership and left their plows in the furrows. Israel Putnam also retired to his farm after his military service, although a paralytic stroke left him with few other options.

39. Honorary members over the centuries have included U.S. presidents Andrew Jackson, Zachary Taylor, James Buchanan, Ulysses S. Grant, Grover Cleveland, Benjamin Harrison, William McKinley, Theodore Roosevelt, Woodrow Wilson, Warren Harding, Herbert Hoover, Franklin D. Roosevelt, Harry S Truman, Ronald Reagan, and George H. W. Bush.

40. "From George Washington to Rufus Putnam, 2 June 1784," *Founders Online*, National Archives, accessed April 11, 2019,

Notes—Chapter Five

https://founders.archives.gov/documents/Washington/04-01-02-0286.

41. Brunelle, Jim. *Maine Almanac.* Guy Gannett Pub. Co., 1979. The State of Maine was originally part of Massachusetts. While there were efforts to promote statehood for the area after the American Revolution, they were unsuccessful until the U.S. Congress voted in Maine as part of the Missouri Compromise of 1820. Maine became the 23rd state and Missouri, a year later, became the 24th. The compromise perpetuated the numeric balance of free and slave states.

42. Cone, *Life of Rufus Putnam* 60.

43. Park Holland was born in Shrewsbury, Worcester County, Massachusetts, in 1752, and died in Bangor, Maine, in 1844 at age 91. Like Rufus Putnam, Holland was a surveyor—surveying Bangor in the late 1700s.

44. Sprague, John Francis. "Stephen Jones 189–190.

45. Putnam, *Memoirs of Rufus Putnam.*

46. Cone, *Life of Rufus Putnam* 61.

47. Earlier, we had mentioned that both Rufus Putnam and his cousin Major General Israel Putnam were each the 11th child in their families. Rufus's fellow Marietta pioneer, General Benjamin Tupper, was the youngest in his family—of eight children. Also, like the two Putnams, Tupper was a native of Massachusetts and a veteran of both the French and Indian War and the American Revolutionary War.

48. *Historical Collections of Harrison County, in the State of Ohio: With Lists of the First Land-owners, Early Marriages (to 1841), Will Records (to 1861), Burial Records of the Early Settlements, and Numerous Genealogies,* Charles Augustus Hanna, Privately printed, 1900.

49. "Military Bounty Land-Bill." *The American Lawyer, and Business-Man's Form-Book Containing Forms and Instructions.* Delos W. Beadle, 1860.

50. For these claimants, the law specified: "Those who engaged to serve twelve months, or during the war, and actually served nine months, shall receive one hundred and sixty acres; and those who engaged to serve six months, and actually served four months, shall receive eighty acres; and those who engaged to serve for any, or an indefinite period, and actually served one month, shall receive forty acres: Provided, That whenever any officer or soldier was honorably discharged in consequence of disability in the service before the expiration of his period of service, he shall receive the amount to which he would have been entitled if he had served the full period for which he had engaged to serve: Provided, The person so having been in service shall not receive said lands, or any part thereof, if it shall appear by the muster-rolls of his regiment or corps that he deserted, or was dishonorably discharged from service, or if he has received or is entitled to any military land bounty under any act of Congress heretofore passed."

51. *Ibid.*

52. *Ibid.*

53. At this time, sixty-year-old Governor James Bowdoin (1726–1790) was in his last year in office. A scholar, as well as a politician and a merchant, Bowdoin was the first president of the American Academy of Arts and Sciences, and the author of a number of scientific papers, including one on electricity that was written with Benjamin Franklin.

54. Pelham, the location of Shays' home, was about 25 west of Rufus Putnam's hometown of Rutland, as the crow flies.

55. "Shays' Rebellion: Letter from Gen. Rufus Putnam to Gov. Bowdoin." Collections of the Maine Historical Society, vol. 2, 1847. 250–254.

56. *Ibid.*, 253–254. The exchange at this point went as follows:

PUTNAM: It is said you are first in command, and it is supposed they have appointed you their General.

SHAYS: I never had any appointment but that at Springfield, nor did I ever take command of any men but those of the county of Hampshire; no General Putnam, you are deceived, I never had half so much to do with the matter as you think for, nor did I order any men to march, except when at Rutland, as I told you before.

PUTNAM: Did you not muster the party to go to Springfield the other day?

SHAYS: No, nor had I any hand in the matter, except that I rode down in a sleigh.

PUTNAM: But I saw your name to the request presented to the justices—that you won't deny?

SHAYS: I know it was there, and Grover put it there without my knowledge; (Born in 1738 in Grafton, Massachusetts, like Rufus Putnam, Thomas Grover served in Captain Ebenezer Learned's Company and Col. Timothy Ruggles' Regiment in the French and Indian War. In 1777, Grover fought at the Battle of Bennington and the Battles of Saratoga. One of the principle leaders of Shays' Rebellion, Grover wasn't pardoned until 1791. He died in 1805.) I wan't got into Springfield when it was done,—the matter was all over before I got there and I had no hand in it.

PUTNAM: But is it a truth that you did not order the men to march to Springfield the other day?

SHAYS: Yes; I was sent to and refused, and told them I would have nothing to do in the matter.

PUTNAM: But why?

SHAYS: I told them it was inconsistent after what we had agreed to petition, as we did at Worcester, and promised to remain quiet and not to meddle with the courts any more, till we knew whether we could get a pardon or not.

PUTNAM: Have you not ordered the men to march to Worcester the 23d of this month?

SHAYS: No. I was sent to from Worcester county to come down with the Hampshire men; but I told them I would not go myself nor order any men to march.

PUTNAM: Who has done it? Hampshire men are certainly ordered to march.

SHAYS: Upon my refusing to act they have chose a committee, who have ordered the men to march.

57. *Ibid.*, 254.
58. *Ibid.*
59. *Ibid.*
60. *Ibid.*
61. *Ibid.*

62. Best known today for his large signature on the United States Declaration of Independence, Hancock (1737–1793) was a wealthy Massachusetts merchant and a prominent supporter of American independence from Great Britain. From 1775 through 1777, he was president of the Second Continental Congress.

63. "Proclamation 5598—Shays' Rebellion Week and Day, 1987: Ronald Reagan Presidential Library—National Archives and Records Administration." *Proclamation 5598—Shays' Rebellion Week and Day, 1987 | Ronald Reagan Presidential Library—National Archives and Records Administration*, www.reaganlibrary.gov/research/speeches/011387b.

64. The Articles of Confederation were superseded by the United States Constitution in 1789. Although modified with many amendments, the latter was still in effect in the 21st century.

65. Also in 1786 Putnam was appointed commissioner to the Penobscot Indians, by Massachusetts.

66. Born in Massachusetts one month before Rufus Putnam in 1738, Benjamin Tupper worked as an apprentice to a tanner at the same time Rufus was a millwright's apprentice. In 1756, Tupper volunteered to serve with the British in French and Indian War. Putnam volunteered a year later. Putnam married his first wife in 1761; Tupper married in 1762. Both served with distinction as colonels during the Revolutionary War. Both served under Washington at the Siege of Boston and under Gen. Horatio Gates at the Battles of Saratoga. Putnam and Tupper attained the rank of brevetted brigadier general at the war's end. Both men in later years went back into service to put an end to Shays' rebellion.

67. A Middletown, Connecticut, attorney, Samuel Holden Parsons was appointed colonel of a Connecticut militia regiment that fought at the Battle of Bunker Hill. In 1776, he was commissioned a brigadier general and his brigade was part of General Israel Putnam's division and participated in the Battle of White Plains. With Return Jonathan Meigs, Sr., Parsons planned one of the most remarkable feats of the war—the Sag Harbor raid. When Israel Putnam was disabled by a stroke in 1779, Parsons took over his command. At the war's end, Parsons was promoted to major general. After the war, he became one of the first settlers of Ohio. In 1789, he drowned in the rapids of Pennsylvania's Big Beaver River.

68. A graduate of Yale College, Manasseh Cutler at age 28 received his license

to preach as a Congregational minister. He had already studied law and had experience as a teacher and businessman. An army chaplain during the American Revolutionary War, he studied medicine and became a medical doctor. An expert in botany and astronomy, Cutler's advice was sought out by many of the leaders of his day. He was a founder of the Ohio Company and drafted the Ordinance of 1787.

69. Drake, Samuel Adams. *Old Boston Taverns and Tavern Clubs.* Boston: W. A. Butterfield, 1917. 33–37. Samuel Adams Drake states that "Three gilded clusters of grapes dangled temptingly over the door before the eye of the passer-by.

70. The plaque also commemorates the site as the location of the founding of the first Masonic lodge in America: "Here on 30th of July 1733—Was instituted under charter from—The Grand Lodge of England—The first regularly constituted lodge—Of Free and Accepted Masons in America—Now St. Johns Lodge of Boston."

71. Sargent was an artillery officer during the Revolution, and like Rufus Putnam, participated in the Siege of Boston (1775–1776) and the Battle of White Plains (1776). The year before he became the Ohio Company's secretary, he had worked at surveying land in eastern Ohio. In 1788, the Confederation Congress appointed him the first Secretary of the Northwest Territory, a post he held for almost ten years. Sargent also served as the first Governor of the Mississippi Territory (1798–1801).

72. In 1787, Varnum (1748–1789) was appointed a judge of the United States Court in the Northwest Territory. The following year he moved to Marietta. A member of the first graduating class at Brown University (then called the College of Rhode Island), he served as a brigadier general in the Continental Army during the Revolutionary War (1777–1779).

73. "Rufus Putnam. An Address by Hon. George F. Hoar, at Rutland, Mass., Sept. 17, 1898." Eighth Annual Report of the Trustees of Public Reservations, Geo. H. Ellis, 1899. 24–42.

74. Crawford, Sidney. "Rufus Putnam and His Pioneer Life in the Northwest." Press of Charles Hamilton, 1899. 10.

75. http://avalon.law.yale.edu/18th_century/nworder.asp.

76. Parton, James. *Life of Thomas Jefferson, Third President of the United States.* Boston: Houghton, Mifflin, 1883. 270.

77. *Laws of the Territory Northwest of the River Ohio: Including the Laws of the Governor and Judges, the Maxwell Code, and the Laws of the Three Sessions of the Territorial Legislature, 1791–1802: with a Sketch of the State of Ohio, the Ordinance of 1787, Etc. Northwest Territory.* 1833. 69.

78. Crawford, Sidney. "Rufus Putnam and His Pioneer Life in the Northwest." *Proceedings of the American Antiquarian Society*, American Antiquarian Society. 1899. 431.

79. Today, the Mason-Dixon Line forms parts of the borders of four states—Pennsylvania, Maryland, Delaware, and West Virginia.

80. *Laws of the Territory Northwest of the River Ohio: Including the Laws of the Governor and Judges, the Maxwell Code, and the Laws of the Three Sessions of the Territorial Legislature, 1791–1802: with a Sketch of the State of Ohio, the Ordinance of 1787, Etc. Northwest Territory.* 1833. 68.

81. *Ibid.*

82. *Ibid.,* 68.

83. *Historical Collections of Ohio: In Three Volumes; an Encyclopedia of the State ... : with Notes of a Tour Over it in 1886 ... Contrasting the Ohio of 1846 with 1886–90, Volumes 2–3,* Henry Howe & Son, 1891. 494.

Chapter Six

1. Cutler, Julia Perkins. *Life and Times of Ephraim Cutler: Prepared from His Journals and Correspondence.* Cincinnati: Robert Clarke & Company, 1890.

2. *Ibid.*, 81.

3. In 1775, the Continental Congress appointed Ireland-born Butler a commissioner in negotiations with leaders of the Delaware, Shawnee, and other tribes in an effort to convince them not to support the British in the war. During the war, he commanded regiments at the battles of Saratoga, Monmouth, and Yorktown. After the war, the Confederation Congress put Richard Butler in charge of Native American

relations in the Northwest Territory. Under his Treaty of Fort Stanwix in 1784, the Iroquois gave up their lands. Butler was 48 years old when he was killed in action in St. Clair's Defeat on November 4, 1791.

4. Butler, Richard. *The New Englander,* Vol. 12. A.H. Maltby, 1854. 395.

5. Ebenezer Sproat (1752–1805), rose to the rank of lieutenant colonel during the Revolutionary War. He later served as surveyor of Rhode Island, and after the founding of Marietta, the first sheriff of the Northwest Territory (of Washington County) from 1788 until 1802. He is buried in Marietta's Mound Cemetery.

6. The son of Ohio Company cofounder Benjamin Tupper, Anselm Tupper was 24 years old at the time of the expedition. Anselm had already traveled with his father to Eastern Ohio in 1786 as part of a surveying mission. However, his life experiences included far more than that trip. In 1775, weeks after the battles of Lexington and Concord, 11-year-old Anselm enlisted in the Massachusetts militia, becoming one of the youngest (if not the youngest) soldier of the Revolutionary War. It's said that when his father was commissioned a major in the militia, he was shocked to discover his young son was a private—not an aide or drummer boy—but a full-fledged soldier. Anselm served for over three years as a private. In 1779, he was promoted to ensign (the equivalent of today's second lieutenant), and in 1780 was commissioned a lieutenant. Until the end of the war in November 1783, he served in Massachusetts regiments. After settling in Marietta in 1788, Anselm worked as a surveyor, became the town's first teacher, and was placed in charge of the defense of Campus Martius. In 1803, Anselm Tupper traveled on the Marietta-built ship *Orlando* when it passed down the Ohio and Mississippi rivers, and crossed the Atlantic Ocean and the Mediterranean Sea. He died in Marietta in 1808 at age 45. "Major Anselm Tupper—The Youngest Soldier of the Revolutionary War," *St. Joseph Gazette-Herald,* St. Joseph, Missouri, 08 Oct. 1888.

7. In the first decades of the Ohio settlements, Devol made incredible contributions in constructing ships and mills. He died about three months after Rufus Putnam in 1824.

8. McCabe, L. R. "Two Noted Pioneers of the West." *Magazine of Western History,* Vol. 9. New York: Magazine of Western History Publishing Co., 1889. 238.

9. Putnam, *Memoirs of Rufus Putnam* 104.

10. For three days, rioters destroyed medical laboratories in the New York Hospital, searched homes for missing bodies, and hunted down medical students. It's said that two of the most prominent people of the day, Alexander Hamilton and John Jay, United States Secretary of Foreign Affairs at the time, tried to reason with the rioters to no avail. Apparently, both were injured by thrown rocks. Jay (1745–1829) would become the first Chief Justice of the United States Supreme Court 17 months later. Revolutionary War general Baron von Steuben came in with militia units who shot and killed between five and eight rioters. Four years later, George Washington was to describe Von Steuben as: "Sensible, Sober & brave; well acquainted with Tactics & with the arrangement & discipline of an Army. High in his ideas of Subordination—impetuous in his temper—ambitious—and a foreigner." "Memorandum on General Officers, 9 March 1792," *Founders Online,* National Archives, accessed April 11, 2019, https://founders.archives.gov/documents/Washington/05-10-02-0040.

11. Putnam, *Memoirs of Rufus Putnam* 104.

12. Rome's ancient Campus Martius, on the bank of the Tiber River, was originally an exercise ground for the Roman legions. In Latin, Campus Martius means "Field of Mars."

13. "A Description of Campus Martius." *American Pioneer,* "a monthly periodical, devoted to the objects of the Logan historical society; or, to collecting and publishing sketches relative to the early settlement and successive improvement of the country." 1842. 84.

14. *Ibid.,* 85.

15. May, John. *Journal and Letters of Col. John May, of Boston Relative to Two Journeys to the Ohio Company in 1788 and*

'89. Historical and Philosophical Society of Ohio. Cincinnati: Robert Clarke & Co. 1873. 37–38.

16. *Ibid.*, 52.

17. *Ibid.*, 54.

18. *Ibid.*, 58.

19. Constructed between 1811 and 1834, the National Road was the first road to be funded by the federal government. Nicknamed "The Main Street of America," the road carried pioneers west and farm produce east. In the late 19th century railroads took over much of the road's business, but it continued to thrive. In the 1920s much of it became Route 40.

20. Stone, Benjamin Franklin. "From Rutland to Marietta: Leaves from the Autobiography of Benjamin Franklin Stone." *New England Magazine: An Illustrated Monthly*, Volume 16. J. N. McClintock, 1897. Stone (1782–1873) began his autobiography at age 78 and finished at about age 90. During his life, Stone was a teacher, the county surveyor of Washington County, Ohio, and clerk of the Ohio militia.

21. Stone, Benjamin Franklin. "From Rutland to Marietta." 210.

22. *Ibid.*

23. Putnam, *Memoirs of Rufus Putnam* 10.

24. *Ibid.*

25. *Reminiscences of Worcester from the Earliest Period, Historical and Genealogical: With Notices of Early Settlers and Prominent Citizens, and Descriptions of Old Landmarks and Ancient Dwellings...*, Caleb Arnold Wall, Tyler & Seagrave, 1877.

26. Stone, Benjamin Franklin. "From Rutland to Marietta" 217. Susanna Putnam Burlingame died in Harmar, Ohio, in 1840 at age 71, and Christopher died in Marietta in 1841 at age 87. Their three sons Edwin, Christopher, and Rufus, and lived to be 91, 87, and 92 or 93, respectively.

27. Stone, Benjamin Franklin. "From Rutland to Marietta" 214–215.

28. Reed, Jonas. *A History of Rutland* 168.

29. Maria later married Benjamin Hubbard.

30. Susanna later married George Corner.

31. John Heckewelder (1743–1823) began his work as a missionary to Ohio River Native Americans when, as a teenager, he assisted missionary Christian Frederic Post in Ohio. In 1778, Heckewelder was ordained a deacon of the Moravian Church. After the American Revolutionary War, he continued his work as a missionary in Ohio, Pennsylvania, and Canada. On May 22, 1792, Secretary of War Henry Knox wrote to Putnam: "I have written to Mr. John Heckewelder of Bethlehem to accompany you, which he has promised to do.... This person superintended one of the Moravian Towns in the Muskingum, and has a general acquaintance with and influence over the Wyandots and Delawares." Heckewelder later was with Rufus Putnam at the Post Vincennes treaty talks. In later life, Heckewelder produced important works on 18th and 19th century Native American culture.

32. Stone, Benjamin Franklin. "From Rutland to Marietta" 215.

33. *Ibid.*

34. *Ibid.*, 216.

35. *Ibid.*

36. *Ibid.*

37. *Ibid.*, 216–217.

38. *Ibid.*, 217.

39. *Ibid.*, 219.

40. *Ibid.*

41. Stone, Benjamin Franklin. "From Rutland to Marietta."

42. *Ibid.*

43. Belpre is located about 14 miles down the Ohio River from Marietta.

44. Stone, Benjamin Franklin. "From Rutland to Marietta" 222.

45. *Ibid.*

46. Hildreth, Samuel Prescott. *Pioneer History: Being an Account of the First Examinations of the Ohio Valley*. Cincinnati: H. W. Derby & Co., Publishers, 1848. 392.

47. White, Larry Nash, and Emily Blankenship White. *Marietta*. Arcadia, 2004.

48. Richard Henderson of Bladensburg, Maryland, was an owner of the Frederick ironworks on the Potomac River.

49. "From George Washington to Richard Henderson, 19 June 1788," *Founders Online*, National Archives, accessed April 11, 2019, https://founders.archives.gov/documents/Washington/04-06-02-0304.

50. The general's son Daniel was by then married with a house of his own in

Connecticut. Israel's youngest son, Peter Schuyler Putnam, and his wife moved in with the elderly general and managed the family farm.

51. *History of the Upper Ohio Valley: With Incidents of Border Warfare...* Madison, Wisconsin: Brant & Fuller, 1891. 814.

52. July 2, 1788.

53. The town's name was later changed to Oldtown, and after that to Harrodsburg.

54. Bancroft, George. *History of the United States of America, from the Discovery of the Continent: In 6 Vols.* I, Edinburgh and London: Fullarton & Company, 1850. 212.

55. Hildreth, *Pioneer History* 504. The United Sates had a 13-star flag from 1777 until Vermont and Kentucky became states in 1795.

56. May, John. *Journal and Letters* 77–78.

57. Hildreth, *Pioneer History* 214.

58. *Ibid.*, 505.

59. *Ibid.*, 507–508.

60. *Ibid.*, 509.

61. May, *Journal and Letters* 62.

62. *Ibid.*, 66.

63. *Ibid.*, 66.

64. *Ibid.*, 83–84.

65. *Ibid.*, 84–85.

66. *Ibid.*, 89.

67. *Ibid.*, 92.

68. Hildreth, *Pioneer History*.

69. On this trip, Israel Putnam Jr. brought along the farming tools, implements and supplies that would be needed to settle his land.

70. Major General Israel Putnam died at his home in Pomfret, Connecticut, on May 29, 1790, at age 72.

71. Hildreth, *Pioneer History*.

72. Stone, Benjamin Franklin. "From Rutland to Marietta" 223.

73. Gilmore, William Edward. *Life of Edward Tiffin, First Governor of Ohio*. Chillicothe, Ohio: Horney & Son, 1897. 75.

74. Hildreth, *Pioneer History* 389.

75. *The Records of the Original Proceedings of the Ohio Company..., Ohio Company (1786–1796).* Marietta Historical Commission, 1917. 89.

76. Shetrone, Henry Clyde. *The Mound-Builders*. New York: D. Appleton and Company, 1930. 9, 13. The Rufus Putnam Papers at Marietta College Library includes a collection of over 1,500 items of Putnam's correspondence, documents, diaries, and memorandums. They were given to the school by Rufus Putnam's descendants.

77. The graves of Willcox, Rogers, Kerr, Moulton, Evans and Goodwin are unmarked.

Chapter Seven

1. *Laws of the Territory Northwest of the River Ohio: Including the Laws of the Governor and Judges, the Maxwell Code, and the Laws of the Three Sessions of the Territorial Legislature, 1791–1802: with a Sketch of the State of Ohio, the Ordinance of 1787, Etc.* Northwest Territory. 1833. 67.

2. *Ibid.*

3. That same month, July 1788, New York officially became a state by ratifying the U.S. Constitution. North Carolina and Rhode Island followed in 1789 and 1790, respectively.

4. Smucker, Isaac. "1788: Our First Court Held A Hundred Years Ago." *Magazine of Western History*, Volume 9. Magazine of Western History Publishing Co., 1889.

5. "First Court in Ohio." *The Western Law Journal*. Vol. 1, Iss. 8, Desilver and Burr, April 1844. 334.

6. *Ibid*. An unusually tall man, Sproat was given the nickname "Big Buckeye" by local Native Americans. Some people believe this is the source of Ohio residents being called "Buckeyes."

7. May, *Journal and Letters* 60.

8. *Ibid.*, 66.

9. *Ibid.*, 68.

10. *Ibid.*, 76–77.

11. *Ibid.*, 83.

12. *Ibid.*, 87.

13. *Ibid.*, 92.

14. Summers, Thomas Jefferson. *History of Marietta*. Leader Publishing Company, Printers, 1903. 69.

15. Putnam, *Memoirs of Rufus Putnam* 412–413.

16. Foster was born in Brookfield, Massachusetts, and died in 1804 at age 44. Another qualified candidate was 31-year-old Return Jonathan Meigs, Jr. Two years later,

Meigs would make it to the territorial court. When Ohio became a state, he was appointed the first Chief Justice of the Ohio State Supreme Court. One of the state's most prominent citizens in the early 1800s, he served Ohio in the U.S. Senate from 1808 to 1810, and as its governor from 1810 to 1814. In 1814, he joined James Madison's presidential cabinet as Postmaster General, in which position he also served President Monroe until 1823. Meigs died in 1825.

17. The Yale College-educated Woodbridge worked as a lawyer and merchant before moving to Marietta. He died in 1823 at age 75 and was buried in Marietta Ohio's Mound Cemetery.

18. In addition to serving in the Massachusetts legislature for many years, Ives rose through the ranks of the Massachusetts militia from captain to major, colonel, brigadier general, and, finally in 1805, major general. He died in 1814 at age 61.

19. A Yale College graduate, lawyer Judd (1743–1804) served in the Connecticut General Assembly. During the American Revolutionary War, he was a captain in Col. Willis' regiment.

20. Putnam, *Memoirs of Rufus Putnam* 411–412.

21. Renick, Felix. "Anecdotes of Jesse Hughs, Pioneer Customs, etc." *American Pioneer,* "a monthly periodical, devoted to the objects of the Logan historical society; or, to collecting and publishing sketches relative to the early settlement and successive improvement of the country," 1842. 274

22. *Ibid.*
23. *Ibid.*
24. Putnam, *Memoirs of Rufus Putnam* 103.
25. Ohio Company Series, Marietta College Historical Collections, Volume 1. Marietta College, 1917. 57.
26. *Ibid.*, 56–58.
27. *Ibid.*, 63.
28. *Ibid.*, 64.
29. May, *Journal and Letters.*
30. Dickinson, *History of the First* 211.
31. *Ibid.*, 210–211.
32. To harvest stinging nettles, gloves are used due to the plant's tiny stinging hairs.

33. *Unionville Republican and Putnam County Journal,* 5 Mar. 1975.

34. During the Revolutionary War, Crary (1748–1812) was a colonel of a Rhode Island regiment.

35. During the Revolutionary War, the Rhode Island-born Greene (1749–1804) was a deputy to the quartermaster general of the Continental Army—Nathaniel Greene—who was his cousin.

36. Massachusetts native Robert Oliver (1738–1810/11) served as an officer from 1775 through 1782 in the Revolutionary War.

37. Hildreth, *Pioneer History.* 248.
38. *Ibid.,* 249.
39. The Scioto River flows 230 miles down the center of Ohio to empty in the Ohio River. It is the longest river that is entirely within Ohio.
40. "To George Washington from Rufus Putnam, 20 December 1790," *Founders Online,* National Archives, accessed April 11, 2019, https://founders.archives.gov/documents/Washington/05-07-02-0056.
41. *Ibid.*
42. *Ibid.*
43. *Ibid.*
44. *Ibid.*
45. "To George Washington from Rufus Putnam, 20 December 1790," *Founders Online,* National Archives, accessed April 11, 2019, https://founders.archives.gov/documents/Washington/05-07-02-0056.
46. State of Ohio, General Assembly, *Journal of the House of Representatives,* vol. 82. 1917.
47. Summers, Thomas Jefferson. *History of Marietta.* Leader Publishing Company, Printers, 1903. 312.
48. McCullough, *The Pioneers* 150.
49. Jackson, Helen Hunt. *A Century of Dishonor: A Sketch of the United States Government's Dealings with Some of the Indian Tribes.* New York: Harper & Brothers, 1881. 322.
50. *Ibid.*
51. *Ibid.,* 322–323.
52. Lincoln, Abraham. *Abraham Lincoln; Complete Works, Comprising His Speeches, State Papers, and Miscellaneous Writings,* Vol 1. The Century Co., 1920. 177.
53. May, *Journal and Letters* 61.

54. *Ibid.*, 88–89.
55. Stone, Benjamin Franklin. *From Rutland to Marietta* 218.
56. *Ibid.*, 219.
57. *Ibid.*, 218.
58. Dickinson, C. E. *A History of Belpre*, Washington County, Ohio. C. E. Dickinson, 1920. 41.
59. *Ibid.* At Belpre, the spies' circuit was "over on to the waters of the Little Hocking river, and up the easterly branches across to the Ohio, striking this stream a few miles above the entrance of the Little Kanawha and thence by the deserted farms down to the garrison. The spies from Waterford made a traverse that intersected or joined their trail, forming a cordon across which the enemy could rarely pass without their signs being discovered. While they were abroad the inhabitants, at work in their fields or traveling between stations, felt a degree of safety they could not have done, but for their confidence in the sagacity and faithfulness of the spies."
60. Putnam, *Journal of Gen. Rufus Putnam* 46.
61. Rogers, Robert. *Journals of Major Robert Rogers Containing an Account of the Several Excursions He Made under the Generals Who Commanded upon the Continent of North America, during the Late War ; from Which May by Collected the Most Material Circumstances of Every Campaign upon That Continent, from the Commencement to the Conclusion of the War*. Albany: Joel Munsell's Sons, 1883. 82–85. As an example, this is rule three: "If you march over marshes or soft ground, change your position, and march abreast of each other, to prevent the enemy from tracking you (as they would do if you marched in a single file) till you get over such ground, and then resume your former order, and march till it is quite dark before you encamp, which do, if possible, on a piece of ground which that may afford your sentries the advantage of seeing or hearing the enemy some considerable distance, keeping one half of your whole party awake alternately through the night." Rule ten is likewise very practical: "If the enemy is so superior that you are in danger of being surrounded by them, let the whole body disperse, and every one take a different road to the place of rendezvous appointed for that evening, which must every morning be altered and fixed for the evening ensuing, in order to bring the whole party, or as many of them as possible, together, after any separation that may happen in the day; but if you should happen to be actually surrounded, form yourselves into a square, or if in the woods, a circle is best, and, if possible, make a stand till the darkness of the night favours your escape."
62. Kilbourn, John. *The Ohio Gazetteer, or, Typographical Dictionary, Being a Continuation of the Work Originally Compiled by ... J.K.* Eleventh Edition. Revised and Enlarged by a Citizen of Columbus. Columbus: Scott and Wright, 1833. 469.
63. Stockwell, Mary. *Unlikely General: Mad Anthony Wayne and the Battle for America*. Yale University Press, 2018. 32. Mary Stockwell is the former chair of the history department at Lourdes University in Ohio and the author of *The Other Trail of Tears: The Removal of the Ohio Indians*.
64. Cone, *Life of Rufus Putnam* 64.
65. *Ibid.*
66. *Ibid.*, 66.
67. *Ibid.*
68. The Wyandot people, also known as the Huron people, are Iroquoian-speaking Native Americans; the Delaware, also called Lenape, are Algonquian-speaking Native Americans.
69. Stone, Benjamin Franklin. "From Rutland to Marietta" 210.
70. *Ibid.*
71. "To George Washington from Rufus Putnam, 8 January 1791," *Founders Online*, National Archives, accessed April 11, 2019, https://founders.archives.gov/documents/Washington/05-07-02-0115.
72. "To George Washington from Rufus Putnam, 28 February 1791," *Founders Online*, National Archives, accessed April 11, 2019, https://founders.archives.gov/documents/Washington/05-07-02-0266.
73. "To George Washington from Henry Knox, 27 March 1791," *Founders Online*, National Archives, accessed April 11, 2019, https://founders.archives.gov/documents/Washington/05-08-02-0010.
74. "To George Washington from Rufus Putnam, 26 December 1791," *Founders Online*, National Archives, accessed April

11, 2019, https://founders.archives.gov/documents/Washington/05-09-02-0206.

75. Hulbert, Archer Butler. *Pilots of the Republic: The Romance of the Pioneer Promoter in the Middle West.* McClurg, 1906. 125–126.

76. Putnam, *Memoirs of Rufus Putnam* 366.

77. "Memorandum on General Officers, 9 March 1792," *Founders Online,* National Archives, accessed April 11, 2019, https://founders.archives.gov/documents/Washington/05-10-02-0040.

78. The site is today near the Ohio-Indiana state border.

79. Fallen Timbers was so named because an earlier tornado had uprooted many trees at the location.

80. Brown, Abram. "The High Crimes and Misadventures of William Duer, the Founding Father Who Swindled America." *Forbes,* Forbes Magazine, 26 Aug. 2019, www.forbes.com/sites/abrambrown/2019/07/04/the-high-crimes-and-misadventures-of-william-duer-the-founding-father-who-swindled-america/#4888479879dc. Educated at England's famed Eton College, 20-something Duer came to the British colony of New York a few years before the beginning of the American Revolution. He joined the cause of American patriots who were working to free the colonies from Great Britain, was a delegate to the Second Continental Congress, a Revolutionary War colonel, a signer of the Articles of Confederation, and the first assistant secretary of the United States Treasury. Less praise-worthy, in later years he also, "conducted a Ponzi-like scheme that took in the rich and poor alike" and "triggered the first financial crisis in American history."

81. An officer in the Revolutionary War, Burnham was present at almost every major battle of the war, from Bunker Hill to Yorktown.

82. Putnam, *Memoirs of Rufus Putnam* 110.

83. Congress made the land grant in March 1795. Putnam *Memoirs of Rufus* 123.

84. On 23 April 1792 bank executive Henry Remsen wrote to his friend Thomas Jefferson: "In every place Duer and his associates are execrated, and it is a remark in every person's mouth, that were they torn to pieces, or hung without undergoing any form of trial, it would be only a necessary example and a just punishment." Several years later, Henry Remsen (1762–1843) served as private secretary to President Thomas Jefferson.

85. Putnam, *Memoirs of Rufus Putnam* 116.

86. A noted orator, Fisher Ames was called by twentieth century writer Russell Kirk "The most eloquent of the Federalists." *The Conservative Mind: From Burke to Eliot.* Washington, D.C.: Regnery Publishing, Inc., 1986. p. 81.

87. Putnam, Rufus. "Why the West will Remain in the Union." *American History Told by Contemporaries ... National Expansion 1783–1845.* Albert Bushnell Hart, editor. Volume III. New York: Macmillan Company, 1901. 106.

88. *Ibid.*, 106.
89. *Ibid.*, 106–7.
90. *Ibid.*, 107.
91. *Ibid.*, 107–108.
92. *Ibid.*, 108.
93. *Ibid.*, 108.
94. *Ibid.*, 109.
95. *Ibid.*, 109.

Chapter Eight

1. "Memorandum on General Officers, 9 March 1792," *Founders Online,* National Archives, accessed April 11, 2019, https://founders.archives.gov/documents/Washington/05-10-02-0040.

2. Stockwell, *Unlikely General* 19.

3. "From George Washington to the United States Senate, 3 May 1792," *Founders Online,* National Archives, accessed April 11, 2019, https://founders.archives.gov/documents/Washington/05-10-02-0216.

4. Putnam, *Memoirs of Rufus Putnam* 125.

5. *Ibid.*

6. Cazier, Lola. *Surveys and Surveyors of the Public Domain, 1785–1975.* U.S. Dept. of the Interior, Bureau of Land Management, 1976. 36–39.

7. Rufus Putnam Letters, William L. Clements Library, University of Michigan.

8. *Ibid.*

9. Buckingham, Jamie. *The Ancestors of Ebenezer Buckingham: Who Was Born in 1748, and of His Descendants.* Chicago: R.R. Donnelley, 1892. 24.
10. *Ibid.*
11. *Ibid.*
12. *Ibid.*, 24–25.
13. *Ibid.* In the fall of 1796, Buckingham worked as a surveyor in Coshocton County, in 1798 he surveyed in Muskingum County, and in 1799 he was joined by a brother on additional surveying work. In September 1799, both of them returned to New York State and convinced almost their whole family to move to Ohio. James Buckingham wrote: "They started in December, 1799, and traveled on sleds as far as Pittsburgh, where they had to wait six weeks for the ice in the Ohio river to break up. The cattle were sent through what was then a wilderness, under the care of Stephen and Milton, to Middle Island, just above Marietta, and the family with their goods and chattels descended the river on a flatboat. Arriving in March 1800, they shortly after, with other families, ascended the Muskingum river, and located at the mouth of Killbuck Creek, near the confluence of the Tuscarawas and Walhonding rivers, which there uniting, form the Muskingum."
14. *Ibid.*, 26.
15. *Ibid.*
16. "To Alexander Hamilton from Rufus Putnam, 19 November 1796," *Founders Online*, National Archives, accessed April 11, 2019, https://founders.archives.gov/documents/Hamilton/01-20-02-0266.
17. Hildreth, *Biographical and Historical* 122. Whipple lived out his last years as a Marietta farmer, "raising barely sufficient of the most common necessaries of life to support him and his aged partner in a very frugal manner, but lacking the most of its comforts, especially comfortable clothing, which was scarce and dear in the new settlements."
18. Dickinson, *History of the First* 164.
19. He had been appointed pastor on August 15, 1798. He died on December 30, 1804, at age 49 and is buried in Marietta's Mound Cemetery.
20. Dwight (1752–1817) had been a good friend of Rufus Putnam's cousin Major General Israel Putnam and 14 years earlier had written the epitaph that appeared on the Israel's table-top grave marker in the cemetery in Brooklyn, Connecticut.
21. Dickinson, *History of the First* 213–214.
22. *Ibid.*, 214.
23. *Ibid.*, 33.
24. Hildreth, *Biographical and Historical* 116–117.
25. *Ibid.*, 116–118.
26. "Cyrus Byington—Missionary and Choctaw Linguist." *Choctaw Nation Website*, www.choctawnation.com/cyrus-byington. Cyrus Byington passed away in 1868.
27. Also known as the Hocking River, it is a 100-mile tributary of the Ohio River.
28. *History of Ohio: The Rise and Progress of an American State*, Volume 6, Emilius Oviatt Randall, Daniel Joseph Ryan, Century History Company, 1912, Vol 6. 565.
29. *A Legal History of the Ohio University, Athens, Ohio: Including Resolutions of Congress, Contracts, Territorial & State Enactments, Judicial Decisions, Etc.* Ohio University. Board of Trustees, Ohio University Board of Trustees, 1881. 123.
30. Cutler, William Parker, et al. *Life, Journals and Correspondence of Rev. Manasseh Cutler.* R. Clarke & Co., 1888. 21.
31. *Ibid.*, 21–22.
32. *The History of Higher Education in Ohio.* George Wells Knight, John Rogers Commons, U.S. Government Printing Office, 1891.
33. "Ohio University: The Historic College of the Old Northwest," Volume 8, Issue 1, Clement Luther Martzolff, The University, 1910—Ohio University.
34. *Legal History of the Ohio University, Athens, Ohio: Comp. from Legislative Enactments, Judicial Decisions, Trustees' Proceedings, Etc.* Press of the Western Methodist Book Concern, 1910. 99.
35. Young's appointment was passed on January 13, 1825. A Zanesville minister, Young served until 1849, and died in 1858. *Legal History of the Ohio University, Athens, Ohio: Comp. from Legislative Enactments, Judicial Decisions, Trustees' Proceedings, Etc.* Press of the Western Methodist Book Concern, 1910. 305.

36. Rufus Putnam's son William Rufus Putnam served on the Board from 1823 through 1842.

37. As of 2019, approximately 24,000 students attended classes at the Athens campus, while about 15,000 were enrolled at other campuses.

38. "History & Traditions." *Ohio University*, 2019, www.ohio.edu/student-affairs/students/history-traditions.

39. Hoar, *Rufus Putnam. An Address* 36.

40. Burnet, Jacob. *Notes on the Early Settlement of the North-Western Territory*. New York: D. Appleton & Co. Publishers, 1847. 353.

41. Cutler, *Life and Times*.

42. http://www.ohiohistorycentral.org/w/Ohio_Constitution_of_1803_(Transcript).

43. *The Biographical Annals of Ohio, 1902–1903: A Handbook of the Government and Institutions of the State of Ohio*. General Assembly, 1892.

44. Section 3 of Article VIII, Bill of Rights.

45. In 1802, the Ohio State Convention, asked the U.S. Congress for admission to the United States and approved the Ohio Constitution. Congress approved statehood but failed to complete one step in the process—the ratification of the state constitution. This was not noticed until 150 years later when some statehood documents could not be located. Technically, Ohio became a state in 1953 when the U.S. House of Representatives passed a law, which was signed by President Dwight D. Eisenhower that retroactively set the date of Ohio statehood at March 1, 1803.

46. The marker also remembers other champions of freedom: "James Davis (1787–1862) was born in Harmar (Marietta) and was the first documented African American born in the Northwest Territory. During his adult life, he became an Underground Railroad activist in Dayton, Ohio. David Putnam, Jr. (1808–1882), a great-grandson of General Israel Putnam, was born and raised in Harmar where he later conducted Underground Railroad activities. Frances Dana (Barker) Gage (1808–1884), daughter of Colonel Joseph Barker, was born in Marietta and became a leading figure nationally with the Abolitionist, Temperance, and Women's Suffrage Movements. Faculty and students from Marietta College became active in the Washington County Anti-slavery Society when it was formed in 1836 at the college. Charlotte Scott, a freed slave living in Marietta at the time of President Abraham Lincoln's assassination suggested placing the Emancipation Monument in Washington DC to honor Lincoln. She donated the first five dollars to raise funds culminating in an 1872 dedication ceremony." The Ohio Historical Marker "Muskingum River Underground Railroad" outside the Ohio River Museum in Marietta.

47. Jefferson had appointed Mansfield to the West Point position two years earlier. It's interesting to consider that when 35-year-old Rufus Putnam was exploring Mississippi River lands in 1773 as the surveyor of a party of French and Indian War veterans, Mansfield was only 13 years old.

48. Jefferson was by no means innocent of contributing to slander and libel at the time. In 1799, he paid scandalmonger James Callender to spread rumors and gossip about President John Adams, who was to be his opponent in the 1800 presidential election. Many consider this to be the beginning of "dirty" politics in the United States.

49. "From Thomas Jefferson to Jared Mansfield, 21 May 1803," *Founders Online*, National Archives, accessed April 11, 2019, https://founders.archives.gov/documents/Jefferson/01-40-02-0312.

50. *Mansfield, Edward D. Personal Memories: Social, Political, and Literary: with Sketches of Many Noted People, 1803–1843*. Cincinnati: Robert Clarke & Co., 1879. 3. Connecticut-born, Yale College graduate Mansfield served as surveyor general for about nine years. He then returned to a teaching position at West Point.

51. Cone, *Life of Rufus Putnam* 70.

52. *History of Washington County, Ohio: With Illustrations and Biographical Sketches*, H.Z. Williams & Bro. Publishers, 1881. 454.

53. Cayton, Andrew R. L. *The Frontier Republic Ideology and Politics in The Ohio Country, 1780–1825*. The Kent State University Press, 1986. 49.

54. Mansfield, Personal Memories 5–6.

55. Rufus Putnam wasn't the only American in his country's service who refused to cut his queue/braid hanging from the back of the head. In 1801, General James Wilkinson ordered military men to cut their queues. One man, Col. Edward Butler, refused. He had worn his hair with a queue since he served in the Revolutionary War. Butler, who could boast of a distinguished military career, garnered the support of future President Andrew Jackson and a number of congressmen. Nevertheless, in 1803, Wilkinson had him courtmartialed, and he was sentenced to be suspended without pay for one year. The sentence was never carried out since Butler soon after died of yellow fever. He never did cut his hair as ordered by Wilkinson. *Life of General Lewis Cass*, Lewis Cass, G. B. Zieber & Company, 1848.

56. Sprague, John Francis. "Stephen Jones 190.

57. Wolcott (1760–1833) served as secretary of the Treasury from 1795 to 1800; later he served for ten years as Connecticut's governor.

58. "From Alexander Hamilton to Oliver Wolcott, Junior, 3 October 1802," *Founders Online*, National Archives, accessed April 11, 2019, https://founders.archives.gov/documents/Hamilton/01-26-02-0001-0046-0001.

59. "From George Washington to Rufus Putnam, 28 January 1798," Marietta College. Special Collections, accessed September 25, 2019, http://cdm16824.contentdm.oclc.org/cdm/search/searchterm/mss002_box03_folder01_item03_17980128.

60. "From Rufus Putnam to George Washington, 17 February 1798," Marietta College. Special Collections, accessed September 25, 2019, http://cdm16824.contentdm.oclc.org/cdm/search/searchterm/mss002_box03_folder01_item04_17980217.

61. Born in Coventry, Connecticut, which was also the birthplace of Patriot hero Nathan Hale, Huntington (1765–1817) was governor of Ohio from 1808 to 1810.

62. Hulbert, *Pilots of the Republic* 125.

63. Kilbourn, *The Ohio Gazetteer* 475.

64. Ibid.

65. Most of Israel Sr.'s children were married and remained in the Pomfret, Connecticut area. Unlike oldest child Israel Jr. who was born in Danvers, Massachusetts, all of the other children were born in Pomfret, Connecticut.

66. Hildreth, *Biographical and Historical* 355.

67. White, *Marietta* 38.

68. "A Journey to Marietta in 1794. The Journal of Israel Putnam." *The New England Magazine*, vol. 13, 1896. 642.

69. Benjamin Dana was the son of Major General Israel Putnam's daughter Hannah Putnam Dana (1744–1820) and John Winchester Dana (1739–1813). Benjamin passed away in Washington County, Ohio, in 1838 at age 68.

70. *Ibid.*, 645.

71. "A Journey to Marietta in 1794. The Journal of Israel Putnam." *The New England Magazine*, vol. 13, 1896.

72. *Ibid.*, 646.

73. *Ibid.*

74. *Ibid.*

75. *Ibid.*

76. *Ibid.*

77. *Ibid.*, 648.

78. *Ibid.*, 648–649.

79. *Ibid.*, 650–651.

80. He and his first wife, Clarina Chandler Putnam (1767–1801), would have six children. With his second wife, Elizabeth Wiser Putnam (1769–1842), he would have seven children.

81. Putnam, Eben. *A History of the Putnam Family in England and America*. Salem Pub. and Print., 1891. 299.

82. Kilbourn, *The Ohio Gazetteer* 470. Kilbourn continues with: "The apple and the peach are most extensively cultivated, and annually the orchards near the rivers, especially the Ohio, furnish thousands of barrels of the choicest kinds of apples both dried and fresh, for the markets on the Ohio and Mississippi rivers. The climate and the soil are so well adapted to the growth of the apple that they often attain a size so great as to weigh from twenty to twenty-six ounces. Pear trees being subject to more diseases, are cultivated with difficulty, but where the trees are healthy, they sometimes afford fruit of the weight of thirty-six, or even forty ounces. Fruit

may be said to be one of the staple productions of the county."

83. The March 7, 1941, edition of the *Zanesville Signal* (page 7) carried the article, "More Than 200 Steamboats Have Plied River Since Voyage Of *The Rufus Putnam*." It listed steamboats by the decades that they made their first appearance on the Muskingum River. In the years after the launching of the *Rufus Putnam*, it shows no others in the 1820s, only two others in the 1830s, 43 in the 1840s, 37 in the 1850s, 26 in the 1860s, 38 in the 1870s, 23 in the 1880s, 24 in the 1890s, and only 10 between the 1900 and 1910. In addition, it lists 18 steamboats under the heading "Miscellaneous." The reason for the dramatic increase in steamboats on the Muskingum after the 1830s is due to both their popularity and the fact that a system of eleven locks and dams was completed on the Muskingum River in 1841, which made it navigable from Marietta to a point where it could connect with the Ohio and Erie Canal (http://www.ohiohistorycentral.org/w/Muskingum_River, http://www.usgenwebsites.org/OHMuskingum/muskfootprints/steamboats.html.)

84. *History of Washington County, Ohio: With Illustrations and Biographical Sketches*, H.Z. Williams & Bro. Publishers, 1881. 379.

85. *Historical Collections of Ohio...: An Encyclopedia of the State: History Both General and Local, Geography with Descriptions of Its Countries, Cities and Villages, Its Agricultural, Manufacturing, Mining and Business Development, Sketches of Eminent and Interesting Characters, Etc., with Notes of a Tour Over it in 1886. Illustrated by about 700 Engravings. Contrasting the Ohio of 1846 with 1886–90. From Drawings by the Author in 1846 and Photographs Taken Solely for it in 1886, 1887, 1888, 1889 and 1890...*, Henry Howe, state of Ohio, 1902.

86. The Marquis de Lafayette, the last foreign-born general of the Continental Army, died in 1834 at age 76. Thomas Sumter, the last surviving militia general of the American Revolutionary War, died in 1832 at age 97. A South Carolina general, Sumter was nicknamed the Carolina Gamecock.

87. The Ohio River Museum in Marietta has the engine room bell from the *Rufus Putnam* in its collection.

88. Dickinson, *History of the First*. These are the words of Sarah Cutler Dawes, who was the granddaughter of one of the most important founders of Marietta, the Rev. Manasseh Cutler. In 1822 or 1823, when she was about 13 or 14 years old, she would visit her friend Sophia Tupper, who lived with her grandfather Rufus Putnam when she attended school in Marietta.

89. *The Sandusky Clarion*. Sandusky, Ohio. 04 Feb 1824. 3.

90. Twenty days later, the United States would see the death of another of its great pioneers: Daniel Boone (on September 26, 1820).

91. Rufus Putnam survived his cousin Israel by about 34 years and George Washington by over 24 years.

92. Monroe would serve as president until March 4, 1825.

93. James, Dana. *Dreams from Our Fathers*. WestBow Press, 2012. 116–117.

94. *A History of the Putnam Family in England and America. Recording the Ancestry and Descendants of John Putnam of Danvers, Mass., Jan Poutman of Albany, N. Y., Thomas Putnam of Hartford, Conn*, Volume 1. Eben Putnam. Salem, Massachusetts: Salem Press Publishing and Printing Company, 1891. 169.

95. *The Boston Patriot*, 28 May 1824.

96. *Gettysburg Compiler*, 09 Jun 1824. 3.

97. Levasseur, Auguste, and Alan R. Hoffman. *Lafayette in America, in 1824 and 1825: Journal of a Voyage to the United States*. Lafayette Press, 2006. 455.

98. Between August 1824 and September 1825, Lafayette visited all 24 American states.

Chapter Nine

1. Brown, John Howard. "Rufus Putnam." *Americana*, Vol. 9. Publishing Society of New York, 1914. 210.

2. "A Description of Campus Martius." *American Pioneer*, "a monthly periodical, devoted to the objects of the Logan historical society; or, to collecting and publishing sketches relative to the early settlement

Notes—Chapter Nine

and successive improvement of the country." 1842. 85–86.

3. *Ibid.*

4. Cutler, *Life and Times* 203.

5. "The Porter family: proceedings at the reunion of the descendants of John Porter of Danvers, held at Danvers, Mass., July 17th, 1895." 44. Ewing himself would be a last survivor—when he died in 1871, he was the last surviving cabinet member of both the William Henry Harrison and John Tyler administrations. He was also the father-in-law of Civil War general William Tecumseh Sherman.

6. "The Porter family: proceedings at the reunion of the descendants of John Porter of Danvers, held at Danvers, Mass., July 17th, 1895." 44.

7. *Ibid.*

8. Cutler, *Life and Times* 9.

9. *Ibid. The New England Historical and Genealogical Register*, Volume 34 New England Historic Genealogical Society, 1880. 102.

10. McCullough, *The Pioneers* 2019.

11. Venable, William Henry. *Footprints of the Pioneers in the Ohio Valley: A Centennial Sketch*. Ohio Valley Press, 1888. 38–39.

12. Bacon, Francis. *Essays*. Woodward & Company, 1893. 279–280. In his essay, "Of Honour and Reputation," English statesman and philosopher Francis Bacon (1561–1626) writes: "The true marshalling of the degrees of sovereign honor are these: in the first place are 'conditores imperiorum,' founders of states and commonwealths; such as were Romulus, Cyrus, Caesar, Ottoman, Ismael. In the second place are 'legislatores,' lawgivers; which are also called second founders, or 'perpetui principes,' because they govern by their ordinances after they are gone; such were Lycurgus, Solon, Justinian, Edgar, Alphonsus of Castile the Wise, that made the 'Siete Partidas': in the third place are 'liberatores,' or 'salvatores,' such as compound the long miseries of civil wars, or deliver their countries from servitude of strangers or tyrants; as Augustus Caesar, Vespasianus, Aurelianus, Theodoricus, King Henry the Seventh of England, King Henry the Fourth of France."

13. Hoar, *Rufus Putnam. An Address* 38.

14. Crawford, Sidney. "Rufus Putnam and His Pioneer Life in the Northwest." Press of Charles Hamilton, 1899. 3–4. Congregational minister Sidney Crawford (1841–1922) served as a pastor in Vermont, Wisconsin, Iowa, Florida, and his native Massachusetts.

15. *The World's Great Classics: Democracy in America*, by A. de Tocqueville. Timothy Dwight, Julian Hawthorne. Colonial Press, 1899. 367.

16. *Benjamin of Ohio: A Story of the Settlement of Marietta, James Otis Kaler*. American Book Company, 1912. Between 1910 and 1913, a dozen of Kaler's "pioneers" stories were published, including *Hannah of Kentucky: A Story of the Wilderness Road, Seth of Colorado: A Story of the Settlement of Denver*, and *Martha of California: A Story of the California Trail*. Today, his best-known work is *Toby Tyler; or, Ten Weeks with a Circus*, which was made into a Disney movie 48 years after Kaler's death.

17. *The Marion (Ohio) Daily Mirror.* 14 September 1907. 9.

18. McKeon, Melissa. "New Signs Honor Marietta as Rutland's Sister City." Telegram.com, 11 Jan. 2014.

19. Flint, Timothy. *A Condensed Geography and History of the Western States, Or the Mississippi Valley*. Vol. 1. E. H. Flint, 182. 364.

20. "Ohio's Centennial." *Omaha Daily Bee*, 22 Apr. 1888, p. 8.

21. Rufus Putnam's cousin, Major General Israel Putnam, almost appeared on a United States postage stamp in 1975. As part of the Bicentennial series, painter John Trumbull's *The Death of General Warren at the Battle of Bunker's Hill, June 17, 1775* was placed on a ten-cent stamp. Unfortunately, the sides of the image of the painting were cropped—including the left side which depicted Israel Putnam, with his sword raised in the air, leading the American forces in an orderly retreat from Breed's Hill.

22. "Report of the Commissioners of the National Centennial Celebration of the Early Settlement of the Territory Northwest of the River Ohio and of the Establishment of Civil Government Therein: Held at Marietta, Ohio, July 15 to 19 In-

clusive, 1888: Including Verbatim Reports and Speeches and Transactions of the Occasion. Ohio. Commissioners of the Old Northwest Centennial Celebration. Westbote Company, 1889. 22–23.

23. "Buckingham, Gen. Catharinus Putnam Obituary 31 Aug 1888." *Chicago Tribune*, August 31, 1888. 3.

24. *Ibid.*, 651.
25. *Ibid.*, 651.
26. *Ibid.*, 652.
27. *Ibid.*, 652.
28. "Reminiscences of Western Men: John Quincy Adams at Marietta." *New York Evangelist.* Vol. 27, Issue 33, 1856. 106.

29. *Ibid.*
30. *Ibid.*
31. *Historical Collections of Ohio*, Volume Three. Henry Howe. Henry Howe & Son, 1891. 500.

32. *James's River Guide: Containing Descriptions of All the Cities, Towns, and Principal Objects of Interest, on the Navigable Waters of the Mississippi Valley*, Uriah Pierson James, Cincinnati: U.P. James, 1871. 98.

Bibliography

Anderson, Bernice May. *Rutland*. Arcadia, 2000.

Andrews, Martin R., and Douglas Putnam. *History of Marietta and Washington County, Ohio, and Representative Citizens*. Biographical Publishing Company, 1902.

Bancroft, George. *History of the United States of America, from the Discovery of the Continent: In 6 Vols*. I, Edinburgh and London: Fullarton & Company, 1850.

Barbour, Lucius Barnes. *Families of Early Hartford, Connecticut*. Genealogical Publishing Company, 1977.

Benedict, William A., and Hiram A. Tracy. *History of the Town of Sutton, Massachusetts, from 1704 to 1876: Including Grafton until 1735; Millbury until 1813; and Parts of Northbridge, Upton and Auburn*. Worcester: Sanford & Company, 1878.

"Bi-Centennial of the Town of Sutton, Massachusetts Official Programme." Central Committee on the Bi-Centennial, 1904.

Bordewich, Fergus M. *The First Congress: How James Madison, George Washington, and a Group of Extraordinary Men Invented the Government*. Simon & Schuster, 2017.

Boynton, Edward C. *History of West Point and Its Military Importance during the American Revolution, and the Origin and Progress of the United States Military Academy*. New York: Van Nostrand, 1864.

"British Colonial Office West Florida Records." David Library of the American Revolution, www.dlar.org/pdf/CO5%20West%20Florida—PDF.pdf.

Brown, John Howard. "Rufus Putnam." Americana, Vol. 9. Publishing Society of New York, 1914. 210.

Bruce, Wallace. *The Hudson: Three Centuries of History, Romance and Invention*. Bryant Union Company, 1907.

Brunelle, Jim. *Maine Almanac*. Guy Gannett Pub. Co., 1979.

Buckingham, Jamie. *The Ancestors of Ebenezer Buckingham: Who Was Born in 1748, and of His Descendants*. Chicago: R.R. Donnelley, 1892.

Buker, George E. *Sun, Sand and Water: A History of the Jacksonville District U.S. Army Corps of Engineers, 1821–1975*. U.S. Army Corps of Engineers, 1981.

Burnet, Jacob. *Notes on the Early Settlement of the North-Western Territory*. New York: D. Appleton & Co. Publishers, 1847.

Buzzaird, Raleigh B. "Washington's Favorite Engineer." *The Military Engineer*, vol. 68, no. 444, 1976. 298–301. www.jstor.org/stable/44575006.

Campbell, John Wilson, and Eleanor W. Doak Campbell. *Biographical Sketches with Other Literary Remains of the Late John W. Campbell ...* Columbus, Ohio: Scott & Gallagher, 1838.

Cayton, Andrew R.L. *The Frontier Republic Ideology and Politics in The Ohio Country, 1780–1825*. The Kent State University Press, 1986.

Cazier, Lola. *Surveys and Surveyors of the Public Domain, 1785–1975*. U.S. Department of the Interior, Bureau of Land Management, 1976.

The Centennial of the United States Military Academy at West Point, New York. 1802–1902. U.S. Government Printing Office, 1904.

Claiborne, J. F. H. *Mississippi as a Province, Territory, and State: With Biographical Notices of Eminent Citizens,* Vol. 1. Jackson, Mississippi: Power & Barksdale, 1880.

Cone, Mary. *Life of Rufus Putnam: With Extracts from His Journal, and an Account of the First Settlement in Ohio.* Cleveland: William W. Williams, 1886.

Cutler, Julia Perkins. *Life and Times of Ephraim Cutler: Prepared from His Journals and Correspondence.* Cincinnati: Robert Clarke & Company, 1890.

Cutter, William Richard. *New England Families, Genealogical and Memorial: A Record of the Achievements of Her People in the Making of Commonwealths and the Founding of a Nation,* Vol. 4. Lewis Historical Publishing Company, 1914.

"Cyrus Byington—Missionary and Choctaw Linguist." Choctaw Nation Website, www.choctawnation.com/cyrus-byington.

Daughan, George C. *Revolution on the Hudson: New York City and the Hudson River Valley in the American War of Independence.* W.W. Norton & Company, 2017.

Dawson, Henry Barton. *Westchester County, New York, during the American Revolution.* New York: Henry B. Dawson, 1886.

Dickinson, C. E. *A History of Belpre, Washington County, Ohio.* C. E. Dickinson, 1920.

Dickinson, C. E., and John W. Simpson. *A History of the First Congregational Church of Marietta, Ohio.* E.R. Alderman, 1896.

Drake, Samuel Adams. *Old Boston Taverns and Tavern Clubs.* Boston: W. A. Butterfield, 1917. 33–37.

Dunkak, Harry M. *Still All around Us: An Illustrated Guide to the American Revolution in Westchester County.* St. Paul's Church National Historic Site, 2001.

Earle, Stephen C. *The Rutland Home of Major General Rufus Putnam.* Gilbert G. Davis, 1901.

"Editor's Table." *New England Magazine: An Illustrated Monthly,* vol. 9. J. N. McClintock and Company, 1894.

Fairbairn, William. *Treatise on Mills and Millwork.* London: Longman, Green, Longman, and Roberts, 1864.

"First Court in Ohio." *The Western Law Journal (1843–1853),* vol. 1, no. 7, April 1844. 334.

Fowler, William Chauncey. *History of Durham, Connecticut: From the First Grant of Land in 1662 to 1866.* Hartford: Press of Wiley, Waterman & Eaton, 1866.

"A Fragment—Putnam's Rock." *The American Journal of Science and Arts,* vol. 5, 1822. S. Converse.

Gibbon, Peter. "Reflections on a Man of Undeniable Character." Baltimoresun.com, 12 Oct. 2018, www.baltimoresun.com/news/bs-xpm-1998-02-16-1998047087-story.html.

Gilmore, William Edward. *Life of Edward Tiffin, First Governor of Ohio.* Chillicothe, Ohio: Horney & Son, 1897.

Griswold, William A., and Donald W. Linebaugh. *The Saratoga Campaign: Uncovering an Embattled Landscape.* University Press of New England, 2016.

Hanna, Charles Augustus. *Historical Collections of Harrison County, in the State of Ohio: With Lists of the First Land-Owners, Early Marriages (to 1841), Will Records (to 1861), Burial Records of the Early Settlements, and Numerous Genealogies.* Privately Printed, 1900.

Hart, Albert Bushnell. *The American History Told by Contemporaries.* New York: Macmillan, 1845.

Hazard, Samuel. *Hazard's Register of Pennsylvania: Devoted to the Preservation of Facts and Documents, and Every ... Kind of Useful Information Respecting the State Of.* Samuel Hazard, 1829.

"Headquarters U.S. Army Corps of Engineers." *Headquarters U.S. Army Corps of Engineers,* 2019, www.usace.army.mil/.

Heitman, Francis B. *Historical Register of Officers of the Continental Army during the War of the Revolution, April, 1775 to December, 1783.* Washington, D.C.: The Rare Book Shop Publishing Company, 1914.

Hildreth, Samuel Prescott, and Ephraim Cutler. *Biographical and Historical Memoirs of the Early Pioneer Settlers of Ohio with Narratives of Incidents and Occurrences in 1775.* Cincinnati: H.W. Derby, 1852.

_____. *Pioneer History: Being an Account of the First Examinations of the Ohio Valley.* Cincinnati: H.W. Derby & Co., Publishers, 1848.

History of the Upper Ohio Valley: With Incidents of Border Warfare. Madison, Wisconsin: Brant & Fuller, 1891.

History of Washington County, Ohio: With Illustrations and Biographical Sketches, H.Z. Williams & Bro. Publishers, 1881.

Hoar, George F. "Rufus Putnam. An Address by Hon. George F. Hoar, at Rutland, Mass., Sept. 17, 1898." Eighth Annual Report of the Trustees of Public Reservations. Boston: Geo. H. Ellis, 1899.

Hoffman, Renoda. *The Battle of White Plains.* Battle of White Plains Monument Committee, 1976.

Hubbard, Robert Ernest. *Major General Israel Putnam: Hero of the American Revolution.* McFarland, 2017.

Hufeland, Otto. *Westchester County during the American Revolution: 1775–1783.* Published for Westchester County by the Westchester County Historical Society, 1926.

Hulbert, Archer Butler. *Pilots of the Republic: The Romance of the Pioneer Promoter in the Middle West.* A.C. McClurg & Co., 1906.

_____. *The Records of the Original Proceedings of the Ohio Company.* Marietta Historical Commission, 1917.

Humphreys, David, Col., *An Essay on the Life of the Honourable Major-General Israel Putnam, addressed to the State Society of the Cincinnati in Connecticut.* Hartford: Hudson and Goodwin, 1788.

_____. *An Essay on the Life of the Honourable Major-General Israel Putnam, addressed to the State Society of the Cincinnati in Connecticut.* Hartford: 1850.

_____. *An Essay on the Life of the Honourable Major-General Israel Putnam. With Notes and Additions. With an Appendix Containing an Historical and Topographical Sketch of Bunker Hill Battle by S. Swett.* Boston: Samuel Avery, 1818.

Jackson, Helen Hunt. *A Century of Dishonor: A Sketch of the United States Government's Dealings with Some of the Indian Tribes.* New York: Harper & Brothers, 1881.

James, U. P. *James's River Guide: Containing Descriptions of All the Cities, Towns, and Principal Objects of Interest, on the Navigable Waters of the Mississippi Valley.* Cincinnati: U.P. James, 1871.

Johnston, Henry P. *The Storming of Stony Point on the Hudson: Midnight, July 15, 1779.* James T. White & Co., 1900.

"A Journey to Marietta in 1794. The Journal of Israel Putnam." *The New England Magazine,* vol. 13, 1896. 642.

Kilbourn, John. *The Ohio Gazetteer, or, Typographical Dictionary, Being a Continuation of the Work Originally Compiled by ... J.K. Eleventh Edition. Revised and Enlarged by a Citizen of Columbus.* Columbus: Scott and Wright, 1833.

Knight, George W., and John R. Commons. *The History of Higher Education in Ohio.* Government Printing Office, 1891.

A Legal History of the Ohio University, Athens, Ohio: Including Resolutions of Congress, Contracts, Territorial & State Enactments, Judicial Decisions, Etc. Board of Trustees, Ohio University, 1881.

Levasseur, Auguste, and Alan R. Hoffman. *Lafayette in America, in 1824 and 1825: Journal of a Voyage to the United States.* Lafayette Press, 2006.

Lincoln, Abraham. *Abraham Lincoln; Complete Works, Comprising His Speeches, State Papers, and Miscellaneous Writings,* Vol 1. The Century Co., 1920.

Livingston, William Farrand. *Israel Putnam: Pioneer, Ranger and Major General, 1718–1790.* G.P. Putnam's Sons, 1901.

Lockhart, Paul Douglas, and George Washington. *The Whites of Their Eyes: Bunker Hill, the First American Army, and the Emergence of George Washington.* Harper, 2011.

Mansfield, Edward D. *Personal Memories: Social, Political, and Literary: with Sketches of Many Noted People, 1803–1843.* Cincinnati: Robert Clarke & Co., 1879.

Martzolff, Clement L. *Ohio University, the Historic College of the Old Northwest.* Ohio University, 1910.

Bibliography

May, John. *Journal and Letters of Col. John May, of Boston Relative to Two Journeys to the Ohio Company in 1788 and '89.* Historical and Philosophical Society of Ohio. Cincinnati: Robert Clarke & Co. 1873.

McCabe, L. R. "Two Noted Pioneers of the West." *Magazine of Western History*, Vol 9. New York: Magazine of Western History Publishing Co., 1889.

McCullough, David. *The Pioneers: The Heroic Story of the Settlers Who Brought the American Ideal West.* New York: Simon & Schuster, 2019.

McKeon, Melissa. "New Signs Honor Marietta as Rutland's Sister City." Telegram.com, = 11 Jan. 2014, www.telegram.com/article/20140111/TOWNNEWS/301119994.

Metterville, Brenda, et al. *Brookfield.* Arcadia Publishing, 2012.

Ohio Company Series, Marietta College Historical Collections, Volume 1. Marietta College, 1917.

"Ohio Constitution of 1803 (Transcript)." *Ohio Constitution of 1803 (Transcript) Ohio History Central*, www.ohiohistorycentral.org/w/Ohio_Constitution_of_1803_(Transcript).

"Ohio Constitutional Convention of 1802." *Ohio Constitutional Convention of 1802 Ohio History Central*, www.ohiohistorycentral.org/w/Ohio_Constitutional_Convention_of_1802.

"Ohio's Centennial." *Omaha Daily Bee*, 22 April 1888. 8.

Paige, Lucius R. *History of Hardwick, Massachusetts.* Boston: Houghton, Mifflin, 1883.

Paine, Thomas. *The American Crisis.* James Watson, 1835.

Parton, James. *Life of Thomas Jefferson, Third President of the United States.* Boston: Houghton Mifflin, 1883.

Philbrick, Nathaniel. *Bunker Hill: A City, a Siege, a Revolution.* Viking, 2013.

"Porter and Bradstreet." *New England Historical and Genealogical Register.* Boston: New England Historical Genealogical Society, 1880.

The Porter Family: Proceedings at the Reunion of the Descendants of John Porter, of Danvers, Held at Danvers, Mass., July 17th, 1895. Higginson Book Co., 1897.

Putnam, A.P. *A Sketch of General Israel Putnam.* Salem, MA: Eben Putnam, 1893.

Putnam, Eben. *A History of the Putnam Family in England and America.* Salem, Massachusetts: Salem Pub. and Print, 1891.

Putnam, Israel, and Rufus Putnam. *The Two Putnams: Israel and Rufus in the Havana Expedition 1762 and in the Mississippi River Exploration 1772–73, Etc.* Hartford, Connecticut Historical Society, 1931.

Putnam, Rufus. *Journal of Gen. Rufus Putnam Kept in Northern New York During Four Campaigns of the Old French and Indian War, 1757 1760: The Whole Copiously Ill.* Albany: Joel Munsell's Sons, 1886.

Putnam, Rufus, and Rowena Buell. *The Memoirs of Rufus Putnam and Certain Official Papers and Correspondence.* Published by the National Society of the Colonial Dames of America in the State of Ohio. Boston and New York: Houghton, Mifflin, 1903.

Randall, E. O. *The Rise and Progress of an American State*, Vol. 6. Century History Co., 1912.

Reed, Jonas. *A History of Rutland: Worcester County, Massachusetts, from Its Earliest Settlement, with a Biography of Its First Settlers.* Worcester: Tyler & Seagrove, 1879.

Rogers, Robert. *Journals of Major Robert Rogers Containing an Account of the Several Excursions He Made under the Generals Who Commanded upon the Continent of North America, during the Late War; from Which May be Collected the Most Material Circumstances of Every Campaign upon That Continent, from the Commencement to the Conclusion of the War.* Albany: Joel Munsell's Sons, 1883.

Rösch, John. *Historic White Plains.* Harbor Hill Books, 1976.

Ross, Charles, and Charles Cornwallis. *Cornwallis. Correspondence of Charles, First Marquis Cornwallis.* London: John Murray, 1859.

Roy, Patricia. "Acclaimed Historian Visits Rutland Home." *The Landmark*, 2 November 2017, www.thelandmark.com/articles/acclaimed-historian-visits-rutland-home/.

Scobey, Frank Edgar, and Burgess L. McElroy. *The Biographical Annals of Ohio, 1902–1903: A Handbook of the Government and Institutions of the State of Ohio.* General Assembly, 1892.

"Shay's Rebellion: Letter from Gen. Rufus Putnam to Gov. Bowdoin." Collections of the Maine Historical Society, vol. 2, 1847.

Shetrone, Henry Clyde. *The Mound-Builders.* New York: D. Appleton and Company, 1930.

"A Short History of the Society of the Cincinnati." The Society of The Cincinnati, www.societyofthecincinnati.org/about/history.

Sprague, John Francis. "Stephen Jones, the First Justice of the Peace East of the Penobscot." *Sprague's Journal of Maine History,* April 1913. 187–191.

Starbuck, David R. *The Great Warpath: British Military Sites from Albany to Crown Point.* Hanover, NH: University of New England, 1999.

———. *Massacre at Fort William Henry.* Hanover, NH: University of New England, 2002.

State of Ohio, General Assembly. *Journal of the House of Representatives,* vol. 82. 1917.

Stockwell, Mary. *Unlikely General: Mad Anthony Wayne and the Battle for America.* Yale University Press, 2018.

Stone, Benjamin Franklin. "*From Rutland to Marietta.*" New England Magazine: An Illustrated Monthly, vol. 16, 1897.

Summers, Thomas Jefferson. *History of Marietta.* Leader Publishing Company, 1903.

Sutton Reconnaissance Report. Massachusetts Department of Conservation and Recreation, 2007.

Temple, J. H., and Charles Adams. *History of North Brookfield, Massachusetts: Preceded by an Account of old Quabaug, Indian and English Occupation, 1647–1676; Brookfield Records, 1686–1783.* North Brookfield: The Town of North Brookfield, 1887.

United States Department of the Interior, National Park Service, National Register of Historic Places, Inventory-Nomination Form, General Rufus Putnam House. Washington: GPO, 1972.

Vandewater, Robert J. *The Tourist, or Pocket Manual for Travellers on the Hudson River, the Western and Northern Canals and Railroads: the Stage Routes to Niagara Falls; and down Lake Ontario and the St. Lawrence to Montreal and Quebec ...* New York: Harper & Brothers, 1841.

Venable, William Henry. *Footprints of the Pioneers in the Ohio Valley: A Centennial Sketch.* Cincinnati: Ohio Valley Press, 1888.

Walker, Paul K. *Engineers of Independence—a Documentary History of the Army Engineers in the American Revolution 1775–1783.* University Press of the Pacific, 2002.

Washington, George. *The Writings of George Washington,* Vol. 10. New York: G.P. Putnam's Sons, 1891.

White, Larry Nash, and Emily Blankenship White. *Marietta.* Arcadia, 2004.

Wood, Gordon S. *Empire of Liberty: A History of the Early Republic, 1789–1815.* The Legal Classics Library, 2014.

Young, Gordon R. "Rufus Putnam." *Professional Memoirs, Corps of Engineers, United States Army, and Engineer Department at Large,* vol. 10, no. 49, 1918. 65–67. www.jstor.org/stable/44580139.

Index

Numbers in ***bold italics*** indicate pages with photographs

Abercrombie, Gen. James 17, 21–23
Adams, Abigail 196
Adams, John 160, 196, 215n48
Adams, John Quincy 186, 198n23
African Americans 34, 106, 109, 111, 122–123, 162–163, 198n10, 215n46
Albany, New York 16–17, 20, 23, 73, 91–92
Alexander, William (Lord Stirling) 55–56, 199n36
Ames, Fisher 147–149, 213n86
Amherst, Jeffrey 23–24
Arnold, Gen. Benedict 61, 67–70, 200n61, 202n95, 202n96, 202n103
Articles of Confederation 88, 100, 103, 206n64, 213n80
Athens, Ohio 158–160, 215n37
Athens County, Ohio 167
Ayers, William 29

Bacon, Francis 181, 218n12
Barnes, Dr. Samuel 117
Belpre, Ohio ***30***, 39, 116–117, 119, 123, 139, 140–143, 171–172, 212n59
Big Black River 35–36, 197n42
Big Bottom 141–142
Blue Jacket, Chief (aka Weyapiersenwah) 145
Boston, Massachusetts 3, 5, 8, 20, 35, 37, 43–48, ***65–66***, 82, ***97***–98, 102, 104, 119, 122, 130, 134, 138, 177–178, 189, 194n50, 198n6, 198n10, 198n16, 198n21, 206n66, 207n69, 207n70, 207n71
Bounty Land 99–100, 205n49, 205n50

Bowdoin, Gov. James 101–102, 105n53, 105n55
Bradstreet, Col. John 21
Breed's Hill 45, 218n21
Brewer's Regiment 43–44
Bronx River 58, 200n66
Brookfield, Massachusetts 11, 20, 26, 29, 32, 155
Brookline, Massachusetts 44
Brooklyn, Battle of *see* Long Island, Battle of
Brooklyn, Connecticut 119, 171, 173, 214n20
Buckingham, Gen. Catharinus Putnam ***185***–186
Buckingham, Ebenezer 31, 152–154, 165, 214n13
Buell, Gen Joseph 125, 183
Bunches of Grapes Tavern 104, 207n69, 207n70
Bunker Hill, Battle of 37, 45, 59, 62, 100, 121, 196n21, 196n25, 198n16, 201n74, 206n67, 213n81
Burgoyne, Gen. John 20, 39, 60–***63***, 72, 79, 81, 184–***185***, 193n32
Burlingame, Christopher ***30***, 111–112, 114, 209n26
Burlingame, Rufus Putnam 187–188
Burlingame, Susanna ***30***, 111–112, 114
Burnham, Maj. John 147, 213n81
Burr, Aaron 166, 196n21
Butler, Col. Edward 216n55
Butler, Gen. Richard 74, 108, 207n3
Byington, Cyrus 156–157

227

228　Index

Cambridge, Massachusetts 43, 44, 170, 178, 194*n*50, 201*n*84
Campus Martius 40, 110, 112, *118*, 126, 128, 131, 133–134, 136–137, 141, 146, 172, 190, 208*n*6, 208*n*12
Captain Pipe (aka Konieschquanoheel) 121
Caribbean Sea 33, 149, 189, 196*n*27
Charlestown, Massachusetts 44, 58–59
Charlestown, South Carolina *65*
Chatterton Hill 58–59
Chester, Gov. Peter 32, 34, 36, 197*n*30
Chief Engineers of the Army 5, 44, 47, 53–54, 198*n*8
Chillicothe, Ohio 159, 163, 168
Choctaws 35–36, 156–157, 214*n*26
Cincinnati, Ohio 141, 159, 175, 179, 186
Cleveland, Ohio 91, 135
Clinton, Gen. George 56, 57, 64, 184, 200*n*53
Clinton, Gen. Henry 57, 60, 70
Clinton, Gen. James 68
Coburn, Phineas 179
Cole, Congressman Ralph 187
Colonial Dames of America *118*, *132*, 134
Commemorative Stamps 183–*185*
Company of Military Adventurers 32, 34, 37–38, 189
Concord, Massachusetts 38, 43, 45, 81, 100, 169, 194*n*50, 195*n*89, 201*n*74, 208*n*6
Cone, Mary 1, 31, 42, 191*n*1
Congregational Church (Marietta, Ohio) 155–156, 186
Connecticut Courant 38
Constitution Island 69, 74, 202*n*94
Constitutional Convention (National) 103, 106
Constitutional Conventions (Ohio) 123, 160–163
Continental Militia Proposal 89–96
Continental Army 3, 5–6, 10, 16, 44–45, 47, 49, 52, 58, *65*–67, 69–70, 72, 83, 85–87, 94, 96, 101, 110, 125, 170, 175–176, 184, 188, 193*n*5, 198*n*8, 199*n*26, 199*n*31, 199*n*36, 200*n*45, 200*n*61, 201*n*75, 203*n*116, 207*n*72, 211*n*35, 217*n*86
Continental Congress 5, 77, 79, 85, 88, 103–104, 146, 183, 193*n*5, 198*n*6, 199*n*31, 206*n*62, 207*n*3, 213*n*80
Cornwallis, Gen. Charles 85, 197*n*60
corporal punishment 16, 129

Crawford, Rev. Sidney 105–106, 181, 218*n*14
Crown Point (New York) 24–*25*, 91, 196*n*17
Cuba 33, 196*n*17, 196*n*25
Cutler, Ephraim 40, 107, 159, 161–163
Cutler, Jervis 107, 179
Cutler, Julia Perkins 107, 179
Cutler, Manasseh 40, 103–104, 107, 119, 128, 158–159, 163, 183–*185*, 186, 206–207*n*68, 217*n*88
Cuyahoga River 91, 204*n*33

Dana, Benjamin 171, 172, 216*n*69
Danbury, Connecticut 71
Danvers. Massachusetts *see* Salem Village
Davis, Lucy Nye 137
Dawes, Sarah Cutler 40–41, 217*n*88
Dayton, Gen. Elias 85, 87
Dearborn, Henry 196*n*21
Delawares 114, 121, 136–137, 141, 143, 145, 207*n*3, 212*n*68
De Tocqueville, Alexis 181–182
Devol, Allen 179
Devol, Capt. Jonathan 109, 123, 208*n*7
Devola, Ohio *118*–119
Dorchester Heights (Boston, Massachusetts) 8, 20, 44–*46*, 47–48, 194*n*50, 198*n*6
Duer, William 146–147, 213*n*80, 213*n*84
Dwight, Timothy 155

Enabling Act of 1802 160–161
Enos, Roger 33–34, 37, 196*n*25
Ewing, Thomas, Sr. 159, 180, 218*n*5

Fairbairn, Sir William: Treatise on Mills and Millwork 28–29
Falmouth, Maine 90
Farmer[apost]s Castle 123, 138–139
farming 6, 8, 28, 31, 49, 79, 81, 101–102, 126, 134–135, 138–139, 154, 170, 189, 204*n*38, 209*n*19, 214*n*17
Febiger, Col. Christian 74
Federalists 160–161, 163, 213*n*86
5th Massachusetts Regiment 61, *63*, 71, 98
Flint, Hezekiah, Jr. 179
Flint, Timothy 183
Fort Ann 52
Fort Boonesborough 120
Fort Box 53, 199*n*38
Fort Carillon *see* Fort Ticonderoga

Fort Clinton (at West Point) 68, 71
Fort Clinton (near Bear Mountain, New York) 70
Fort Constitution 53
Fort Defiance 53
Fort Edward 12, *14*–16, 23, 52, 60
Fort Greene 53, 199n39
Fort Harmar 99, 124, 128, 140, 142, 168
Fort Lee 49, 53, 59–60, 200–201n70
Fort Massac 91, 204n31
Fort McIntosh 99
Fort Meigs 68
Fort Michilimackinac 204n30
Fort Montgomery 52, 70
Fort Pitt 92–93, 99, 204n32
Fort Stirling 53
Fort Ticonderoga (Fort Carillon) 20–21, 23–24, 27, 45, 47–48, 60, 100, 193n32, 196n17
Fort Vincent 99
Fort Washington (New York) 49–50, 53, 59, 200n40, 200–201n70
Fort Washington (Cincinnati, Ohio) 141
Fort Webb 68
Fort William Henry 15–16, 23, 193n22
Fort Wyllis (Wyllys) 68
Franklin, Benjamin 104, 183, 187, 205n53
Freemasonry 49, 168, 207n70
French and Indian War 10–27, 31–34, 36–37, 39, 44, 49, 57, 61, 73, 86, 91, *97*, 131, 140, 165, 175, 188–189, 191n1, 193n32, 196n17, 196n25, 198n2, 198n4, 198n6, 199n26, 200n61, 202n98, 203n116, 204n30, 204n32, 205n47, 206n56, 206n66, 215n47
Frye, Col. Joseph 12, 193n5
fugitive slaves 163
Fuller, Jonathan 8–9
Fulton, Robert 174

Gage, Gen. Thomas 21
Gallia County, Ohio 147
Gallipolis, Ohio 140, 146–147, 168, 177
Gates, Gen. Horatio 60–62, 64, 71, 78, 96, 184, 206n66
Gilman, Benjamin Ives 163
Gilman, Joseph 129–130
Gnadenhutten Massacre 137–138
Goodrich, Capt. Wait 33–34, 37–38
Grant, Ulysses S. 4, 68–69, 161, 191n2, 198n4, 204n39
Great Comet of 1744 7, 192n8, 192n9
Greaton, Gen. John 85, 87, 184
Green, Capt. Daniel 174

Greene, Griffin 125, 135, 141, 154, 159, 211n35
Greene, Nathanael 56, 96, 184, 187, 192n11, 199n31, 199n37, 202n88
Greeneville, Treaty of 145
Greenwich, Connecticut 72
Gridley, Col. Richard 44, 47, 54, 198n8

Hale, Nathan 6
Halifax, Nova Scotia, Canada 45, 48, 90
Hall, the Rev. David 7
Halleck, Gen. H.W. 186
Hamilton, Alexander 42, 58, 96, 154, 166, 187, 208n10
Hancock, John 103, 199n26, 199n30, 199n34, 206n62
Hardin, Col. John 141
Harlem Heights 51
Harlem Heights, Battle of 54, 58
Harrison, William Henry 145, 196n29, 218n5
Hart, Capt. Jonathan 124
Hartford, Connecticut 37, 39, 108, 111
Havana, Cuba 148, 193n32, 196n17, 193n25
Heath, Gen. William 47, 158, 194n50, 199n27
Heights of Abraham, Battle of (also known as the Battle of Plains of Abraham) 70, 202n98
Hessians 57–58, 62, 77, 179
Hildreth, Dr. Samuel Prescott, Jr. 39–40, 110, 120, 122–123, 170, 178–179
Hildreth, Dr. Samuel Prescott, Sr. 125
Hitchcock, the Rev. Enos 62
Hoar, George F. 4, *8*, 10, 40, 104, 161, 178, 181
Hockhocking River (aka Hocking River) 91–92, 139, 157, 212n59, 214n27
Holland, Park *97*–98, 205n43
Hopewell people 124
Horseneck 72
Howe, Gen. George 20–22
Howe, Adm. Richard 21
Howe, Gen. William 21, 48, 54, 56–57, 59–60
Hull, Maj. William 74
Humphreys, David 22, 87, 192n11, 196n21
Huntington, Jedediah 87
Huntington, Gov. Samuel H. (Ohio) 159, 168, 216n61

Ingersol, Lt. Col. Joseph 23

Index

Jamaica 33
James, Thomas 35–36
Jefferson, Thomas 41–42, 52, **65**, 84, 103, 105, 119, 160–161, 163–165, 187, 198*n*22, 213*n*84, 215*n*47, 215*n*48
Johnson, Lt. Col. Henry 73, 77
Jones, Stephen 19, 98, 165, 194*n*44

Kentucky 107, 119–120, 138, 140–141, 165, 182, 198*n*22, 210*n*55
Knox, Henry 45–48, 85, 87, 96, 141, 143, 184, 187, 198*n*16, 209*n*31
Kosciuszko, Thaddeus 52, 64, 67

Lafayette, Marquis de 16, 100, 147, 175, 177, 184, 217*n*86, 217*n*98
Lake Champlain 13, 91–93, 193*n*32
Lake Erie 86, 91, 154, 204*n*33
Lake George 10, 15, 21–22, 24–**25**, 52, 92, 196*n*17
Lake Huron 204*n*30
Lake Michigan 204*n*30
Learned, Capt. Ebenezer 11–13, 15, 17–18, 20, 61, 194*n*50, 206*n*56
Lee, Gen. Charles 44, 53, 77
Leicester Academy 82, 203*n*8
Lexington, Massachusetts 38, 43, 45, 100, 169, 194*n*50, 195*n*89, 196*n*21, 201*n*74, 208*n*6
Library of Congress 49, **80**
Lincoln, Abraham 4, 138, 147, 178, **185**, 191*n*2, 192*n*21, 198*n*22, 215*n*46
Lincoln, Benjamin 61, 96, 102, 131, 151, 184, 201*n*73
Lindley, Jacob 159
Little Miami River 167
Little Turtle, Chief (aka Weyapiersenwah) 141, 145
Long Island, Battle of 53, 179, 199*n*36, 200*n*45, 200*n*75; *see also* Brooklyn, Battle of
Lopez, Aaron 82
Louisiana Purchase 166
Lyman, Phineas 13, 31–33, 38, 196*n*17
Lyman, Thaddeus 32–34, 36–37

Machin, Thomas 70
Madison, James 42, 187, 210–211*n*16
Malbone, Christopher [qm]Kit[qm] 122–123
Manhattan Island 5, 53–54, 57, 200*n*45
Mansfield, Edward 164–165
Mansfield, Jared 163–165, 215*n*47, 215*n*49, 215*n*50

Marie Antoinette 119
Marietta, Ohio 1, 39, 41, 62, 83, 85, 95, 104, 107–**113**, 115, 117–**118**, 119–**132**, 133–144, 146, 149, 152, 155–156, 159, 163, 165, 168–183, **185**–188, 190, 191*n*1, 192*n*6, 195*n*12, 205*n*47, 207*n*72, 208*n*5, 208*n*6, 211*n*17, 214*n*13, 214*n*17, 214*n*19, 215*n*46, 217*n*83, 217*n*87, 217*n*88, 218*n*18, 218–219*n*22
Marietta College 124, 144, 168, 187, 210*n*76, 215*n*46
Marietta Earthworks 124–126, 131, 172, 177
massacres 15–16, 137–143
Matthews, Daniel, Jr. 9, 192*n*18
May, Col. John 110–111, 120, 122, 128–129, 134, 138
Mayflower (riverboat) 109, 175, 180
McClellan, Gen. George **185**–186
McCullough, David 1, 4, 40, 49, 137, 180
McDougall, Alexander 58, 64–**65**, 71, 73, 200*n*61
McIntire, John 163
Meigs, Return Jonathan, Jr. 183, 186, 210–211*n*16
Meigs, Return Jonathan, Sr. 68, 74, 108, 117, 206*n*67
Middletown, Connecticut 38, 206*n*67
Mifflin, Thomas **51**, 199*n*31, 201*n*84
Millwright 3, 9–10, 24, 26, 28–29, 36, 126, 188, 190, 193*n*23, 206*n*66
Mississippi (boat) 33
Mississippi (river) 10, **14**, 32, 34–39, 86, 95, 103, 107, 148–149, 164, 166, 176, 182, 189, 197*n*42, 208*n*6, 215*n*47, 216*n*82
Mississippi (state) 67, 157, 196*n*19, 197*n*42
Mississippi (territory) 207*n*71
Missouri Compromise of 1820 205*n*41
Monmouth, Battle of 207*n*3
Monroe, President James 176, 187, 211*n*16, 217*n*92
Montreal 27, 195*n*89
Moravian Church 114, 137, 209*n*31
Morgan, Daniel 60, 62, 78, 184, 187, 201*n*72, 201*n*78
Mound Cemetery (Marietta, Ohio) 124–125, 172, 177, 188, 208*n*5, 211*n*17, 214*n*19
Murray, Col. John 81
Muskingum Academy 156, 187
Muskingum River 91, 93, 99, 107–108, 110–111, **113**, 117–120, 123–125, 138,

142–143, 146, 154, 163, 165, 168–169, 172, 174, 181, 188, 209n31, 214–215, 217
mutiny 88

Natchez, Mississippi 32, 35, 38
Native Americans 15–16, 34–37, 39, 60, 65, 73, 87, 89, 90–91 95–96, 99–100, 105–106, 108–110, 114, 116–*118*, 123–126, 128–129, 131, 133, 135–149, 152, 154, 156–157, 170–172, 180, 183, 189–190, 195n78, 207–208n3, 209n31, 212n68
New Orleans 34–36, 148
New Rochelle, New York 55
New York Times 53, 70
Newburgh Conspiracy 85–88
Newburgh Petition 85–88
Newport, Rhode Island 44–45, 49, 203n8
North Brookfield, Massachusetts 9–10, 28–*30*, 43, 82, 176, 189, 192n18
Northwest Ordinance of 1787 103–106, 127
Northwest Territory 1, 3–4, *80*, 83, 87, 89, 91, 95, 99, 103, 104–107, 117, 120, 127, 130, 134–135, 141–143, 145–147, 149, 152, 157, 159–160, 163, 165, 166–167, 169–170, 175, 180, 182, 187–190, 191n1, 196n29, 207n71, 207n72, 207–208n3, 208n5, 215n46
Nye, Arius 137
Nye, Minerva T. 137

Ohio Archaeological and Historical Society 137
Ohio Company Land Office (Marietta, Ohio) *132*, 134, 172
Ohio Company of Associates *80*, 103–104, 107, 146, 154, 159
Ohio Constitution of 1803 160–163, 215n45
Ohio River 11, 39, 85, 91–93, *97*, 99, 103, 106–108, 111, *113*, 115–117, 123–124, 134–136, 138–140, 142, 146–147, 154, 167, 170–172, 177, 181–182, 186, 204n31, 209n31, 209n43, 211n39, 214n13, 214n27
Ohio University 157–160, 189
Oliver, Robert 135, 154, 211n36
orchards 126, 174, 183, 216n82
Oxford, Massachusetts 20

Paige, Capt. William 23, 26–27, 195n86
Paine, Thomas 200–201n70

Parsons, Samuel Holden 103–104, 127–128, 131, 186, 206n67
Paterson, Gen. John 61, 83, 87, 204n16
Patton, Gen. George 69, 198n4, 199n26
Paulding, James Kirke 69, 202n93
Penobscot County, Maine 90
Penobscot People 131, 206n65
Pensacola, Florida 34, 36, 148, 197n30
Philadelphia 52, *65*, 88
Pickering, Timothy 129, 152
piracy 33
Pomfret, Connecticut 32, 122, 166, 169, 210n70
Porter, Amos, Jr. 179–180
Pratt, Edward 6
Princeton, Battle of 199n26, 199n36, 200n58
prison ships 199n39
Pulaski, Gen. Casimir 184
Putnam, Aaron Waldo 123, 139, 171
Putnam, Amos (Rufus' brother) 23, 195n68
Putnam, Ann Holyoke (Rufus' great-grandmother) 193n24
Putnam, Catharine (Rufus Putnam's daughter) 153–154
Putnam, Daniel 32–33, 196n21
Putnam, David 156, 187
Putnam, Deacon William Rufus (Rufus Putnam's son) *30*, 77, 172, 186, 215n36
Putnam, Eben 177
Putnam, Edward (Rufus' grandfather) 10
Putnam, Elisha, Jr. (Rufus' brother) 6–7, 10
Putnam, Elisha, Sr. (Rufus' father) 6–8
Putnam, Elizabeth Ayres (Rufus' first wife) 29
Putnam, Hannah Pope 169
Putnam, Huldah (Rufus' sister) 9, 192n18
Putnam, Israel 1, 5, 10–*14*, 15, 20, 22, 32–38, 50, 57, 59, 62, 64, 72–73, 87, *118*–119, 122, 166, 169, 171, 175, 187, 189, 192n11, 193n24, 196n21, 196n25, 198n4, 201n75, 201n84, 202n104, 204n38, 205n47, 206n67, 209–210n50, 210n70, 214n20, 215n46, 216n65, 216n69, 217n91, 218n21
Putnam, Israel, Jr. *118*, 122–123, 169–170
Putnam, Israel, III 169, 171–174
Putnam, Persis (Rufus' second wife) 29, 31–32, 77, 81, *113*, 155, 176, 195n12
Putnam, Peter Schuyler 210n50

Index

Putnam, Rufus: American Revolutionary War 3, 5–*8*, 10, *14*, 19–20, 24, 28, 38, 41, 43–90, *97*–99, 151, 175–176, 178–179, 181, 184–186, 188–190; apprenticeship 9, 10, 188, 206*n*66; the Battle of Saratoga 20, 49, 61–62, *185*, 206*n*66; birth 7–*8*; brigadier general appointments 40, 85, 107, 151, 189, 206*n*66; Chief Engineer of the Continental Army 5, 50, 53–54, 188, 198*n*8; childhood 7–10, 39–40, *97*, 188; death 175–177; designs Marietta[apost]s Congregational church 156; education 4, *8*–10, 106, 112, *153*, 157, 181, 188, 192*n*21; elected to the Massachusetts General Assembly 98; farmer 1, 3, 28, 31, 79–83, 86, 126, 189–190; *Father of Ohio* 83, 150, 187, 190; forms bible society 156; fortification of Dorchester Heights *8*, 44–48; fortification of Newport, Rhode Island 45, 49; fortification of the Hudson River *8*, 52–54, 60, *63*–*75*, 82–83, 90, 92–93, 189–190, 202*n*93; freemason 49, 168, 207*n*70; justice of the peace (Massachusetts) 82, 104; Maine surveys 85, *97*, 99, 130–131, 176, 189; Marietta (Ohio) home 40, 133–134, 136–137, 152–*153*, 156–157, 172; marriages 29–32, 77, 81, *113*–115, 176, 195*n*12; millwright 3, 9–10, 24, 26, 28–29, 36, 126, 188, 190, 193*n*23, 206*n*66; opposition to slavery 2–4, 62, 106, 122, 150, 161–164, 181, 190; physical appearance 39–42, *63*, *97*, *153*, 172, *185*; religion 29, 41, 62, 83, 105–106, 155–157, 168; settlement of Marietta, Ohio 107–*113*, 114–*118*, 119–*132*, 133–147, 149–160, 176–177, 183; Rutland (Massachusetts) home 29, 79, *80*, 81- 83, 101, 104, 106, 112–114, 126, 176, 182, 189, 203*n*11, 205*n*54; Shays' Rebellion 101–102, 205*n*54, 205–206*n*56, 206*n*66; spying 5–6, 49, 55–57; surveyed land for Ohio University 160, 189; territorial judge 3, 84, 107–108, 127–130, 143, 150, 166, 190; trustee of Ohio University 158–159; U.S. Surveyor General appointment 41, *51*, 84, 126, 129, 145, 151–*153*, 163–165, 167, 189; West Point *8*, *63*–*75*, 82–83, 90, 92–93, 189–190, 202*n*93
Putnam, Sarah Waldo 169–171
Putnam, Susannah Fuller (Rufus' mother) 6

Putnam, Thomas (Rufus' great-grandfather) 193*n*24
Putnam, William Rufus (Rufus Putnam's grandson) 186
Putnam County, Ohio 187
Putnam Street (Marietta, Ohio) 168
Putnam's Rock 62–64

Quebec 60, 70, 91, 148, 202*n*98
Queen's Rangers 57

religion 6, 29, 31, 33–34, 41, 62, 83, 105–106, 114, 129–130, 137, 155–157, 159, 162–163, 168, 180, 186–188, 192*n*6
religious liberty 31, 105–106, 162–163
Revere, Paul 195*n*12
Rice, Zebulon 29, 195*n*12
Rogers, Robert 22, 57, 140, 212*n*61
Rogers Rangers *25*, 140, 212*n*61
Roxbury, Massachusetts 43, 44, 47, 50, 198*n*10
Rufus Putnam (steamboat) 174–175, 217*n*83
Rufus Putnam Birthplace House site (Sutton, Massachusetts) *8*, 192*n*10
Rufus Putnam House (Marietta, Ohio) 40–41, 133–134
Rufus Putnam House (Rutland, Massachusetts) *80*–83, 203*n*11
Ruggles, Col. Timothy 20, 23, 206*n*56

Sadler, Capt. John 9, 112
St. Clair, Gov. Arthur 96, 110, 117, 119, 121, 127, 129–130, 139, 141, 143–144, 161, 208*n*3
Salem Village, Massachusetts (now Danvers) 6, 8–10, 108, 131, 169, 179–180, 191*ch*1*n*3
Saratoga, Battle of 20, 49, 60–*63*, 72, 79, *185*, 201*n*73, 201–202*n*88, 206*n*56, 206*n*66
Saratoga, New York 12
Sargent, Rowena Tupper 135
Sargent, Winthrop 104, 135, 167, 207*n*71
Schuyler, Philip 184
Scioto Company 146–147
Scioto Valley, Ohio 135
Scott, Gen. John Morin 57
Sharples, James, Sr. 40, *153*
Shaw, Benjamin 179
Shawnees 145, 207*n*3
Shays, Daniel 19, 100–103, 205*n*54, 205–206*n*56

Index

Shays' Rebellion 19, 100–103, 204n16, 205–206n56, 206n63, 206n66
Shepard, Col. William 83–84, 203n15
Sherman, William Tecumseh 4, 69, 191n2, 198n4, 218n5
Simeral[apost]s (Simerill's) Ferry (West Newton, Pennsylvania) 108, 115
6th Massachusetts Regiment 61
Skene, Capt. Philip 17, 24, 193–194n32
slavery 2–4, 62, 105–106, 122, 150, 161–164, 181–182, 190, 215n46
smallpox 33, 117, 171, 198n6
Society of the Cincinnati 96, 121, 204n38
Spencer, Gen. Joseph 57
Sproat, High Sheriff Ebenezer 87, 99, 108–109, 125, 128, 140, 208n5, 210n6
Stacy, Col. William 125, 134
Stark, John 87, 184, 187
steamboats 174–175, 183, 188, 217n83
Stone, Benjamin Franklin 111–117, 123, 138–139, 141–142, 209n20
Stony Point, the Battle of 68, 72–75, *76*–78, 144
Stony Point, New York 90
Story, Rev. Daniel 155, 159
Sullivan, John 57, 184
Sumter, Gen. Thomas 217n86
surveying 28, 32, 34, 41, *51*, 67, 84–85, 97–99, 108–109, 126, 129, 140, 145, 149, 151–154, 157, 163, 165, 167, 172, *185*, 189, 198n22, 205n43, 207n71, 208n5, 208n6, 209n20, 214n13, 215n47, 215n50
Sutton, Massachusetts 6–*8*, 20, 23, 192n6, 192n10, 195n68

3rd Connecticut Regiment 68
Thomas, Gen. John 43–44, 48, 198n6
Thoreau, Henry David 198n22
Throg's Neck (in Bronx, New York) 54, 58
Tories 56–57, 73, 196n21
Treaty of Paris (1763) 11
Treaty of Paris (1783) 84, 91
Trenton, New Jersey 198n16, 200n45
True, Dr. Jabez 117, 125
Trumbull, John (painter) 39–40, 62–*63*, 87, 167, 192n11, 218n21
Trumbull, Jonathan George Washington 167
Trumbull, Jonathan, Jr. 166–167
Trumbull, Jonathan, Sr. 167
Tryon, William 72–73
Tupper, Anselm 87, 108, 125, 208n6

Tupper, Gen. Benjamin 3, 87, 98–99, 103, 107, 125, 127–128, 130–131, 135, 186, 205n47, 206n66
Tupper, Sophia 40, 217n88
Tuscarawas River 91, 214n13

United States Constitution 103, 105–106, 109, 121, 162, 192n11, 206n64, 210n3

Valley Forge 87, 194n50
Varnum, James Mitchell 104, 120–121, 127–128, 131, 186, 207n72
Venable, William Henry 180
Verplanck, New York 72–77
veterans of the American Revolutionary War 3, *80*–81, 86, *97*, 99–101, 103, 121, 125, 149, 157, 163, 166, 178–179, 196n21, 198n4, 215n47
veterans of the French and Indian War 31–32, 34, 36–37, 39, 157
Von Steuben, Friedrich Wilhelm (aka Baron Von Steuben) 96, 184, 208n10

Wampas, John 6
Washington, George 3–6, *8*, 10, 41–42, 44–*51*, 52–60, 64–*65*, 67–68, 70–77, 83–*97*, 104, 107, *118*–119, 121, 135–136, 142–144, 146, 151–*153*, 158, 160–161, 163–167, 170, 177–178, 181, 183–184, 187–189, 192n11, 194n50, 196n21, 198n16, 198n22, 198n23, 199n26, 199n27, 200n45, 200n70, 201n75, 201–202n88, 204n38, 206n66, 208n10, 217n91
Washington County, Maine 194n44
Washington County, Ohio *30*, 125, 140, 156, 161, 163, 174, 179–180, 208n5, 209n20, 215n46, 216n69
Wayne, Anthony 68, 73–77, 140, 144–145, 184, 212n63
Webb, Gen. Daniel 15–16, 193n22
Webster, Daniel 106
West Florida (British colony) 31–32, 34, 36–38, 197n30
West Point *8*, *63*–65, *66*–75, 82–83, 90, 92–93, 164, *185*, 189–190, 200n61, 201–202n88, 202n90, 202n93, 202n95, 202n96, 202n97, 202n103, 215n47, 215n50
West Point Chain 69–70
West Point Museum 71
Whipple, Abraham 125, 154–155, 183, 186, 214n17

Whitcomb, Capt. Joseph 20, 194*n*51
White, Maj. Haffield 108–109, 131
White, Peletiah 179
White Plains, Battle of 5–6, 54–60, 206*n*67, 207n71
Willcox, Gen. Joseph 125, 210*n*77
Wolcott, Oliver, Jr. 152, 166, 216*n*57
Wolfe, Gen. James 202*n*98
Woodbridge, Dudley 125, 129, 159, 211*n*17

Wyandot Indians 136, 141–143, 145, 209*n*31, 212*n*68

Yale College 129, 155, 187, 192, 196*n*17, 206–207*n*68, 211*n*17, 211*n*19, 215*n*50
Young, the Rev. David 159

Zanesville, Ohio 111, 154, 165, 174–175, 214*n*35, 217*n*83

www.ingramcontent.com/pod-product-compliance
Lightning Source LLC
Chambersburg PA
CBHW032039300426
44117CB00009B/1116